PETER EDWARDS AND KEVIN LORING

LYT

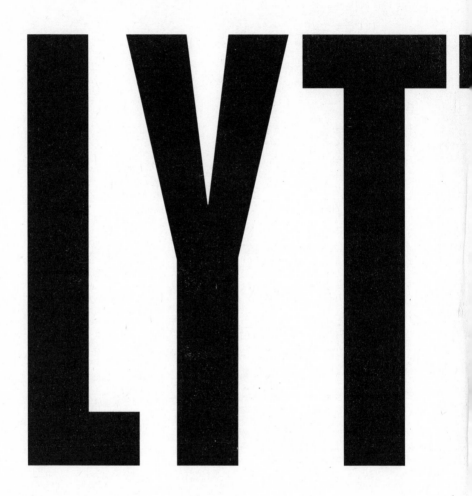

RANDOM HOUSE CANADA

TON

CLIMATE CHANGE, COLONIALISM AND LIFE BEFORE THE FIRE

PUBLISHED BY RANDOM HOUSE CANADA

Copyright © 2024 Peter Edwards and Kevin Loring

All rights reserved under International and Pan-American Copyright Conventions. No part of this book may be reproduced in any form or by any electronic or mechanical means, including information storage and retrieval systems, without permission in writing from the publisher, except by a reviewer, who may quote brief passages in a review. Published in 2024 by Random House Canada, a division of Penguin Random House Canada Limited, Toronto. Distributed in Canada and the United States of America by Penguin Random House Canada Limited, Toronto.

www.penguinrandomhouse.ca

Random House Canada and colophon are registered trademarks.

Library and Archives Canada Cataloguing in Publication

Title: Lytton : Climate Change, Colonialism and Life before the Fire / Peter Edwards and Kevin Loring.
Names: Edwards, Peter, 1956- author. | Loring, Kevin, 1974- author.
Description: Includes index.
Identifiers: Canadiana (print) 20230560512 | Canadiana (ebook) 20230560717 | ISBN 9781039006157 (hardcover) | ISBN 9781039006164 (EPUB)
Subjects: LCSH: Lytton (B.C.) | LCSH: Lytton (B.C.)—History. | LCSH: Lytton (B.C.)—Social conditions. | LCSH: Lytton (B.C.)—Ethnic relations.
Classification: LCC FC3849.L98 E39 2024 | DDC 971.1/72—dc23

Jacket and text design: Matthew Flute
Jacket design: Matthew Flute
Jacket photo: courtesy of Brayden Sawatzky
Additional textures: dannyeve, jennaduffy / both Unsplash; and Adobe Stock
Typeset by Terra Page

Printed in Canada

10 9 8 7 6 5 4 3 2 1

Penguin
Random House
RANDOM HOUSE CANADA

To Winona and Ken Edwards.
Thanks a million for raising us in the Centre of the Universe.
PETER EDWARDS

To my N'kshayt'kn, my friends and family,
and to all Lyttonites past, present and future.
The story of this special place continues.
KEVIN LORING

CONTENTS

INTRODUCTIONS

THIS BOOK BEGINS with a confession. I rolled the school bus down a hill by my home, crashing it into the Sam family's fruit trees in Lytton, British Columbia, when I was ten years old.

I was never brought to justice, but I'm sure I was suspected. I don't say this to boast or to relieve myself of any guilt, but rather in an attempt to jazz up this book. I also assume that I'm protected by some statute of limitations and that my tender age at the time of the crime protects me legally.

Besides, Lytton has burned down since then—twice. The evidence has been destroyed, along with my old family home.

The book that follows is written out of love, not for any form of repentance.

It was not written in easy times, and there was another fire in the area when the book was in the editing stages. Still, the book got written and I am confident that Lytton will rebound yet again. I continue to message with my old childhood friends like Robert Bolan, Donny Glasgow and Tommy Watkinson, as well as my mom's great friend Kareen Zebroff. They're all survivors. Lytton is the home of survivors. The community at the junction of the Fraser and Thompson Rivers has been around for thousands of years and has always rebounded in the past. I can't imagine the world without it.

The Lytton that was the centre of my universe in the 1950s and 1960s had no skyscrapers, elevators, escalators, parking lots, bookstores, public libraries, fast-food franchises, drive-throughs, malls or even traffic lights. It also didn't have great school bus security.

My family moved into a modest old stucco house on Fraser Street, across the street from the Lytton Hotel and its lively beer parlour, which we could smell from the street. When we occasionally camped on the front lawn and slept under the stars in sleeping bags, patrons lobbed salt shakers at us before heading home. Our house was also just a stone's throw from the Anglican parish hall and the Catholic church, and a monument to the great nineteenth-century Chief Cexpen'nthlEm (also known as Sexpinlhemx, Cexpen'nthlEm, Cixpen'ntlam, Shigh-pentlam and David Spintlum) of the Nlaka'pamux* people. Just a block from our home in another direction, overlooking the Fraser River, was the train station where a young Queen Elizabeth II once stopped long enough to shake hands with a few of the locals.

Years later, I learned that the land where the CNR site was built was also where Chief Cexpen'nthlEm negotiated a peace back in 1858 to stave off a war with American gold miners. If not for the Chief and the Nlaka'pamux of the Lytton area, what is now British Columbia could well be part of the United States, and Canada would not stretch from coast to coast to coast.

I didn't know any of this history while growing up, just that the view from our yard was spectacular and that the monument to the

---

* Nlaka'pamux is sometimes spelled "Nlakapamux," "Nlha7kápmx," "Nlakapamuk" or "N'lakapamux" and is pronounced *Ing-Kla-paw-muck*. This book took the spelling from the Lytton First Nation's website, https://lfn.band/language.

Chief overlooking the river and the CNR station was formidable and mysterious.

My dad, Dr. Kenneth Edwards, was the only physician in the area and he got to make the rules in St. Bartholomew's Hospital, which was a few minutes' walk from our home. Much later I heard that he made a rule immediately after he started work at the old Anglican hospital: everyone got to come in and leave through the front door. Up to that point, Indigenous people had to come in through a side entrance, even though they were the overwhelming majority in the area and had lived there much longer. I also learned from my brother David that Dad sometimes scaled cliffs, dangling by a rope, to treat victims of car crashes. I marvel at the thought, as he was no great athlete. After a dozen years there, we moved to Windsor, Ontario. You can be a doctor in a place like Lytton for only so long. Dad's responsibilities were 24/7 and relentless. He had delivered almost every kid at Lytton Elementary who was younger than me, and he pronounced their relatives dead when their time came, often through car accidents. In a place that size, many had been his friends as well as his patients, and I know that hurt him. This was before Canada had universal health care, and Dad loved it when Indigenous people would show up at the door of our house to pay him in freshly caught fish. Perhaps that's why, to this day, I love the taste of salmon.

At the end of a hectic day, Dad would bunker himself away in his den, relaxing with a beer and a book, two closed doors away from us kids and the TV, which he dismissed as "the Idiot Box." He was surrounded by books in his den, and I sometimes felt I was competing with them for his attention. Perhaps that's why I became a writer.

Our mother, Winona Edwards, was the first real writer I knew, although I'm sure she was too modest to think of herself as one. She influenced me enormously. She loved reading as much as my father, and her world shone brightly whenever Agatha Christie published a new mystery. They both loved the British philosopher Bertrand Russell, but Agatha Christie was Mom's own special favourite. A comment from Christie I'll never forget was about the moment she felt she had turned professional. Christie said that a real writer writes "even when you don't want to." Without Mom's influence, this book would never have been written.

The older I get, the more blessed I feel to have spent my first dozen years in the shadow of Jackass Mountain, a two-kilometre-tall peak to the south. In a community that wasn't just the centre of my universe but the centre of countless universes for generations before and after me, the name typified the local sense of humour, fitting for a place where anything that endures is bound to be loved but nothing is really precious. Mom and Dad raised me and my three siblings—Jim, David and Melanie—in a happy and defiant little cocoon. I never really saw limits. In the Lytton of my childhood, we felt we could see forever and be anything we pretended—and aspired—to be. I have since learned that not everyone had it so good.

We were unaware as children of the horrors that existed for other children who were starting their lives nearby. We almost never saw any kids from St. George's Residential School, set on farmland just four kilometres from my home. We never visited or were invited to visit St. George's. Lytton was the centre of their universe too, but the view for them was often very different.

The community now known as Lytton was at the centre of the Nlaka'pamux universe long before the settlement on their territory was named after a much-ridiculed British writer, who was also a senior official in British Columbia's nineteenth-century colonial government. Tiny, confident Lytton once aspired to be the provincial capital, but mostly it has been a place of refuge and countless new beginnings and fresh starts. The family of an Olympic gold medallist got its Canadian start there in the nineteenth century. Another Olympic champion hid out here to get away from life's pressures and recharge his emotional batteries.

Lytton was home to about 550 people when I grew up there, but it had shrunk to 249 before it burned down in the summer of 2021. The Lytton Creek Fire wasn't the first to ruin downtown Lytton, but unlike the fires before it, that one in June 2021 destroyed pretty much everything, including my old family home on Fraser Street. That was the same street that was once home to another career writer, playwright Kevin Loring of the Nlaka'pamux of Lytton First Nation. I learned that Kevin's dad even lived for a time in our old family house. This wasn't some great serendipity, as there were only a half-dozen or so streets and a limited number of homes in town.

The book you're reading is an attempt to explore and understand Lytton—and all that we lose when places like Lytton are destroyed by wildfire—brought to you by two homegrown writers from different generations and different backgrounds. I'm a few years older than Kevin. I went to school with his aunt, Shiela Adams, who was one of the top students and athletes in my grade. I was great friends with one of his cousins, Donny Glasgow, whose family gave Lytton its smile and swagger for generations. Donny was authentic before that term became trendy. Shiela and Donny are now two among many living symbols of Lytton's resilience as it faces its greatest threat in over a century.

The fire that levelled my former family home was mentioned by Canadian prime minister Justin Trudeau and teenaged Swedish activist Greta Thunberg and others around the world as an example of the danger and brutality of climate change. People once went to Lytton to heal their bodies and souls in its dry, intense heat. Now it's a canary in the mine shaft for the future of our planet. Saving Lytton could offer lessons for saving countless other communities.

Lytton was struggling to pull itself up from its knees when another massive wildfire swept through the area in the summer of 2022, and even more fires in the summer of 2023. As this book was being completed, other Canadian communities were suffering the ravages of climate change in the form of uncontrollable wildfires. Yet the people of Lytton are struggling to rebuild yet again—stronger than ever.

This book is also an attempt to explore and understand Canada, as Lytton is a quintessentially Canadian place—for all the good and bad that this entails. William Blake said that you can find the meaning of life by studying a grain of sand. I think you can also find much of the soul of Canada by studying sandy Lytton.

Despite the many earnest themes this book will touch on—the environment, the legacy of colonialism, Indigenous rights, the hope (and threat) of technology, religious imperialism and race relations—we also want you to be moved to laugh and cry and appreciate a community worthy of your attention, just as I did while growing up in it.

We didn't have such weighty concerns when growing up in Lytton before it all burned down.

Our little universe seemed as though it would last forever.

Hopefully, it still will.

Peter Edwards
September 2023

THE STORY OF the village now known as Lytton, BC, located at the confluence of what we now call the Fraser and Thompson Rivers, didn't begin during the gold rush era, when it was given the name of the British

Secretary of State for the Colonies in 1859. And contrary to Prime Minister Justin Trudeau's remarks at the COP 26 climate summit in Glasgow, late in 2021, when he said, "There was a town called Lytton," it didn't end on June 30 of that year, when the village was burned to the ground during the hottest week ever recorded north of the forty-ninth parallel.

The story of this special place at the heart of the Nlaka'pamux Nation is many thousands of years old. My own family comes from both those early settlers who emigrated there during the gold rush and the Nlaka'pamux, who have always called this place home. I am from there, in the most elemental sense. I was born and raised there. I have made my life's work as an artist telling stories that come from this place, which my people called ltKumcheen,* meaning, in essence, "where the rivers meet" or, as I was told, "the place inside the heart where the blood mixes."**

Lytton has been my muse and my passion. I draw on it as a source for artistic creation and inspiration. My first published play is called *Where the Blood Mixes*, a reference to when n'Shinkayep, the Coyote, the Trickster, was destroyed by a powerful transformer. His heart was thrown into the junction of the rivers. His heart is still there now, turned to stone, and exists today as a massive heart-shaped boulder just below town. This place is the heart of the Nlaka'pamux Nation and home to the largest First Nation in the tribe. Even now as we recover from the devastation and trauma of the 2021 fire, and the terror that subsequent fires and floods have brought, I am still inspired to create and tell the story of

---

* The Nlaka'pamux name for the site at the junction of the Fraser and Thompson Rivers has been alternately spelled Camchin, Shilkumcheen, Thlikumcheen, Tl'cumjane, Clicumchin and Kumsheen.

** Various translations include "cross mouth," "shelf that crosses over" and "where the rivers meet."

this special place, and the people who have—and who still—call it home.

Since burning down as the world watched, Lytton has become syn-onymous with the effects of climate change. In the months and years following the fire, everywhere I went, the story of the little town that burned to the ground was ever-present. Not only that, but the video most often used to depict the tragedy always ended with the ruins of my mother's yard, the home I grew up in, where the only thing left standing was the beautiful treehouse my stepfather made for the grandkids. The most absurd example of this occurred when I travelled to Dubai in my role as the director of Indigenous Theatre at the National Arts Centre of Canda, to participate in an Indigenous forum at the World Expo in November that year. As I was checking into my hotel room I turned on the TV, and there on the BBC was the video of my burnt-out backyard playing on repeat, with the ruins of everything my mother and step-father, friends and family had owned as a graphic example for the world of the climate catastrophe we all must reckon with. Having just travelled halfway around the globe to talk about the importance of telling Indigenous stories in the era of climate change, I couldn't shake the dark irony or the karmic guilt of my own carbon footprint. All while an atmospheric river of torrential rain was washing away highways and communities and reshaping the traditional territory of my people on a level not seen since the last glaciation.

In my lifetime I have witnessed the battles over the environment from both sides of the conflict, and I've witnessed the changes to the ecology. There once was a small glacier on the eastern slope of Klowa Mountain on the west side of the Fraser. Even during the hot summers of Canada's hotspot, that bright white patch of ice was ever visible throughout my childhood. However, I noticed in my early teens that every summer it was getting smaller and smaller, until one year, when I was about nineteen, it was gone. It never returned.

The heat brought us more than fire. Pine beetle infestations caused by the warmer winters have been evident throughout the BC Interior since the late 1980s, turning millions of hectares of evergreen pine forests orange with dead trees. There has been much speculation that the devastating floods from the atmospheric river that inundated the region in the fall of 2021 were exacerbated by the extensive clearcutting of bug-killed trees.

Sockeye salmon stocks, which my family relies on for sustenance, are threatened and continue to dwindle every year from extensive commercial fishing, habitat loss, disease from fish farms and overheated river systems. The coho stocks are now listed as threatened, and the Fraser River steelhead are on the verge of extinction.

Concern for the environment in relation to colonization and resource extraction has been a central issue since the gold rush. The massive influx of miners washing the riverbanks into the river in search of gold and competing for space on the river with the First Nations hampered the annual salmon harvest. This ultimately sparked a little war between the Nlaka'pamux and the miners, the outcome of which may have saved western Canada from being annexed by the United States.

But what truly makes Lytton the special place that it is, as it once again builds back from fire, is the people—the remarkable stories of the individuals who collectively helped to shape the character and legacy of this little town. These unique characters and how they relate to one another, their journeys and where they end up, help us see how and why this little village on the side of the Trans-Canada Highway matters.

I was born in that humble little town on November 24, 1974, at St. Bartholomew's Hospital. Dr. Edwards and his family had moved away by then. I grew up on Fraser Street, just down from Peter's childhood home. Only, for me, Peter's childhood home was the Haugens'. It was my great-aunt Rita and her husband Laurence "Haugie" Haugen's house. Our Yaya, our matriarch, my great-grandmother, also lived there. And so to me that house was also Yaya's house.

One of the treasures I lost in the fire was my father's Shakespeare book. My cousin, John Haugen, the current owner of the property, gave it to me a few years ago. It had been in their basement for decades. My father had made notes in it and had left it there after a period in his life when he was studying to be an actor. He passed away in 1994, so little treasures that remind me of him, particularly of him as an artist, are special.

Before we moved to my mom's current property at Fourth and Fraser, my parents owned a trailer at the southernmost end of town, overlooking Hobo Hollow. We had a perfect view of the Winch Spur and the CN trestle bridge and Lytton Creek, where the fire began. We lived there until I was eleven. The trains pass through town about every half-hour—and with the CP and CN tracks running parallel above and below town, trains came through all day long. Our little trailer would shake like there was an earthquake. And when they blasted their horns, it sounded as if the trains were coming right through the front end of the trailer. I grew up hearing the sound of screeching brakes and the *badooom-pa-thump* rhythm of the railroad ties beating the ground like a drum, day in and day out. At night, lying in my bunk bed, tucked in and tired from playing all day outside, it was the rhythm of the passing trains that put me to sleep.

We had so much freedom in those days. I remember walking down Main Street when I was maybe eleven, wearing a fully loaded bandolier of 40/10 shotgun shells with my shotgun in hand, to go hunt grouse along the ridgeline above Botanie Valley Road—with only so much as a "Hey, Kev, where ya headed? Good hunting!" from the adults on the street.

The smells of the timber on a hot day. The crickets and the grasshoppers, the birds and coyotes across the river. The constant wind in the days and evenings and the weird stillness that would settle in at twilight. The familiar faces chatting on the street. The friendly waves to people as they drove along Main Street. The Christmas and May Day parades. The street dances with my uncle's band, Little Ritchie and the Fendermen, rocking the oldies. These are the memories of Lytton that I cherish.

The name *ltKumcheen* has been anglicized to Kumsheen, which is the name of a local rafting company and resort. It was also the name of the high school—a fact that was often made fun of by opposing high school sports teams. Our team mascot was a cougar; we were the Kumsheen Cougars. It was always funny until we kicked their asses. Lytton is a competitive town.

Is. Was. My family home was the dead centre of town. Across the street from Caboose Park, the swimming pool, the town hall, the Legion, the bank, the medical clinic, and a quick stagger to the Lytton Hotel and Buds and Suds pub. Lytton is about the size of a city block. The rez at the end of town makes it feel a bit bigger, but not by much.

Since the fire, the residents, the Lyttonites, are displaced. In hotels and at the homes of friends and family. Most residents are low-income earners or pensioners. Many have spent their entire lives in Lytton. Many are uninsured or underinsured. Some have moved on to other communities, too defeated or too heartbroken or too old to wait out the long rebuild ahead.

When you live on the rez, it's a different story. Even if you can afford it, it can be difficult to purchase homeowners' insurance on a house that is collectively owned. Insurance is purchased en masse for houses on reserve because land and the majority of the housing is collectively owned by the First Nation.

Since the fire, the Lytton First Nation has built a temporary tiny home village for those band members who lost their homes, in a field at the old St. George's Residential School property that we call the Battlefield. I was always told by my mother that the reason it's called the Battlefield is that we used to have epic battles with the Lil'wat there, on that field. I don't know if that's true, but everyone calls it the Battlefield. There are old pit houses there, remnants from a time long before there was a Lytton.

As Lyttonites, we've all been wounded, disappointed and lost. It is my sincere hope that this book will help to illuminate how special our little town is. That it will help inspire those who still carry its spirit in their hearts to rebuild and continue the story of Lytton. And now it is our honour to share with you this ancient little village off the side of the highway, in the heart of the canyon, at the Centre of the Universe.

Kevin Loring
September 2023

CHAPTER 1

CENTRE OF
THE UNIVERSE

Humalth

NLAKA'PAMUX TERM FOR "KEEP LIVING,"
AGREEMENT OR AFFIRMATIVE. USED FORMALLY AS A SALUTATION.

IN THE BEGINNING, at the end of the last ice age, there were the early Nlaka'pamux people.

As mastodons, mammoths, sabre-toothed cats and giant beaver were exiting the planet thousands of years ago, the first humans were appearing in North America, and some of them settled at the junction of two large rivers, the Ntekw Tekw (meaning, accurately enough, "muddy water") and qwu.mix, the Thompson.

These were the opening days of the longest continuous human settlement in North America. The early Nlaka'pamux community flourished long before the construction of the Great Pyramid of Giza in Egypt or the Great Wall of China, or the invention of the printing press. Jesus Christ, William Shakespeare and Albert Einstein were still far over the horizon. These first inhabitants called their village the Centre of the World.

Over millennia, fuelled by a seemingly never-ending supply of fish, especially salmon and trout, berry fields and root-digging grounds, the village at the eastern end of the Stein Valley became a vibrant community with its own economy, legal and social systems, and relationships with other long-standing Indigenous communities among the mountains at the continent's edge. This was a society with its own deeply held spiritual beliefs and creation stories, which tied people to the land, as well as systems for dealing with social issues, from child care to marriage.

The Nlaka'pamux lived in pit houses known as *sheestkns*, round subterranean houses that were dug into the ground and roofed with timbers that were then covered over with dirt and a large notched pole extending out of a central hole at the top of the mound, which was used as a chimney for the hearth. These dwellings were typical of the tribes throughout the central Interior. Sheestkns provided warmth and protection through the winter and much-needed cool in the summer. Construction of sheestkns also helped foster a sense of community, as neighbours worked together to build them and extended families lived within them. Larger communal pit houses gave people someplace to gather away from the valley's intense summer heat and to hold ceremonies away from the ferocious winter winds. Thousands of years after the earliest ones were dug into the Stein Valley soil, the mound-shaped homes were copied by prospectors drawn to the area by the nineteenth-century gold rush. Throughout the central Interior of modern British Columbia, all that remains of these village sites are the telltale bowl-like craters marking where the many pit houses once stood.

After archaeologists studied large burial grounds in the area, some fine stone carvings ended up in museums like the Royal Ethnographic Museum in Berlin. Dr. George M. Dawson studied the area in 1877 and 1888–90, and the things he found remained on the continent at least, in Montreal specifically, at the museum of the Geological Survey of Canada. Dr. Charles Hill-Tout of Vancouver, an archaeologist with the Jesup North Pacific Expedition, made a trip to the area in the summer of 1897, and north of the river junction, in a hill, he found remnants of an underground house that appeared to have been five hundred feet long and two hundred feet wide. Nearby were the remnants of hearths and more sheestkns. There had been a lot of people here, and their accomplishments weren't modest.

The Nlaka'pamux Nation extended to several places outside ltKumcheen. There was a village a kilometre south, in land later bisected by the CPR railway and now known as the Skuppa Reserve. A third community, called Nicomen, was established in a marshy area three kilometres north of present-day Lytton. Six kilometres north of the junction was a fourth community, overlooking Stein Creek, whose name translates roughly to "the hidden river." The remains of another village sit on the north side of the Stein, overlooking the point where the creek empties into the Fraser. Though there's little there today, it's easy to imagine that these villages were special places once. Because nowhere is more sacred in the Nlaka'pamux universe than the Stein Valley, which winds west through the mountains from this junction where the clean waters of the Stein Valley watershed flow into the silty Fraser. The Nlaka'pamux were raised to have reverence for things around them, from air to water and fire and the sun, moon and stars. Noted shookna.am, or shamans, created vibrant red ochre paintings of their visions and dreams on rocks in the valley, evoking supernatural forces. Medicine men trained there. Youth went there on vision quests, hoping to become warriors, hunters or healers. This was where the Coyote, the Trickster, is believed to have sent his son down to Earth. The Stein is like the womb of the Nlaka'pamux, just as ltKumcheen is the heart.

For the Nlaka'pamux, the land isn't an inanimate thing meant to be conquered. Animals and trees are fellow beings. Time isn't linear, as in Western culture. History is everywhere, blending the present with the past. Even verb tenses in the Nlaka'pamux language make the past the present. Pronouns don't distinguish gender, and the rain and mist are living things—the breath of ancestors.

Lawyer Darwin Hanna of the Nlaka'pamux Nation well knows the value of language. With Elder Mamie Henry, he compiled and edited a book called *Our Tellings*, a collection of local stories. His father, Herbert Hanna, was fluent in the Nlaka'pamux language, as were many of his relatives. Darwin Hanna notes that the Nlaka'pamux language has no word for goodbye. Instead, people say *humalth*, which translates to "keep living." There's also *palique*, which means "working together as one." Such words are essential to appreciating the Nlaka'pamux culture, as is the land. "How can you claim land when you don't have the language?" Hanna says. "How can you be a people without a language?"

The first documented visit by white people to ltKumcheen was led by fur trader Simon Fraser. He and his small band of explorers set foot at the junction of the Fraser and Thompson Rivers on Sunday, June 19, 1808. In his journal, Fraser speaks of the hospitality he received when he arrived with two clerks, sixteen voyageurs and two Indigenous guides. Some twelve hundred Nlaka'pamux men and women were gathered at the junction to see Fraser that day. "I had to shake hands with all of them," Fraser grumbled. It was a friendly visit. Fraser spurned a feast of boiled fish offered by the Nlaka'pamux. Instead, his men chose to chow down on six of the local dogs, much to the shock of the hosts.

Fraser could see he had arrived at the capital of the local Nation, and that the Nlaka'pamux had already made contact with Europeans. "Seeing the Indians in possession of white traders' goods, Fraser realized that he had encountered the ancient line of communication that, for centuries, had followed the river from the seas," author Bruce Hutchison writes in *The Fraser*. "The Thompson Indians called their village Camchin,* the largest center of habitation in the interior," he continues. "Fraser regarded its people as more enlightened than any he had met farther north and he consulted with them at length about the route ahead. As usual, he was told that it was impassable by water and this time, though he did not believe it, the Indians spoke the truth."

The Chief invited Fraser to dine with him in his lodge and instructed a band member to tell the explorer what to expect downriver. "One of the old men, a very talkative fellow, and we understood a great warrior, had been to the sea: saw great canoes and white men there," Fraser noted in his field journal. The Elder confirmed Fraser's suspicion that, although he was the first white explorer in ltKumcheen, the Nlaka'pamux had themselves passed over some forbidding terrain to travel far from their lands.

Fraser was a newcomer to this land, but he was no stranger to difficult times and adventure. His family had escaped a tough economy and hostile government to move from Scotland to America three years before his birth, in 1776 in Mapletown, New York. His father, Simon Fraser Sr., had joined British forces during the American Revolution and was captured at the Battle of Bennington. He died a prisoner of war in the Albany, New York, jail.

His widow fled north after she was harassed by the victorious Americans. Young Simon settled in Montreal in 1790 to live with his uncle, a judge. Two years later, he became an apprentice with the North West Company, and in 1793 he was sent, as a teenager, to isolated outposts in Athabasca to learn his trade. By his mid-twenties he was a

---

* Alternative spelling of ltKumcheen.

Hudson's Bay Company partner, and his task soon became the expansion of the company's fortunes west of the Rockies. At age thirty-two, he set out to find a transportation route to the Pacific. His arrival in ltKumcheen had been prophesied by a local Elder.

The story of that prediction and Fraser's arrival was later recounted by Wa'xtko, a woman from Spences Bridge, about thirty-five kilometres up the Thompson River to the northeast. She heard the story from others, as she was born around 1830. In her account, she uses the ripeness of berries to gauge what time of year it was:

> When Kw-tina-u came to Lytton, Tcexe'x was Chief of the Spences Bridge band. He was a prominent Chief and a great orator. He had one eye. He never practised as a shaman, but was more powerful than most shamans. I am directly descended from him. He had a large family, and was an elderly man at the time when these whites came to Lytton. It was in midsummer. The berries were just ripe in the river-valley; and many of the tribe were assembled at Botany, digging roots and playing games. Some Thompson men, who had been up at La Fontaine on horseback, came back quickly with the news of the approach of these people. Tcexe'x was at Botany* with others from Spences Bridge. He hurried down to Lytton, and was there when the whites arrived. The Chief of the latter we called "Sun." We did not know his name. Several Chiefs made speeches to him, but Tcexe'x made the greatest speech. His speech so pleased Sun, that he gave him a present of a large silver brooch, or some other ornament, which he had on his person. On special occasions Tcexe'x used this attached to his hair in front,

---

* The Botanie Valley (and Botanie Creek, which runs through it) comes south to intersect with the Thompson River about two kilometres upriver from Lytton, to the east of town.

or on the front of his head. When I was a girl, I saw it worn by his sons. One of his sons inherited it; on his death, his brother obtained it; and it was probably buried with the third brother who had it, as it disappeared about the time of his death. The last-named died at Lytton as an elderly man, and his body was buried on the north side of the Thompson River at Drynoch, about seven miles below Spences Bridge.

When Fraser's men paddled away, they had left an iron axe behind by mistake. A local boy chased them down and returned it.

Fraser moved on, but before he got too far, he had to find his way through Hells Gate. It wasn't called that yet. Fraser's reaction to traversing the Nlaka'pamux route south is the reason this dangerous stretch of the Fraser River got that name. A Chief recalled by Fraser only as "Little Fellow" guided them south to the treacherous canyon, over the cliffs and down a spiderweb of ladders to get past the inpassable rapids. Fraser wrote in his journal that "no man should ever pass through here it was truly like passing through the Gates of Hell!"

Delivered safely, he and his men spent the night in Spuzzum, in all about seventy kilometres downriver from ltKumcheen. "We had to pass where no human being should venture," Fraser recalled of his cliffside adventure. He marvelled at how comfortably the Nlaka'pamux had navigated the ladders suspended over the precipice: "But we, who had not the advantages of their experience, were often in imminent danger, when obliged to follow their example."

Fraser left the area feeling good about the Nlaka'pamux people. That wasn't surprising for anyone familiar with the community. Nlaka'pamux culture stresses hospitality to visitors, with the assumption that the visitors will eventually leave.

CHAPTER 2

GOLD FEVER

. . . he was quaffing from the stream when he perceived a shining pebble which he picked up and it proved to be gold.

BC GOVERNOR JAMES DOUGLAS

THERE WERE GRAND PLANS in 1857 to set up a Hudson's Bay Company post five kilometres downstream from ltKumcheen and call it Fort Dallas. The fort was to be named after Hudson's Bay Company agent Alexander Grant Dallas, son-in-law of Governor James Douglas of Vancouver Island. Establishment of the inland fort would mean the HBC could restrict access to the valleys around ltKumcheen by outsiders, which was ironic since the agents of the HBC weren't exactly locals themselves.

Then somebody found gold. Suddenly, no one cared about fur trading and forts. A mad rush of newcomers followed, and they cared even less than the colonial agents about asking permission from the Nlaka'pamux to be there. Soon, things got ugly enough that the future country of Canada nearly didn't happen.

The Nlaka'pamux already knew about gold in the area. They'd found some of it around 1855 near the Nicomen River, a tributary that meets the Thompson about fifteen kilometres upstream from where the Thompson joins the Fraser,* and they had taken the sample to Hudson's Bay Company chief trader Donald McLean in Kamloops. McLean was startled by the ore and rode out to inspect the source for himself. He then wrote to Roderick Finlayson, chief factor at Fort Victoria: "They [the Nlaka'pamux] pick it out with knives, or . . . use their fingers for that purpose." McLean asked for "iron spoons to be used by the Indians for the purpose of extricating the nuggets from the crevices in the rocky beds of the creeks."

Excitement ramped up after a huge nugget was found on the Thompson River, downriver from the Nicomen River. "Gold was first found on Thompson's River by an Indian ¼ of a mile below Niconim [*sic*]," Governor Douglas wrote in his diary. "He is since dead. The Indian was taking a drink out of the river. Having no vessel he was quaffing from the stream when he perceived a shining pebble which he picked up and it proved to be gold. The whole tribe forthwith began to collect the glittering metal."

The mysterious discoverer of the shining pebble was never identified, nor were the circumstances of his death. Nonetheless, excitement percolated through 1857 amongst the newcomers. "We had just now received very favourable accounts from Thompson's River," Douglas wrote. "About 209 ounces of gold have been traded from the Indians since the sixth of last October. I am forming a transport corps for the purpose of pouring supplies into the interior by Fraser River . . . and we shall probably form a depot at the junction of Thompson's River with Fraser's River."

---

* Simon Fraser accidentally named Hells Gate, but the renaming of the whole river—Ntekw Tekw—after him was entirely on purpose.

Soon, frenzied headlines screamed across US publications. One California article claimed that, on just one spot of the Thompson River, "the gold was lying as thick as pebbles on the bottom of the stream, and they could have dipped it up in a thin cup, had not the Indians objected." Those stories hit just as the California rush of 1848–49 was fading into memory. Some 400 California miners rushed north into Fort Victoria on April 25, 1858, ready to head up the Fraser Canyon. They were joined by some 10,000 more American miners between May and June. Their ranks hit 25,000 by the fall of 1858 and an estimated 50,000 by 1859. Most were of white European background, but there were also Hawaiians, African Americans and Chinese. Many of the gold seekers brought handguns to ltKumcheen, along with American notions of frontier justice.

Sir James Douglas feared the ultra-aggressive newcomers would push the American government to annex the mainland of what had just formally become the colony of British Columbia. He also recognized that the stampede of Americans was unstoppable. Douglas wrote to British prime minister Edward Stanley on May 19, 1858: "I am now convinced that it is utterly impossible, through any means within our power, to close the gold districts against the entrance of foreigners, as long as gold is found in abundance, in which case the country will soon be over-run."

Up to this point, the opening of the Canadian West to non-Natives had been far more orderly than the bloody free-for-all to the south. White law had generally arrived in the north in the form of massive British trading companies. Douglas himself was a product of that system. The trading companies needed co-operation with Indigenous peoples for furs and survival, while the American push west had led to centuries of disastrous Indian wars, still raging by the late 1850s. The gold discovery near ltKumcheen marked a change in the British colonies, though. Indigenous co-operation wasn't needed for gold mining.

The gold rush jeopardized the Nlaka'pamux salmon fishery, which was central to their economy and diet. Waters were diverted and muddied as miners washed gravel through mining sluices. It seemed just a matter of time before tensions turned to bloodshed. "It will require I fear the nicest tact to avoid a disastrous Indian war," Douglas had written to London on June 15, presaging the arrival in the Interior of the violence that marked the American West.

Fishing sites were particularly vital during the late summer salmon run, and by August disruptions to the rivers were escalating tensions. The summer had already been a lean one for salmon, and the added pressure put on the salmon run by the hungry gold miners risked making for an even leaner winter. In an attempt to put a British stamp on the area, the Crown Colony of British Columbia was established on August 2, 1858, effectively underlining the fact that Douglas, its first governor, considered the Fraser Canyon* area to be British soil. The name Lytton was chosen by Douglas for the settlement at the junction of the Fraser and Thompson Rivers, as a "merited compliment and mark of respect" for his boss, Sir Edward George Earle Bulwer-Lytton, Secretary of State for the Colonies.

The newly arrived Americans had been calling ltKumcheen "The Forks," "Great Forks" and "Grand Forks," in apparent reference to the coming together of the Thompson and Fraser Rivers. That they called it after the geography and not by its actual name says a lot about their

---

* Where the south-flowing Fraser River cuts deep into the mountainous BC Interior, from just north of Lytton to the Lower Mainland of BC, is known as the Fraser Canyon.

attitude towards whoever else thought they were in charge. This place that had been the centre of the Nlaka'pamux universe for millennia was changing, much too quickly for the liking of Chief Cexpen'nthlEm.*

Cexpen'nthlEm was at the peak of his influence in 1858. He was an impressive man who carried himself as someone born to lead, which was in fact the case, as his father and grandfather were Chiefs before him. Their influence extended to the neighbouring Lillooet, Shuswap and Okanagan areas, where they were treated with deference in Indigenous communities. As a young man, he had led war parties against other Indigenous groups, and even against his mother's people from the Lillooet area. He had several wives and hundreds of horses, as befitted a man of his status. He had become Chief of the Nlaka'pamux in 1850, and brought massive Potlatch celebrations to the ltKumcheen area. He held them every three or four years, displaying and sharing his wealth by giving gifts like blankets, dried salmon and deer hides to everyone who attended. The Chief made it clear that "Lytton" was at the centre of the land of his family and people. He wasn't about to let it be overrun.

Meanwhile, the new gold miners were increasingly uneasy. The reality of the Fraser Canyon seldom matched up to the frenzied headlines and the stories of gold lying as thick as pebbles on the bottom of streams. Many of the newcomers were already struggling, as reflected by the name for a spot near neighbouring Lillooet: "Horse-beef Bar."

* Also called Sexpinlhemx, Cexpen'nthlEm, Cixpen'ntlam, Shigh-pentlam and David Spintlum.

CHAPTER 3

CANYON WAR

Every one of the White men had loaded rifles,
ready to shoot the people of Lytton.

NLAKA'PAMUX ELDER MARY WILLIAMS

FORT YALE, AT THE FOOT of the Fraser Canyon, had become a suburb
of San Francisco by the summer of 1858. Thousands of gold-hungry
foreigners from all over the world poured into the Fraser Canyon, most
of them via steam-powered paddlewheelers chugging their way up the
Pacific coast from northern California. Governor Douglas didn't have
much of a military force at hand, but he did have the only navy on the
Pacific coast, in the form of two gunboats. He had previously used them
to levy a landing tax on anyone coming into the mainland, despite not
actually having the authority to do so.

Far upstream, in Lytton, tensions between the camps of miners
and the Nlaka'pamux trying to fish on the rivers grew heated. Things
exploded after two Nlaka'pamux women were sexually assaulted by a
group of French miners below the village of Spuzzum, downriver from
Lytton. A Hudson's Bay Company official delicately called it "insulting
there [*sic*] women." Some Nlaka'pamux from Spuzzum struck back,

killing two French miners, cutting up their bodies and dumping them into the Fraser. Their body parts were found swirling in the Fraser near Yale, a warning to other newcomers that was impossible to ignore.

Roughly four dozen American miners grabbed their rifles and headed up the Fraser towards Lytton. Jason Allard, the son of an HBC trader at Fort Yale, wrote that "troops started for vengeance, in military formation, the stars and stripes at their head." It was a head-snapper to see Americans so up in arms over violence to the French. However, they were all white and it was a convenient excuse to attack the Nlaka'pamux.

Vigilantes burned the village of Spuzzum to the ground and hanged several of the Chiefs, wounding and killing an untold number of Nlaka'pamux. Survivors of the raid retreated upriver to Lytton.

At Yale, various militias formed. One group of American miners was called the New York Pike Guards and led by Captain Henry M. Snyder, a miner and newspaper correspondent for the *San Francisco Evening Bulletin*. Snyder made an alliance with an Austrian mercenary named Captain Rouse and his heavily armed men. On August 17, 1858, Snyder led his men up the Fraser River towards Kumsheen to settle things with the Nlaka'pamux, "by peaceable means if we could, and by force if we must."

Another militia wanted to take an even more aggressive approach than Snyder. An American miner referred to as Captain Graham wanted to kill "every [Nlaka'pamux] man, woman and child they saw." He was the leader of a militia made up mostly of Southerners called the Whatcom Company, named for a trail in the northwest United States.

As the New York Pike Guard and the Whatcom Company were headed out to engage the Nlaka'pamux, they met each other on the trail just outside Fort Yale and fell into a heated argument about their intentions. This led to a skirmish between the two heavily armed militias, with Snyder's men beating back Graham's Whatcom Company. Graham and his men weren't deterred, and they continued upriver on the opposite side of the canyon.

Lytton was their destination, and it served as the centre of resistance for the Nlaka'pamux Nation, which was then allied with the Secwepemc (Shuswap), Sylix (Okanagan) and other Nations. Some thought it was time to take a stand and go to war against the miners, noting recent unprovoked attacks, including the murders of several Indigenous people by Okanagan Lake miners just a few months earlier. The Nlaka'pamux war chief Cuxcux'elt (*Shook-shook-elt*) Grizzly Paw wanted to wipe out the miners, while Chief Cexpen'nthlEm still held out hope of peaceful coexistence.

On August 22, 1858, thousands of warriors were waiting in the mountains nearby as Snyder approached the Nlaka'pamux war council. He was met by Chief Cexpen'nthlEm and eleven other Chiefs at Lytton. Snyder must not have known the size of the assembled forces ready to fight, because history suggests the conversation didn't go well.

Governor Douglas was racing from Victoria to try to quell the violence, but he wasn't needed. The war was largely over by the end of the month, when Douglas arrived in the Fraser Canyon with thirty-five armed men, "in hopes that early measures will be taken by Her Majesty's Government, to relieve the country from its present perilous state." He planted a British flag on the riverbank outside Fort Yale and announced that the mainland was now a colony of the British Empire, without having established treaties with any of the tribes there and without any authority from England to do so.

Snyder had hastily fastened a white flag to a stick to signify that a peace accord had been reached. It was sent down the canyon to alert the other miners that peace was at hand. Graham wasn't ready to stop the aggression, however. Upon being met by the flag-bearers, he tossed the flag to the ground and trampled on it. Then he had the men who carried it beaten and tied up.

That night, there was a mysterious exchange of gunfire within the Whatcom Company that didn't involve the Nlaka'pamux. A credible theory is that a loaded rifle accidentally fell over, having been propped against a tree, and discharged, sending the camp into a panic. They apparently shot at each other, thinking they were under attack. Curiously, both Graham and his lieutenant were shot dead in the confusion, effectively decapitating the leadership of the Whatcom Company. Their men disbanded in sheer terror in the pitch black of night, with some running off cliffs to their deaths. Another theory is that the leadership was assassinated, which also would have decapitated the maurading militia and immediately prevented further conflict in the canyon.

In less than a month, an estimated thirty-six Nlaka'pamux, including five Chiefs, were killed by the miners. Many others were wounded and three Nlaka'pamux were taken as prisoners. Exact numbers are impossible to determine, but it was known that Nlaka'pamux villages were burned to the ground and some individuals were shot while fishing alone. The Americans reported that thirty-six of their men were killed that August, including several accidentally shot by their fellow miners and militia.

Chief Cexpen'nthlEm said that Nlaka'pamux territory was defined by four posts:

At Lytton is my centrepost. It is the middle of my house, and I sit there.
All the country to the headquarters of all the streams running into the
valleys between these posts is also our territory in which my children
gather food. We extend to meet the boundaries of the hunting

territories of other tribes all around this country I have spoken of, I
have jurisdiction. I know no white man's boundaries or posts. If the
whites have put up posts and divided my territory, I do not recognize
them. They have not consulted me. They have broken my house
without my consent. All Indian tribes have the same as posts and
recognize boundaries, and the chiefs know them since long before
the first whites came to the country.

Through it all, back in London, Sir Edward Lytton was oblivious
to the state of hostilities in his namesake community. In 1858, it took
about six months for a letter to go from Fort Victoria to London. He
didn't realize until long after the final shots had been fired that British
authority in the Fraser Canyon could easily have been lost to the
Americans, if not for the Nlaka'pamux.

In all its years of existence, tiny Lytton never lacked in ambition, which
made it a source of curiosity in the centres of power. That's reflected in
the media of the time, including these words from the *Victoria Gazette*,
published May 14, 1859:

LYTTON "CITY"

The "City" of Lytton is beautifully situated on a high plane of green
sward, as level and smooth as a carpeted floor. There are four fine
plateau before reaching the foot-hills, which here are much lower and
more open than further down the river. The town numbers twenty-six
houses, built mostly of logs, one or two being nicely furnished. The
Government House, which has been erected for the reception and

occupation of His Excellency Gov. Moody,* who is expected to visit this point soon is a substantial building, 51 by 22 feet, and 14 in the clear high, made of sawed and planed logs, eight inches thick, at a cost of $2,500, and is an ornament to the place [but in our opinion an extravagant and unnecessary outlay. EDS GAZETTE]. Just above the level on which the town is located, Thompson River empties its clear cold flood into the murky Fraser, presenting a singular contrast as the two streams flow side by side along the front of the town. The street (There being but one at present) is laid out North and South, wide, and I think eventually will become a thorough business street, as residences are built for families, of which there are several, away from the traders on the nice grass plot. Most of the heavy stock of goods . . . [is] packed on mules, and they must be replenished by mule trains from below almost immediately.

The war now years behind him, on May 29, 1861, Governor Douglas set out on horseback to explore the village he had renamed before see-ing it. It would take ambition for the governor just to get there. "His impressions, set down in his diary, indicate the dimensions of the task he had set himself—the construction of a road where the Indians had crawled for centuries on their dizzy ladders, where even now a mule traveled with difficulty and danger," George Hutchison wrote in *The Fraser*. Douglas reached Lytton two days later.

The little community was a source of fascination but also ridicule. In years to come, the butt of many jokes was its namesake, Bulwer-Lytton,

---

* Richard Clement Moody became the first lieutenant-governor of BC on Christmas Day, 1858. He and Douglas promptly began feuding, as their powers overlapped. Douglas, who had more real power, wasn't as endearing to British high society, as he was of mixed race and a merchant.

and his enthusiastic writing style. Bulwer-Lytton's contributions to
literature include coining the phrases "the pen is mightier than the
sword," "the almighty dollar" and "a wrinkle in time." Bulwer-Lytton is
best known in literature, however, for the beginning to his 1830 novel
Paul Clifford. The story opens with these words:

> It was a dark and stormy night; the rain fell in torrents—except at
> occasional intervals, when it was checked by a violent gust of wind
> which swept up the streets (for it is in London that our scene lies),
> rattling along the housetops, and fiercely agitating the scanty flame
> of the lamps that struggled against the darkness.

That passage literally dogged Bulwer-Lytton. A century later, the beagle
Snoopy from Charles Schultz's *Peanuts* cartoon strip, when struck with
writer's block, would sit on his doghouse and type "It was a dark and
stormy night" repeatedly. Lytton's connections to the world of literature
weren't its source of pride.

Back in the fall of 1866, mockery followed the short-lived and ultimately futile attempt to have Lytton named the capital of the newly
amalgamated colonies of British Columbia. Victoria would win out
over New Westminster, but not before Lytton village officials put up a
fight. Their ambitions annoyed the editorial board of the *Victoria
Colonist*, which huffed on October 13, 1866:

> The argument that can be advanced in favor of Lytton as the capital, is
> that its location is central. In every other respect, there is not a hamlet
> on the Lower Fraser that does not possess advantages superior to those
> it has to offer. For nearly four months of the year the town is almost
> unapproachable from the lower country, and until a railroad has taken
> the place of the wagon road, and the iron horse has superseded the

patient pack animal, it is folly to imagine that the prayer has any chance of success, besides, supposing that Lytton be an excellent location for the capital, there are no government buildings for the accommodation of the officials, and the financial state of the country is such that it cannot afford to erect the necessary buildings.

As the push to make Lytton the colony's capital fizzled, problems continued with the community's name. Colonel R.C. Moody, the first lieutenant-governor of British Columbia, wrote a friend in 1869 that he just wasn't comfortable with Douglas's rebranding of the town:

> It will require much perseverance and determination on our parts
> to prevent "Lytton" becoming fixed at "Lyttonville" or "Lytton City."
> The latter is not bad, if it was not so intensely American. The Governor
> has given the name to a town which will become very important at the
> junction of the Thompson & the Fraser. The first large bold mountain
> to which it will apply well I shall call "Mount Bulwer." Bulwer is a good
> sounding name for a Mountain. Lytton would be appropriate to a
> River, the Lytton . . .
>   I shall do all I can to persuade the Governor to consent to the
> Thompson River being called the Lytton & give Mr. Thompson
> something else. It is not too late.

The Thompson River is still the Thompson. The town name of Lytton stuck, despite Moody's discomfort. For all the ridicule the name invited, someone named a mountain to the southeast Lytton as well. Never underestimate Lytton.

CHAPTER 4

WATKINSONS ARRIVE

I must tell you I can't keep it any longer I love you.

WILLIAM KANE OPENS HIS HEART TO SUSAN WATKINSON

FREDERICK JOSEPH (JOE) WATKINSON had little hope of advancement, let alone a comfortable life, if he continued to live in what his great-grandson Tommy Watkinson later called "the ancient and perpetually poor town" of Lostwithiel, Cornwall, in southwestern England.

Joe was born there in 1835, the fourth of seven children. By his early twenties, everyone in Cornwall seemed to be looking for a way out. Joe's older brother, William John Watkinson, and his family immigrated to Strathroy, Ontario, while two of his younger brothers, Thomas and Philip, went to Australia.

Joe Watkinson was equally adventuresome. He braved the oceans to sail for San Francisco, then caught a steamboat to Victoria, BC, arriving in early 1858. From Victoria, Joe headed to the Yale area at the mouth of the Fraser River, where he fell in with a small group of men from Cornwall who shared his dreams of finding gold on the Fraser Canyon riverbeds. Along the way, he befriended members of the Nlaka'pamux and Secwepemc.

Joe Watkinson arrived just as the Canyon War was about to explode. He wisely exercised caution. He didn't want to be mistaken for one of the aggressive Americans flooding the Hill Bar area, south of Yale. The Americans seemed to think they could act the same way they did in California, which often meant killing Indigenous people like animals. They had little respect for other miners either.

The winter of 1858 was particularly harsh. The Fraser River was covered with ice, blocking steamboats from delivering supplies. Joe and his associates huddled in newly built cabins and canvas tents. Icebound in this strange new land, some miners tried to walk up the frozen river to Hope to get supplies, only to fall through the ice and die. Their gold was strapped to them in "pokes," or small leather bags, which only dragged them down, quickening their deaths. Others were blinded by snow and walked in circles until they collapsed and died.

Joe Watkinson survived to mine the Fraser Canyon near Yale until the late spring of 1860. Then he and seven other miners walked upriver to Lytton, arriving on June 1, 1860. From there, it was on to Lillooet by foot, north along the Fraser Canyon.

Life remained tough for Joe and his fellow Fraser Canyon miners. The mining bars at Lytton were largely picked over by the fall of 1860, and the climate was merciless. There was, however, alcohol. Halifax-born newspaperman David W. Higgins was among the people rushing into the area, after trying his luck in the California gold rush. He called his liquor "oh! be-joyful" and only ventured north from Hope once, writing:

The cold grew sharper and the wind fiercer. We were fairly well wrapped in woollens. There was one fur coat in the party, and the wearer of it, young Talbot, who was not at all robust, seemed to feel the cold more keenly than the other three. Several times he paused

as if unable to go on, but we rallied him and chafed him and coaxed
him, until he was glad to proceed.

Joe Watkinson's get-rich dreams of striking gold cooled as he realized there was also a living to be made providing goods and services
to fellow miners. Joe soon became a model of adaptability and resilience, making him the sort of settler who could reasonably expect to
found a family in the area without any roots of his own. He and partners Richard Harris and Richard Hoey built the first flour mill in the
Lytton–Lillooet area, near where Cayoosh Creek leaves Seaton Lake.
Watkinson and Harris also dug a ten-kilometre ditch from Fountain
Creek to the flats at Parsonville, on the banks of the Fraser River opposite Lillooet. Miners needed plenty of water to sift for gold, and they
were soon in business.

Joe Watkinson also recognized that the land had agricultural
potential, if they could just add some water. So did Arthur Bushley,
county clerk for Justice Matthew Baillie Begbie, BC's first chief justice.
On April 5, 1859, Bushley travelled from Lytton to nearby Fountain
Flat and wrote in his diary: "The scenery along is very fine and we
passed a good many agricultural patches of land—rolled a tree down
and put it to fire. We passed Foster Bar [*sic*] and struck away from the
Fraser River."

Joe Watkinson's business partner Richard Harris meant more to him
than simply friendship and money-making opportunities; he eventually became family. Harris had brought his adopted teenaged daughter
with him to BC. Catherine Lewis Harris was said to be the child of an
Indigenous Chief from Walla Walla, near Spokane, Washington. Joe
was roughly seventeen years older than Catherine, which made him
about twice her age. They married and moved to Foster's Bar, between
Lytton and Lillooet. Joe and Catherine lived in a tent for more than

a year before they completed their six-bedroom, two-storey log house in 1865. Catherine gave birth to their first child, Susan, there on August 24, 1866, setting off an exhausting string of childbirths.

There was plenty of travel up and down the canyon while they worked to turn their new home into a travellers' destination. The dream of striking gold had long passed, but by 1866 the Barnard's Express (BX) stagecoach was bringing passengers to enjoy the Watkinsons' hospitality and using their home as a spot to refresh their teams of horses. The latter meant an opening for the Watkinsons to provide blacksmithing and stable services. Stagecoach horses at the time were bred for speed, not endurance. Teams had to be changed, on average, every twenty-nine kilometres to keep the coaches moving quickly.

The Watkinson ranch became known as 24 Mile because it was about twenty-four miles (thirty-nine kilometres) from both Lillooet and Lytton. Joe's great-grandson, Tommy, later wrote in a family history:

> The standard rate for a meal or a bed was fifty cents and the food was outstanding. Nearly every dish was produced on the ranch since the nearest store was either Lytton or Lillooet and both towns were about 24 miles away. Large gardens supplied fresh vegetables and root cellars provided a year-round supply of root crops and canned goods. Milk cows supplied fresh milk and cream. Beef, pork, chicken and duck were all from the farm. Breakfasts included oatmeal porridge and a jug of fresh milk. All meals included steaks, fried potatoes, vegetables, and eggs. Sometimes, there was fresh-baked bread and pies too . . . During very cold weather, guests were brought a pre-breakfast hot toddy to warm their insides.

The area was opening up to outsiders. Below the new Watkinson ranch, on the Fraser River, steamboats and barges carried supplies. Oxen and horses pulled freight wagons up the steep climb from the river to the road. Soon, Joe was making enough money to hire help for chores such as irrigating and harvesting crops and looking after animals.

Catherine was still a teenager when their second child, Frederick Watkinson, was born on January 1, 1868. For most of her adult life, Catherine seemed to be giving birth or recovering from giving birth or getting pregnant again. By 1884, when she was just in her mid-thirties, she had eleven children, ranging from an eighteen-year-old to a newborn. The couple's older boys helped with the animals and in the fields. Their older girls worked in the kitchen, tended the gardens and looked after the younger children. They also waited upon the guests, some of whom were primly dressed young ladies on their way to take up teaching positions in one-room schools. Others were young men looking for adventure.

Guests at 24 Mile had a chance to relax, soaking in the gorgeous sunsets on the west-facing porch in the evenings. The older Watkinson girls, Alice, Elizabeth and Emily, served up generous slices of freshly baked pies—cherry, peach or apple, depending on the season. There was also hot coffee or tea as the guests were refreshed, renewed and reinvigorated in the crisp, clear air of the evening.

Joe Watkinson hadn't struck gold, but he had survived, and that was a victory in itself. The Fraser River's current helped the early Watkinsons ship their produce downriver to Lytton. A century later, there were still traces of the trail used by "pullers" on the riverbank, Lorraine Harris writes in her local history, *Halfway to the Goldfields.* "In some places, mules or horses were attached to lines which hauled the boat against the current; in other areas, Chinese were hired to pull the lines," she writes.

The Watkinsons' first-born child, Susan, grew up to become a local beauty with dark, curly hair. She was especially stunning in the eyes of Billy Kane, who lived on a neighbouring ranch on the Lillooet–Lytton road. Billy was the son of Captain James Kane, an Irishman who arrived on the coast in 1860 after an extraordinary trek across the Atlantic, around Cape Horn and north from the southern end of Chile. In BC, Captain Kane bought a vessel, the *Scuddy*, to move freight upriver from New Westminster to Yale. Business was brisk. Yale boosters boasted that the settlement had suddenly become the biggest city west of Chicago and north of San Francisco, with a tent city, boarding houses, plenty of newly created saloons and just one magistrate.

In Yale, Captain Kane met an Indigenous woman named Christine. They soon married, and in September 1863 Christine gave birth to Billy. When Billy was two years old, his father moved north alone, drawn by the feverish excitement of the gold rush. The plan was for James to get rich and return home, but that never happened. In time, Christine heard that James Kane did indeed strike gold and then was murdered for his new-found fortune. "This news was never substantiated, and his grieving wife waited three years for him to return," Lorraine Harris writes.

Billy was five years old in 1868 when his mother finally stopped waiting for her man to come back and married a freighter named Richley, who ran his business with a string of mules. Richley needed pasture for his animals and bought ranchland close to the Watkinsons' place; it became known as Pine Grove Ranch or 14 Mile. Billy was fourteen when he moved to his stepfather's ranch.

At eighteen, Billy struck out on his own, buying nearby 20 Mile Ranch and building a sturdy log house. He was already smitten with his neighbour Susan Watkinson, who was three years his junior, and was sending her letters and poems. One letter included a silk handkerchief and these words:

> *I don't know what you will think of me, but I must tell you I can't keep it any longer I love you . . . if you only knew how dearly I love you.*

I am sure you would . . . we are made to get married why should not get married, I never would think of no one else but you, and you are the first one and the only one.

Signed
Yours respectfully
Wm Kane

It wasn't Shakespeare, but it worked. Billy Kane and Susan Watkinson were married in 1882 at the Watkinson home, when Billy was nineteen and Susan sixteen. Harris notes that Susan worked hard to make her wedding a success:

Susan made her own wedding dress of rust-coloured embroidered silk.
The hand-made buttonholes on this elegant dress are a work of art,
a fact her granddaughter can attest to, for she has worn it on many
special occasions. Because of her skill at sewing, Susan never discarded
an article of clothing. Even clothes given to her for use in quilt-making
were more often returned to the owner beautifully mended. Susan Kane
washed, carded, and spun all the wool from their sheep, and when in
later years she could no longer handle her spinning wheel, she continued
to card and spin wool by hand onto a stick spindle. Although money was
not a plentiful commodity, she kept her daughter beautifully dressed,
and knit all the socks and sweaters for her husband and seven sons.

Billy thrived in their union. He was constantly looking out for equine stock, and his string of horses grew in value. One set the Canadian record for the half-mile, and Billy raced his stock in competitions large and small across the country, even on the streets of tiny Lillooet and Lytton. His horses usually won.

Joe and Catherine's tenth child—and sixth daughter—was Jane, who was born November 22, 1882. Jane and her husband, Antonio Cenname, operated an apple orchard and owned and ran a motel/service station at Gladwin, ten kilometres east of Lytton. Their son Carmen, the second-oldest of their six children, died at age eleven when a tree branch he was playing on broke, dropping him into the swift-moving Thompson River.

For settlers trying to make a go of it in and around Lytton, the Fraser Canyon was tough terrain. And its developing economy was hardly predictable. The stream of guests to 24 Mile House began to decline in 1887, as travellers now had the choice to take the newly built Canadian Pacific Railway into the Interior. Fire was a constant threat, too. The dry, dusty environment aside, many of the stopping houses in the BC Interior were destroyed in fires caused by faulty chimneys and overturned oil lamps. The Watkinsons' log home at 24 Mile House burned to the ground in the spring of 1912. The ranch house was rebuilt, but the stagecoaches no longer stopped there, ending a glorious forty-six-year run.

The farm and its surrounding area were the entire universe to the Watkinson children in the late nineteenth century. Susan's sister Lilia was born on the ranch and baptized at St. Paul's Church in Lytton, just behind the future Edwards family home. Lilia lived and died at the family ranch, passing away at age fifteen. Then she became the first person to be buried in the family graveyard on the ranch, overlooking the Fraser River.

Joe died on January 29, 1914, at the ranch, and was buried under the largest headstone in the family cemetery. His wife, Catherine, died January 23, 1920, at the age of seventy-one and was buried next to him. Joe was on the ranch for fifty years, while it was Catherine's home for fifty-six years.

Joe and Catherine's second child, Frederick R. Watkinson, had been married at the ranch in 1895 to Lucy Roberts, from the neighbouring McGillary Ranch, which eventually became known as the Halfway Ranch.

Frederick was twenty-seven and Lucy fifteen when they married, settling on the farm where he was born.

Billy and Susan Kane remained on their neighbouring ranch on the Lillooet–Lytton road for life. There was no price to put on a home, which was just as well. Billy Kane sometimes told of how his stepfather offered to sell his ranch at 18 Mile to his brother-in-law, Fred Watkinson, for four dollars, which was the outstanding amount of taxes owed on the property. "Fred's answer was: 'I wouldn't give my hat for it!'" Harris reported.

Fred and Lucy had fifteen children, including one who was stillborn. All were born on the ranch. One of those Watkinson children was Thomas, born on October 13, 1914. He was the father of co-author Peter's childhood friends Tommy and Harvey Watkinson.

> We didn't have summer camps back then. Not that our
> parents didn't fantasize about even a few hours of quiet
> in a house full of four furniture-breaking, constantly
> chattering kids. In Lytton, the idea of cottages and getting
> away seemed oddly exotic and a bit redundant.
>
> And where would we go to get away from Lytton?
> We already were away. Where would we go to unwind
> when we already lived in a community with no traffic
> lights, elevators or escalators? Boston Bar? Spences
> Bridge? Spuzzum?
>
> There was, however, the Watkinson ranch. The high
> point of my summers was to go and play cowboy there
> for a week or so. It was probably the high point of my poor
> mother's summer too, although she had the good grace
> not to say so. Whenever she saw the Watkinsons, however,
> she looked particularly grateful and awestruck, the way
> a person must look when encountering a saint.

My big brothers Dave and Jim were the Edwards kids
who were really invited to the ranch, but I was allowed to
tag along. Perhaps I was thrown into the deal as a break
for my mother. Whatever the case, I got a serious pair of
cowboy boots so I would blend in.

Peter Edwards

Locals farmers like the Watkinsons propped up Lytton with their
business but remained distinct. The Watkinsons clearly considered
themselves farm people who felt on display when venturing into town.

There was a sense of excitement as they shined their shoes
and boots for a trip into town. Their clothes were neatly
ironed, even though it was a skill and no small job to
use an iron made of cast iron, heated on the stove. Once,
their father wouldn't come into our house because he was
embarrassed to be wearing high-top canvas running shoes.
He remained in the car and spoke to my parents through
the car window.

Peter Edwards

As you can see, it's hard to tell the story of Lytton without jumping
ahead to the time when we were growing up there. It's hard to think of
the landscape of our youths being just ashes now, though hopefully to
be rebuilt again. We've skipped a few things and jumped ahead. You
can't blame us. You would want to be back there too, if you'd known it
the way we did.

CHAPTER 5

THE HARANGUING JUDGE

Was the wretched place depopulated by a plague,
or was the listless population all asleep?

EARLY VISITOR TO LYTTON

IT'S A SAFE BET that Judge Matthew Baillie Begbie was the only man in the area sporting a smartly waxed moustache, pointed Vandyke beard and wide-brimmed velvet hat when he walked over Jackass Mountain and into Lytton in March 1859. He was certainly the only one bringing a long white judicial wig and red legal robe. That was a relatively modest getup for the judge, who had been routinely cutting a more dramatic figure back in his new hometown of Victoria. "He often walked to official functions in Victoria dressed like an Elizabethan courtier, complete with velvet breeches, flowing cape and big-buckled boots, leading a pack of spaniels," author Donald J. Hauka notes in *McGowan's War: The Birth of Modern British Columbia on the Fraser River Gold Fields*. Begbie was just thirty-nine, but he looked older, as his hair and beard were already greying. Just four months earlier, he had stepped off a ship from

England in Esquimalt, near Victoria. He arrived in the colony to take up the post as the first judge in British Columbia. In addition to a lavish Victoria home, Begbie kept a cabin in Richfield, in the Cariboo region of the Interior. He travelled throughout the province by foot, horse and canoe, often sleeping in tents and eating freshly killed game, which he sometimes shot personally. He wrote many of his legal decisions from atop a horse.

There is a backstory to Begbie's relocation from England, although it's in some dispute. The story goes that his brother, Thomas Stirling Begbie, "had supplanted a lady's affections," in the words of Sydney G. Pettit in the *British Columbia Historical Quarterly*, or had "just stolen his fiancée," as Bruce Hutchison writes in *The Fraser*. Whatever the case, the judge was without a significant other when he went looking for a fresh start, which brought him to Lytton. A third student of Begbie's life, author/lawyer David R. Williams, has serious doubts about the stories that the newly minted judge was newly jilted. "It has been suggested that Begbie accepted a colonial appointment because he had lost his fiancée to [his brother] Tom. By 1858, when Begbie left London, Tom had been married eleven years, had had seven children, and remained married for at least thirty years more."

It's just as likely that Begbie had grown restless. He was born at the Cape of Good Hope, South Africa, in 1819, and seemed to have thrived on travel ever since. "He once told an audience at Richfield that he could scarcely remember a time when he had not been travelling from one place to another, and that his earliest recollection of childhood was of being on board a Dutch vessel bound for Antwerp," Pettit writes.

Whatever brought him to the Fraser Canyon, one thing that *is* clear is that Begbie didn't want to become a soldier like his father, a colonel in the British army. Begbie couldn't stand the thought of taking a human life. That said, as a judge, he was regularly called upon to consider sentencing prisoners to death by hanging. However, that all may have seemed too abstract to worry about as he descended from Jackass Mountain into dusty little Lytton.

Begbie cared about justice, but he wasn't a stickler for legal fine points. "It seems that he never cared for the law," Pettit wrote in the *British Columbia Historical Quarterly*. Precision wasn't a major requirement in the new post, as the closest court of appeal was a continent and an ocean away, in London. But he certainly looked judicial, and he exuded the confidence to back up his elaborate dress. He possessed a quick, curious mind, with interests that included mathematics, meteorology, cartography, history, literature, music, art and the outdoors. He was fluent in French and Italian, and quickly set about learning the Indigenous languages of his new surroundings.

As eager as Begbie the traveller appeared while in the Interior, it was at his large estate in Victoria that he seemed most in his element, tending rose bushes and hosting tennis parties. "His tennis parties are still remembered by a few early Victorians, and the cherries his Chinese servant picked from the tree and tied to the shrubbery so that the guests could eat them conveniently," Hutchison wrote in 1950. "Though he never married, he was pre-eminently a ladies' man and was greeted over the teacups everywhere as 'Dear Sir Matthew.'" He sang in the St. John's Church choir in Victoria, with a surprisingly high voice considering his massive physical stature. "On Saturday nights—for he was an inveterate debater in theology—he entertained the clergymen of the town at dinner to discuss abstract problems of religion over the port," Hutchison notes, "but he ushered the ecclesiastical company out at nine o'clock and ushered in the town bloods to play cards all night."

The refined quiet of Begbie's Victoria estate might have seemed to contrast sharply with his Saturday nights, but his card games had nothing on the social mood of the Fraser Canyon, flooded still with aggressive, gold-hungry white Americans. Begbie dismissed many of them as the "refuse of California," according to a quote attributed to him in the March 15, 1860, London *Times*. "B.C. was then on the verge of anarchy, with the influx of American prospectors, and Begbie and Douglas were bent on the territory not falling under the rough justice of Bowie knives and pistols," author/lawyer David Ricardo Williams has written.

The idea was to bring the area to heel beneath British law, so much so that it could never become American. Too much violence or chaos and the newcomers would look south for help, and a second war might not go as decisively in favour of the locals and the British—with whom the Nlaka'pamux at least had trading relationships—as the first. "That meant imposing the British law system in an area where there were few lawyers or courthouses," Williams wrote. "Begbie personified British law." The judge's bearing lent itself to an air of authority. A miner in 1862 said of him: "By God, he was the biggest man, the smartest man, the best looking man, damndest man who ever came over on the Cariboo trail." Begbie described his own arrival in Lytton from Fort Yale in March 1859 in a letter to Governor James Douglas. By his own account, Begbie was accompanied by "an Indian servant, and seven other Indians carrying our tent, blankets and provisions . . ."

It is perhaps in Begbie's comfort with servants as he crossed the Interior that he begins to distinguish himself from the governor, Douglas, and to reveal just how much they were very different men. For starters, Begbie was a white man trained in law at Cambridge, England. Douglas was born in Guyana to a Scottish father and a mother of mixed Barbadian-Creole ancestry. Douglas had worked almost his entire life as a wilderness fur trader for the Hudson's Bay Company, where he did business with a diverse group of Indigenous trappers, including Métis, Orkney Islanders, Hawaiians and Scots.

There was still plenty of snow on the ground when Begbie entered Lytton. He likely was hungry. There were only a few restaurants along the way, the last almost thirty kilometres before Lytton. "We found it would have been an extreme inconvenience to have been without a tent and without a sufficient supply of provisions for the entire route," he wrote Douglas, describing the trail between Fort Yale and Quayome/Boston Bar as "utterly impassable for any animal, except a man, a goat, or a dog."

The judge's first impressions of Lytton weren't positive: "Lytton does not appear a well-chosen site for any town," he explained to Douglas, "it is one the higher of two benches, parallel to each other and to the River Fraser, the lower one being the narrowest, both terminating in a very steep descent, as steep as a man can descend without using his hands, to the River Thompson."

Lieutenant Richard C. Mayne, the man hired to make a road survey from Yale to Lytton and on to Kamloops, adds to Begbie's portrayal of the little town. No more impressed than the judge, Mayne wrote in *Four Years in British Columbia*: "Lytton, at the time I saw it (in May 1859) consisted of an irregular row of some dozen wooden huts, a drinking saloon, an express office, a large court-house—as yet unfinished—and two little buildings near the river, which had once belonged to the Hudson Bay Company, but which were now inhabited by the district magistrate."

Begbie's Lytton visit was by no means a random stop along the Fraser Canyon trail. He was hoping it would bring him in contact with Captain Oswald T. Travaillot, known as "Captain" even though he hadn't held that rank in the army, police or anything else. He had been a sailor and a gold miner, and was considered prominent enough to land the title of "commissioner" for Lytton, which made him a tax collector and all-purpose judge.

The commissioner was nowhere to be found. "It was a great disappointment to us that Captain Travaillot absented himself from Lytton during the whole of our three days' sojourn there," Begbie wrote Douglas. Perhaps Travaillot was in hiding from Begbie and a harsh assessment of his work to date. Whatever the case, he had vanished. "There were many complaints as to the manner in which decisions had been made by him, but in my opinion they did not involve any amount of corruption; but the errors (if any) were such as might reasonably arise from inexperience, and the absence of books or advice," Begbie wrote. "It was a great inconvenience to have no access to any books or plans of the town, which were all locked up." Nor could he easily call anyone who might know the whereabouts of Travaillot or some means to unlock the town records.

The Lytton that Begbie walked into was full of Americans, as he noted to Douglas, describing "the great preponderance of the Californicised element of the population, and the paucity of British subjects," as well as "the absence of all means of communication, except by foaming torrents in canoes, or over goat-tracts on foot . . ." A portion of the old Lytton Hotel on Main Street, across the street from the future Edwards house, was reserved for the judge and his party. He met with Chief Cexpen'nthlEm of Canyon War fame to pick up fresh horses. Begbie stood over six feet tall and it was a challenge to find a mount to fit him.

The Nlaka'pamux already had a justice system that had served them for generations. Local resident Nathan Spinks told author Darwin Hanna for his book *Our Tellings* that, in this system, the Chief would act as the judge, saying, "It would be up to the captain and the watchmen of the tribe to carry out the sentence. This really worked well for our people—they respected these leaders. Most of the time they only had to go to court once in their lifetimes." The arrival of thousands of Americans—many of whom were packing handguns—had upset this balance, and the Americans would certainly challenge Begbie as he ventured up the canyon.

Begbie was approached by two Chiefs in the neighbouring community of Cayoosh, on the road to Lillooet. He noted:

> They complained of the conduct of the citizens of the United States in preventing them from mining, in destroying and carrying away their root-crops without compensation, and in laying wholly upon the Indians many depredations on cattle and horses which these Indians informed me were in part, at least, committed by "Boston men." On the other hand, many cases of cattle-stealing were alleged by the whites of all nations against the Indians; and stealing, indeed, of anything which could by possibility be eaten. For even the cattle which Indians stole they did not attempt to sell or make use of otherwise than as food, and it was admitted on all hands that many hundreds of Indians had died of absolute starvation during the winter. The Indians said that the salmon had failed them now for three years together.

Overall, the judge was impressed with the Indigenous people he encountered as he ventured up the canyon. Honesty was apparently a virtue in their culture:

> It was the uniform practice of storekeepers to entrust these Indians with their goods, generally 100 lbs., of flour, beans, or pork, and provisions for their own sustinence [sic]. Thefts were said to be unknown, and great care taken of their burdens. And these individuals who work we found extremely fleshy and hearty. My impression of the Indian population is, that they have far more natural intelligence, honesty, and good manners, than the lowest class—say the agricultural and mining population—of any European country I ever visited, England included . . .

A British journalist* ventured into Lytton to see Begbie in July 1859. The London *Daily News* correspondent clearly wasn't tickled by the assignment, writing: "Why this infernal thoroughfare is called the Jackass Pass I am unable to conjecture, unless it is from having been designed by some unmitigated donkey, too dull to see its difficulties and too stupid to appreciate the danger." The correspondent went on to complain of the "nerve-tearing dangers of the Jackass Pass." His story had the grand place-line "LYTTON CITY, FORKS OF FRASER," but "Lytton City" clearly was no metropolis. "It is composed of two struggling strings of shapeless unsightly log hovels, stretching along a bleak barn hill site, flanked by some squalid Indian warrens, composed of rags and tatters," the correspondent wrote. "There was not a soul to be seen as we descended towards it." There were a few dogs, who raised their hackles upon the newsman's arrival. "Was the wretched place depopulated by a plague, or was the listless population all asleep?" the correspondent wondered.

Not long after that, he saw the object of his quest, Judge Begbie, who was impossible to miss, with his towering frame and natty attire. The newsman referred to Begbie as the "tall gentleman in the semi-Zouave suit and comical hat." He also met Chief Cexpen'nthlEm, who had many wives and modes of dress. The *Daily News* correspondent's copy reflected the racist world view of the time. "One day he is dressed in a complete civilized costume and appears perfectly at ease in it," the journalist wrote, as if intending a compliment. "The next he will assume the grotesque trappings of the barbarian potentate, and demean himself like an unsophisticated savage."

Despite his apparent unease with the town's cultural heritage, he found Lytton then to be on an upward swing, even if where it was heading confounded him: "The government is expending a large sum on a

*   The journalist's name was left off the article. Probably for the best.

large public building here, but for what purpose it is intended, I am unable to conjecture."

The village was becoming a legal centre of sorts. Its namesake, Sir Edward Bulwer-Lytton, got a letter in June 1859 from H.M. Ball, the village of Lytton's Justice of the Peace, saying he would like permission to buy a cabin so that it could be refitted as a jail. The British Columbia Provincial Police (BCPP) had been set up in 1858, partly in response to the influx of American gold miners. Aside from law enforcement, early officers were expected to collect taxes and act as postmasters in the isolated colony.

Ball's request was granted that October. The new jail was a sturdy log cabin with two cells and another room for storage, as well as a kitchen. As soon as the cabin became a jail, prisoners began breaking out of it. In 1862, a prisoner named Christian Homan bolted while awaiting trial on charges of maliciously and feloniously setting fire to the establishment of Eugene Comber & Co. at Kanaka Bar, just south of Lytton on the Fraser River. Homan's previous criminal record included stealing a tin pot holding ten cents' worth of beans. He bolted before trial, cutting his way to freedom with a hatchet and a large pair of scissors that had somehow been smuggled inside. When he was recaptured, he was slammed with a ten-year sentence.

The incident prompted another letter from Ball to Bulwer-Lytton. Security at the Lytton jail clearly had to be tightened. This time he requested a set of handcuffs and leg irons. (Years later, when it was decommissioned, the jail became a doghouse for the terrier-like Tahltan bear-hunting dogs owned by a local police constable.*)

---

* Raised by Indigenous people of the west coast for centuries for running down bear, the work done by this tough little breed was eventually replaced by hunting rifles, and it went extinct in the late twentieth century. ckc.ca/en/The-Dish/July-2020/The-Tahltan-Bear-Dog.

Judge Begbie's first criminal trial involving Lytton was scheduled to begin in October 1858. It was his task to resolve a dispute that broke out in the saloon of the Lytton Hotel. A gambler from California named William Hartwell had been drinking through the afternoon, and by the evening he was particularly pugnacious. He objected to the change he received from a twenty-dollar piece at the rondo table. Matthias Niel, a gold prospector from Amador County, California, was among the eight miners at the table, and he also had been imbibing from afternoon into the evening. Hartwell uttered fighting words, calling Niel a "damned old liar," and then fired a shot at him, to show that he was serious. He missed. Niel pulled out his gun and shot back three times, killing Hartwell. Under California law at the time, this was perfectly acceptable. There was no "duty to retreat" when someone drew a gun. British law was different. It required a subject to seek every way possible to escape before opening fire.

The only thing Niel escaped was Lytton, but he was soon arrested downriver at Yale. His trial, presided over by Begbie, came up in 1859 at Fort Langley. The trial became nothing less than a public showcase for the supremacy of British law and order over Californian notions of frontier justice. Begbie sentenced the prisoner to a four-year term for manslaughter, trying to set an example for other American miners.

Niel didn't think it was fair to try him under British law. He wrote to his family. In a letter printed in the *San Francisco Evening Bulletin*, he declared his sentence a miscarriage of justice. "I want some of my friends in California to get up a petition and get my friends to sign it and send it to the Governor," Niel wrote. A petition calling for his release drew more than five hundred signatures from residents of El Dorado and Amador Counties in California, as well as other Americans in British Columbia. Signees even included a county court judge.

Little Lytton's barroom trial even made the news across the ocean, as the *Times* of London reported on it on March 15, 1860, describing Begbie's new circuit as

> wild and almost pathless (certainly roadless) . . . with a population
> that is generally pointed at as the refuse of California—with a magistry
> weak in numbers, weaker in their great inexperience, from the
> judge downwards, everyone of them new to judicial and magisterial
> business—with a police never 20 in number, and never more than
> four or five in one place—the population all armed, and all engaged in
> the most exciting and demoralizing pursuit (namely, gold hunting).

Governor Douglas caved in to public pressure. He overturned Begbie's sentence.

Back in Lytton, Louis Hautier appeared before Judge Begbie, charged with shooting, but not killing, the town's burly butcher, Patrick Kilroy. Kilroy's backstory wasn't common knowledge to his peers. Lytton was and continued to be home to a stream of outsiders who ventured into the Fraser Canyon to hide out or reinvent themselves. Originally from Philadelphia, Kilroy dropped off about US$650 at the Philadelphia Saving Fund bank on Walnut Street and then never looked back or touched the money. Years later, on December 15, 1869, the bank wrote that it had not heard from him in three years. His brother-in-law, John Duncan, swore that Kilroy had died intestate in 1861 and said he spoke as Kilroy's next of kin. Then Duncan withdrew and spent the money, dying penniless five years later.

Meanwhile, in Lytton, Kilroy was very much alive. One day, Hautier heard that Kilroy had made some insulting remarks about his family. Burning with indignation, Hautier stuffed a revolver into the right pocket of his coat and grabbed a thick stick with his left hand. Then he crossed the street to Kilroy's butcher shop.

Kilroy was standing in the doorway when Hautier arrived. "The butcher was a bit of a bully and did not like being 'called down' by a man half his size and, wrenching the stick out of Hautier's hands, proceeded to batter him with it over the head and shoulders," Dr. M.W. Wade wrote in the Vancouver *Province*. Without drawing his gun, Hautier fired a shot from inside his pocket. The bullet glanced off Kilroy's forehead, knocking him to the ground. Through it all, Hautier never showed his gun, although a witness saw a puff of smoke come out of his coat.

Bill McWha, proprieter of the Lytton Hotel, ran off to get a doctor. The local medical man was leery about whether Kilroy would pay him, as he had a reputation for being cheap. "I'll see that you get paid, Doctor," McWha reportedly said, and that was enough for the doctor, McInnes, to take a look at Kilroy. A couple of days later, McInnes presented a bill for three hundred dollars. By this time that fee seemed high, as Kilroy wasn't too badly hurt. But McWha paid the bill anyway.

The trial was to be held in Yale before Begbie. The only witness of the violence from start to finish was Chief Shall-lou, and in the words of Wade, "Kilroy had . . . to win the Indian's good opinion. All the meat he wanted to had [*sic*] for the asking and during the interval between the hearing before the magistrate and the assizes, Shall-lou lived, literally, on the fat of the land." Shall-lou listened closely to all his new benefactor had to say in exchange for many free meals. He wasn't the only potential witness Kilroy primed for their appearance at trial. By the time they all appeared in court in Yale, Kilroy was brimming with confidence.

Wade describes the Chief's testimony: "Shall-lou proved to be an excellent witness and told a straightforward story: all the butcher's bribes and blandishments, and the suggestions had failed to induce him to deviate one iota from the facts as he knew them. He told of the vicious attack Kilroy had made upon Hautier with the club, of the shot and the smoke from Hautier's coat."

When Kilroy took the stand himself, deflated no doubt by the key witness's inerrant truth-telling, he left out the detail about beating Hautier with the club. Hautier's lawyer flatly asked, "Did you hit Hautier on the head with a stick?"

Kilroy dodged the question. The reporter Wade wrote that Kilroy would begin his responses "Well it was this way" and "then go off at a tangent."

Begbie grew impatient. "Now, Kilroy, I want a straight answer, yes or no: did you beat Hautier with the stick?" the judge asked.

Kilroy dodged the direct question again.

"Kilroy, I am going to ask you that question three times and if you don't answer yes or no, I shall commit you for contempt of court," the judge warned.

Kilroy dodged some more and Begbie sent him to jail for six hours, then acquitted Hautier on the grounds of self-defence.

Begbie became somewhat proficient at Indigenous dialects, and at a trial in Lytton in 1860 he acted as his own court interpreter. He defended the rights of Chinese immigrants and didn't enforce a law that forbade Potlatches, or Indigenous feasts. In one instance, he seemed to ignore the colonial attitudes of the white village locals, who weren't shy about offering the judge pointers. A letter dated November 1, 1861, and signed by local Lytton notables, including Marcus Nutting, C. de Nouvenvon, George Wilson, B.C. Sampson, John Hill, Charles Coleman, Richard Deighton, John Buie, G.W. Peterson, E. Harris, and the aforementioned Alexander McWha and butcher Patrick Kilroy, suggested the legal system adopt a new policy on haircuts: "We would call your attention to a system that is adopted in the prison, viz cutting the hair off prisoners previous to conviction." That would presumably make the prisoners more recognizable, should they escape, and also cut down the transmission of head lice. There is no record of the judge adding hair care to his duties.

More serious disputes found their way before Begbie. In one case, a Nlaka'pamux man claimed to have become engaged to a ten-year-old Indigenous girl by giving, according to Aboriginal custom, presents to her parents. He tried to take her away with him, but her parents objected, arguing that she hadn't yet reached puberty. When they refused to return his wedding gifts, the man became enraged and stabbed his would-be bride, deeply and repeatedly. In her final moments, she whispered, "Mother, I am going to die."

Court heard testimony from Chief Cexpen'nthlEm's brother, who said the man had acted correctly, according to local custom. The court found the accused guilty, but the jury recommended mercy. Judge Begbie opposed this, and the Nlaka'pamux man was hanged.

Begbie sat in judgment of another Nlaka'pamux man at a murder trial in October 1860 in Lytton. The Crown's chief witness was a young Nlaka'pamux girl. When lawyers questioned her about the date of the death, the girl described how flowers hadn't left the fruit and how the Fraser River was running fast from melting snow, so that canoes could not be safely put into the waters. The case ended with the Crown winning a guilty verdict from the jury, and with the Nlaka'pamux man losing his life on a makeshift gallows.

Begbie presided over 52 murder trials between 1859 and 1872, resulting in 38 convictions, 27 of them ending in hangings. This was a time of an automatic death sentence if a jury found the accused guilty of murder. Begbie, who often kept the company of a chaplain for personal support, seemed to find the legal process tilted against non-white defendants, as he routinely appealed for mercy to Governor Douglas for Aboriginal and Chinese accused; he was successful 11 times.

Begbie encouraged juries to be lenient with Indigenous defendants, describing what he saw as their "natural intelligence, honesty and good manners." He also allowed oaths to be sworn on sacred objects and not just the Bible. What seems to have been respect for the Nlaka'pamux went the other way in the case of American miners. He convicted one of assaulting a Nlaka'pamux man, drawing only from the evidence of Indigenous witnesses. The judge's decision had a ring of irony to it, as Indigenous people weren't allowed to give evidence in California courts.

When juries decided against his own judgment, Begbie didn't hold back on saying what he thought of them or their decisions. After one acquitted a man of assault, Begbie said it was his hope that the former prisoner would now assault the jury. In another case, Dr. W.W. Walkem noted how the judge erupted when a jury returned a verdict that fell short of Begbie's belief that the prisoner on trial was guilty of murder. Walkem recorded the irate judge as saying:

> Prisoner: It is far from a pleasant duty for me to have to sentence you only to imprisonment for life. I feel I am, through some incomprehensible reason, prevented from doing my proper duty (in a voice of thunder). Your crime was unmitigated, diabolical murder. You deserve to be hanged! Had the jury performed their duty I might now have the painful satisfaction of condemning you to death and you, gentlemen of the jury, you are a pack of Dallas horse thieves and permit me to say, it would do me great satisfaction to see you hanged, each and every one of you, for declaring a murderer guilty only of manslaughter.

Much of what the judge said was more theatre than law as he fought to make it clear that British law was in force in BC. In the case of the "unmitigated, diabolical murder," he was more restrained in his report on it to Governor Douglas. Begbie wrote Douglas, with his notoriously bad spelling, that the verdict was "not perhaps an altogether unsatisfactory result":

> This wod have been of course "death by misadventure" in California—
> in British Columbia it is not perhaps an altogether unsatisfactory result
> that Gilchrist was convicted of manslaughter & sentenced to penal
> servitude for life, while his friends (who are well know to the police
> and to me) have left the Colony and are not, I think likely to return.

It wasn't until after his death on February 27, 1905, that he was nicknamed BC's "Hanging Judge," although that moniker is more often than not contradicted by his record of preferring non-lethal sentences. Perhaps more accurately, a Barkerville newspaper noted his tendency to lecture jurors, and called him the Haranguing Judge.

> In more recent times Lytton and the surrounding communities have produced Nlaka'pamux lawyers who have ascended to the role of judge. Madam Justice Ardith Walkem, from nearby Spences Bridge, fifteen minutes upriver from Lytton, was the first Indigenous woman appointed to the BC Supreme Court, in 2020. The Honourable Judge Raymond Phillips, from Lytton, was appointed to the Kamloops provincial court in 2019. When Judge Phillips was a practising lawyer in Lytton, one of his clients didn't have enough money, and he paid Raymond for his legal services in *stwen*, wind-dried salmon, which is a traditional Nlaka'pamux currency.

> *Kevin Loring*

CHAPTER 6

THE CHURCHES

Those who frequent such dens of iniquity have no shame . . .

EARLY MISSIONARY SHOCKED TO FIND
A BROTHEL IN LYTTON

DECADES BEFORE BEGBIE was asserting British law on the Fraser
Canyon to save it from American-style frontier justice, early missionaries were spreading the gospel. Most churches usually require a certain
commitment from the newly converted, but the same civility and good
manners of the Indigenous population that would one day so impress
the judge was confounding overseers in the corridors of denomina-
tional power. Governor George Simpson of the Hudson's Bay Company
wrote to his masters in London in 1841 that "the country is studded
with missions." The number of missionaries went up each year after
1841, church historian Joan Weir writes, adding:

So did each denomination's enthusiasm for converts. Had anyone
taken the trouble to add up the numbers, a wildly distorted picture of
population figures must have emerged, for the native population had
no wish to insult any of the visiting missionaries and were quite willing

to be baptised by the Anglicans one day, the Roman Catholics the next, and by the Methodists or Baptists the third.

The faiths divvied up the spiritual real estate. Lytton became largely Anglican missionary turf in exchange for the Church of England's backing off on Kuper Island in the southern Gulf Islands, leaving souls there to the Roman Catholics. There were atrocities committed on both sides. In July 2021, Penelakut First Nation of Kuper Island (now called Penelakut Island) announced the discovery of more than 160 unmarked and undocumented graves on the grounds of and near the remote residential school there, which operated from 1889 to 1975 and became known as "Canada's Alcatraz." Meanwhile, the switch paved the way for the Anglicans to bring St. George's Residential School to the Lytton area and to establish All Hallows' Residential School downriver in Yale.

Anglican Reverend James Gammage reached Lytton on June 4, 1859, just a few months after Begbie (but after the snow had melted). He estimated the community had twenty-two houses and "a population of about thirty." Gammage immediately set about trying to save souls in the town, even if those souls didn't ask for his form of saving. The day after his arrival, he reported:

On Sunday, June 5th, 1859, I held two services here, one in the morning and the other in the afternoon. Twelve attended in the morning, and nine in the afternoon. I do not think I should have had even that number if I had not gone to each house half-an-hour before the service, and invited the people to attend.

Anglican Reverend William B. Crichmer was in Lytton in the summer of 1860 and pondered a troubling metaphor when he looked out over the village:

Below the cemetery is the junction of the two rivers, the Fraser and

the Thompson: the former, large and discolored: the latter, clear as

crystal,—an emblem of the two races of Whites and Indians, now in

God's providence, united. And truly, the type stops not here; but, if

the truth must be told, the larger, more fierce, rolling and filthy stream

of the sinful White, after flowing for a short space apart, gradually

pollutes, absorbs, and destroys the unsophisticated children of nature.

Author and academic Brett Christophers draws upon this quote in his insightful—but cheekily titled—book *Positioning the Missionary: John Booth Good and the Confluence of Cultures in Nineteenth-Century British Columbia*, writing: "Here, as Crichmer intimated, was a microcosm of colonialism at large—Europeans and Natives had collided in a cramped canyon space and, together with immigrant Chinese, had crafted a pluralistic society in which ill will reigned."

Christophers focuses on John Booth Good, who was a missionary to the Nlaka'pamux from 1867 to 1883. Good arrived in Lytton at the invitation of some of the Nlaka'pamux. Mystery clouds that invitation. Mainstream historians generally draw only from white narratives, making their stories thin, if not misleading, no matter how well-intentioned their authors may be. "We must appreciate, of course, that powerful prejudices filtered white comment on Natives," Christophers writes. "All colonial knowledges are situated in one way or another, and must be read as tainted evidence."

That said, there were some Nlaka'pamux people who reached out to the Anglicans, presenting Good with what he considered an opening that was blessed by God. Good was eager to answer what he considered a divine calling. At the time of Good's arrival, the Nlaka'pamux were reeling from a colony-wide smallpox outbreak in 1862 and sorely required medical help. They also desperately needed mediators who could speak for them to the crush of outsiders flooding into the area. And there was a feeling that the Nlaka'pamux were losing faith in the Roman Catholic Oblates, who visited the community only every few months. "It seems that they turned to him [Good] as their experience of Catholicism soured," Christophers writes.

Good was in his late thirties when he arrived in Lytton in June 1867. He set up the St. Bartholomew's missionary headquarters in Lytton as the Anglicans began in earnest to connect with the Nlaka'pamux. Lytton was far from his childhood roots in Lincolnshire, England, where he was born in 1830. Lytton was also far from the place of his training, as he had been educated at Lincoln College, Oxford, and then St. Augustine College, Canterbury, studying medicine, math, science and theology.

Good first set up shop in an empty store. He drew from the work of the missionary William Duncan, whom author Geoffrey York called "the most aggressive and influential Protestant missionary in the early days of white settlement in British Columbia." Duncan wanted to reach into the souls of Indigenous people and remake them. He wrote with pride of some of his Indigenous students: "They can sing hymns and are learning God Save the Queen. . . . They have learnt how to speak in terms of civility to their fellowmen and have had several of their ways corrected."

Good wanted Lytton to become an Anglican missionary centre, and did his best to connect with Indigenous people. He even wrote a primer on how to speak their language, called "A Vocabulary and Outlines of Grammar of the Nitlakapamuk [sic] or Thompson Tongue: The Indian Language Spoken Between Yale, Lillooet, Cache Creek and Nicola Lake, Together with a Phonetic Chinook Dictionary, Adapted for Use in the Province of British Columbia."

Converting the Nlaka'pamux to Anglicanism meant undermining the very structure of their society. For instance, to be eligible for baptism in Good's church, a married person had to be in a monoga-mous relationship. Polygamy was part of Nlaka'pamux culture, but now Nlaka'pamux men had to reject all their family members with the exception of their first wife and the children from their first wife. That left many women and children in tenuous circumstances, deprived of family and clear social status within their own community.

Good wasn't too impressed with many of the local whites either. Some were a prickly challenge for a man of God to embrace, prompting him to use terms like "white savages" and "white barbarism." They were almost always male and often rough. An 1860 emigration report said that 98 percent of the five thousand non-Indigenous residents in BC were male. Good wrote in his diary in 1868 that he had been shocked to discover a brothel in town, or, as he put it,

> One of those vile institutions in which White men and the worst
> class of Indian women meet, has just been opened and still nearer the
> Mission School premises. Those who frequent such dens of iniquity
> have no shame, and invoking the assistance of the laws in putting it
> down must be allowed its swing and only one of the many signs that
> this is an unhappy spot.

The presence of this den of iniquity in Lytton helped explain why Good laid the groundwork for St. George's Indian Residential School four kilometres outside town. The school was purposely planned to counter the "evil influences" of the village. Tragically, though, it would become home to far more evil influences.

On February 9, 1868, Good officiated at the first Indigenous baptism in Lytton. Men and women filed into the church, with men on one side and women on the other. Good wrote in his diary:

As they proceed, they sing and the sacred melody, when taken up by the whole line, swells out and occasionally into quite a glorious burst of song. The services of the sanctuary are as they can well be made, and worshippers realize that they are there for prayer and praise.

This is no light work, nor make-believe, but a serious exercise of ecclesiastical discipline and to many it would doubtless appear strange that it is submitted to by a race of people to whom such obedience is as foreign as it is repugnant to naturally insubordinate dispositions.

Good's biggest success came in 1872, when Chief Cexpen'nthlEm was baptized in St. Paul's Church. The Chief had protested that his land had been divided without his agreement and that his people had been deprived of their water rights. Good supported their claims for self-government, with no success. But he still brought the most powerful Chief in the region into the Church.

Good moved downriver to Yale in 1873, bringing with him painful memories from Lytton. The previous year, his four-year-old daughter Elizabeth Booth Good had died in Lytton from a brain inflammation after a fall:

A child of rare beauty and singularly attractive winning ways, and to me she was so precious that perhaps nothing could have been taken from me that would have been harder to surrender than this holy and blessed child, and not less dear was she to her mother, whose name was the last upon her lips before they were closed in death on October 1, 1872. We buried her within the fence of our Indian Church, just opposite the east window, and can thus see her little grave from the parsonage.

In July 1879, Good was back in the Lytton area along with Indian Commissioner Gilbert Malcolm Sproat for a gathering of about a

thousand Nlaka'pamux men and women on the reserve. A large building with a canvas roof was erected for the occasion, with lots of greenery
for decorations. Observers were suitably impressed, including a reporter
from the *Mainland Guardian* of New Westminster, who made it sound
as though the Nlaka'pamux weren't welcome in town overnight. He
wrote, with more than a touch of condescension: "The Indians are
remarkably well behaved, and not a single one of them has been seen
in town after dark. These Indians have assembled for the purpose of
making arrangements for the better management of their people and
reserves." The reporter seemed stunned that the event could be so
peaceful, purposeful and respectful: "Several townspeople besides
myself watched the proceedings, and were much pleased with the
orderly manner [in which] things were conducted."

Thirteen councillors and a Chief were elected to three-year terms, to
be served "subject to the Queen's pleasure." The new Chief was Meshall,
from Spuzzum, who had spent some time as Sproat's interpreter. There
would continue to be hereditary Chiefs, who would hold power until
their deaths and then not be replaced. There would also be a top spot
for the Indian agent, who represented the Queen.

The first policy priorities concerned education. A school would be
built in Lytton with a tax levied on the people, and a teacher of arithme-
tic and reading would be hired.

The second policy priorities concerned health. A white doctor
would be hired, and paid from a medical tax. Drunkenness and gambling would be banned. Cole Harris writes in *BC Studies*:

> There would be fines for drunkenness, potlatching, gambling, and
> animal trespass; villages would be "made to look well." The duration of
> fish traps and hunting seasons would be regulated, useless dogs would
> be killed, women would not work in the fields while men idled. . . .

Land on the reserve would be divided fairly. No one would be gaoled; punishments would be fines or confiscations. Everyone was to respect the Council's decisions and help enforce them.

The reaction from the provincial seat of government in Victoria was strong and negative. Much of it came from journalist and former premier Amor De Cosmos, who had been born in Windsor, Nova Scotia, with the far less memorable name of William Alexander Smith. He renamed himself while working as a photographer in the California goldfields around the community of Mud Springs. His inspiration for the name change came when Mud Springs opted to change its name to the far more uplifting "El Dorado." If a town can change its identity in such a mellifluous and optimistic way, why couldn't a person do the same? He said his new name of Amor De Cosmos—Love of the Cosmos—"tells what I love most . . . order, beauty, the world, the universe."

There was nothing whimsical, though, about his reaction to the new policy announcements for Lytton. De Cosmos wrote that they were reckless and a threat to white settlement. He added that Indigenous people could not be trusted. More practically, he wrote that a strong, unified Indigenous voice was a threat to accessing their water and land. Aboriginal title to land had never been extinguished in British Columbia, so taking that land was a delicate topic, one that would be complicated by a unified Indigenous voice. "Singly the Indian tribes are easily dealt with, but once bind them together by ties, whether political or social, and they will be much more difficult either to coerce or persuade," De Cosmos wrote.

And so the great attempt at Lytton to use white law to protect Indigenous people died on the vine, but not for lack of effort. "The year of planning, the number of people present, and the ceremony to welcome Sproat and his surveyor indicate that the meeting was of considerable importance to the Nlha7kápmx," Cole Harris concludes. "Its failure reflects neither Sproat's domination nor Nlha7kápmx indifference, but a vitriolic response from Victoria that Ottawa was not prepared to counteract." Ottawa knew what was happening and refused to step in. "By refusing to endorse the efforts of the Nlha7kapmx in the face of provincial opposition, the federal government dropped the ball. In doing so it shattered what might have become a relationship based on trust and the rule of law."

Begbie had asserted British law in the 1860s, and now, at the end of the 1870s, there was a chance to genuinely put it to work in the interest of protecting the Nlaka'pamux from the political upper hand of the newly settling whites. This Indigenous attempt at governance was wholly realistic about their changing circumstances with respect to the Crown and settlers, but even that bid died when Ottawa went mute. As Harris sums up, "An important window of opportunity in White-Native relations in British Columbia was closed."

CHAPTER 7

THE HOSPITALITY BUSINESS

It's a long walk to the Cariboo. Here will be
a town, and we will build a hotel.

EARLY HOTELIER ALTERS PLANS AND SETTLES IN LYTTON

LITTLE ALPHONSE K. HAUTIER arrived at the junction of the Fraser and Thompson Rivers in the summer of 1859, strapped into a basket on the back of Lasha, a beloved Indigenous woman who worked for Alphonse's parents, Louis Constant and Josephine. Little Al was just three months old, having been born en route to Lytton on April 2, 1859.

Lasha was reportedly born in 1816, eight years after Simon Fraser paddled into town. She was a survivor and a witness to major events that had a huge impact upon her people. Lasha had survived a measles epidemic in 1848, and the Fraser Canyon War of 1858. She had known Judge Begbie and was a devout Catholic by the time Anglican missionaries reached town. She was forty-three when she carried baby Alfonse into town, making him the first non-Indigenous infant in the area. Lasha would be fifty-four when smallpox—called "spotted death"—swept the area and killed a third of her family. She would be seventy-four when smallpox hit again, killing a quarter of her family and community.

Baby Alphonse's parents, Louis and Josephine Hautier, were originally from Belgium. Louis was a medical practitioner of sorts who gathered herbs, bark and roots to treat the sick. This was a sought-after skill
in the area, where mainstream doctors were rarer than gold.

The Hautiers left San Francisco in early 1858, going first to Victoria
and then by boat to Yale. There, the Fraser River becomes too rough to
boat any farther, so they set off along a trail. Their intended destination
was the Cariboo, where gold was said to sparkle in the shallow creeks.

Lytton was little more than a sprawl of wooden huts and tents, an
express office and a saloon when the Hautiers walked in. Local legend
has it that Louis surveyed the activity by the junction of the Fraser and
Thompson Rivers and then announced, "It's a long walk to the Cariboo.
Here will be a town, and we will build a hotel." And that was that.

The wave of newcomers into the old Indigenous land continued as
transportation routes improved. Governor James Douglas reported to
the Duke of Newcastle in October 1859 that the Canadian colonies
in the east were developing a proper route across the Rockies to the
Pacific. The Duke served as Queen Victoria's principal Secretary of
State for the Colonies:

> From Lytton, a natural pack-road now exists leading to Red River
> Settlement by the Coutannais Pass, through the Rocky Mountains,
> and from thence following the valley of the Saskatchewan, chiefly
> over an open Prairie Country of great beauty, and replete with objects
> of interest to the tourist and sportsman; a settler may then take his
> departure from Red River in spring with his cattle and stock, and reach
> British Columbia by that road in course of the autumn following. This
> is no mere theory, the experiment having been repeatedly made by
> parties of Red River people travelling to Colville, from whence there
> is a good road to Lytton; so much so that one of those persons assured

me that the whole distance from Lytton to Red River, with the exception of the Coutennais Pass, which is thickly wooded, may be safely
travelled with carts. If the Canadian government would undertake
to open a road from Red River to the borders of Lake Superior,
which really represents no very formidable difficulties, the connection
between British Columbia and Canada would be complete, and the
whole distance might, I think, be travelled on British soil.

Louis, Josephine, little Alphonse and his two-year-old big sister had a
new home. The hotel they built was called the Globe. The Hautiers settled
on a plot of land on the old Fort Dallas site, and farmed alfalfa and vegetables. Produce from their gardens was served in their hotel, to rave reviews.

At the hotel, Josephine sometimes displayed her fine singing voice, a
reminder of her pre-Lytton days as a concert singer. She sometimes
sang duets with Judge Begbie, whose oddly high-pitched vocals revealed
surprising talent. The Hautiers' hotel hosted other notables, including
Sir James Douglas, the province's governor. Douglas had appointed the
Indigenous magistrates and often travelled to the Interior in an attempt
to reassure First Nations people they would not be harshly treated, the
way Indigenous peoples were in the United States.

In time, the Hautiers had six children. Louis Hautier supported
them all by sometimes doubling as a surgeon of sorts. In 1927, Alphonse
recalled that his father was the go-to man for pioneers suffering from
maladies of the foot:

My father won for himself the reputation of having considerable surgical
skill at that time when medical men were few and far between . . .
Particularly was he famed for his skill in removing corns, which was
a source of great misery to everyone at that time. The governor of the
territory, James Douglas, was a great sufferer in this respect.

One day the governor remarked to a friend that he would give a great deal to be relieved of his corn trouble. The friend happened to know that my father was in Victoria at the time, so he was called in to see the governor. James Douglas had five particularly bad corns which father undertook to remove for the sum of $5 each.

After the operation was performed, the governor said he thought $20 was sufficient for the job. Father accepted the money and went away. A short time afterwards my father was again called in to see the governor. One of the corns had reappeared. The governor asked father if he had not guaranteed that the corns would not return.

"I did," my father replied, "but after I had done the job you only paid for four. Of course one grew again." My father removed the corn and collected all his money.

Louis Hautier's medical treatments aside, the Globe Hotel was also known for its beer parlour. At the end of its long bar was the detention room, a private jail where overly enthusiastic imbibers were held until they were sufficiently sober. The wooden jail on Main Street was hardly its equal for strength. The bar jail was the prison of choice when some desperadoes were apprehended in 1866, wanted for stealing a stage-coach's cargo of flour and beans. Such was their offence that they were tracked down by a very serious posse, which the *North Kamloops News Advertiser* described as "armed to the teeth with rifles, six-shooters, pick handles, pokers, and all kinds of deadly weapons."

Business was robust. In 1872, a second hotel was built in Lytton, this one by George Baillie, who ran it until his death in 1887.

The next generation of Hautier boys became famous in the area as freight and stage drivers. One boy, known as "Lulu," became super-intendent of Wells Fargo in Alaska and the US.

Lasha, the woman who had carried baby Alphonse into town years before, lived until February 1919, dying at age 103. She was beloved by the First Nations and non-Indigenous communities alike and was one of the first Indigenous people to teach white people to speak the local language. Even in her senior years, Lasha would walk into town twice a year with her kerosene can for refilling.

It was said that Lasha never forgave the local police for a misfortune that befell her son. He was walking by the jail one day when he spotted some keys on the ground. There were four men in the jail at the time and they asked Lasha's son what he had found. He held up the keys and threw them to the prisoners when they called for them. Not long after that, they walked to freedom while Lasha's son was sentenced to two years in prison for abetting their escape.

Transportation routes in and out of Lytton were perilous. Jackass Mountain, looming over the Fraser Valley about fifteen kilometres to the south, got its name for the unfortunate mule train members who tumbled to their deaths there en route to the Cariboo goldfields. Its rugged granite reaches 365 metres, and a fall means almost certain death. Looking down the side of the mountain from the Cariboo Trail wasn't much fun either.

The stretch of the trail along the canyon between Yale and Lytton was completed by the Royal Engineers in 1863, but it remained unnerving. The trail was eighteen feet wide, spacious enough for a wagon to pass, but travellers really didn't want to meet one coming in the opposite direction. Mules were a better fit, but they were no treat. Spences Bridge resident Jessie Ann Smith noted that a local man with the last name of Megan struggled mightily to move a covered wagon out of Lytton for a local minister:

When they came to a steep hill the mules would not pull and it seemed like they would be left there all day. The driver asked the minister if he minded him using his lash and his own language. The minister said that if that was the trouble, go ahead. Mr. Megan raised himself in his seat and, uttering a stream of curse words, brought the lash down on the poor little mules with such force that they started ahead, seeming to understand the awful language the driver used.

Locals were open to new ideas, and camels were brought into Victoria on May 2, 1862, destined for the Fraser Canyon. The twenty-three camels cost three hundred dollars each in San Francisco, twice the cost of a mule, but they were bigger, faster and considerably stronger. Still, a camel in the mountains can present problems. Their feet might be great on desert sand, but they couldn't handle the rough granite of the Fraser Canyon, even when they were outfitted with rawhide booties. Worse yet, the camels emitted a ghastly stench that lingered even after they had passed, profoundly troubling the local horses. There was an attempt to perfume the camels, to no avail. Further, the animals have the habit of spewing dirty water from their nostrils when agitated. They even dismayed Judge Begbie, who had a flair for the exotic. "Judge Begbie was riding his cayoosh leisurely along when the cayoosh espied the camel train and despite the most strenuous efforts on the part of the rider carried the judge into the jungle, making havoc of his unmentionables," the Vancouver *Province* reported.* Exactly what constituted his "unmentionables" was not mentioned.

Soon, stagecoach drivers sued to get the camels off the rocky roadways. "I believe the camels proved to be unsuitable for the purpose

---

* The newspaper mistakenly used the word *cayoosh*, a geographic place name in BC derived from *cayuse*, a stocky western horse.

intended," Lytton area rancher Thomas Earl understated. Impractical as they were, those animals became something of a local legend, even after they were cut loose east of Cache Creek. The last reported camel sighting was in 1905. One ended up in a stew after being shot by a miner named Grizzly Morris. It reportedly appeared in a Fraser Canyon eatery under the heading "Grizzly's Bear."

There was also a local ferry business, which was started by Byron Karnhaw, a Yorkshireman who settled in Lytton in 1862 after moving to San Francisco at age ten. That route, from California to Victoria to British Columbia, had so often ended in Lytton. Improved transportation brought in even more outsiders, including dance-hall girls with plenty of makeup and prospectors with plenty of guns. There were slick card players and impressive trains of up to twenty pack animals—including bulls—yoked together, the heavy-wheeled transport trucks of the day. In time, the ferry became popular with local dogs as well, some of whom crossed the river on it unattended.

CHAPTER 8

PLAGUES

. . . the stench peculiar to the disease was simply awful.

NEWSPAPER DESCRIBES SMALLPOX HITTING LYTTON AREA

SMALLPOX ARRIVED WITH the early European visitors to the northwest Pacific coast during the late 1700s. By the time ltKumcheen was being called Lytton, the populations of Indigenous people all over British Columbia had plummeted. One historian estimates that within a century of Euro-American contact, the Indigenous population in the Pacific Northwest dropped from a conservative estimate of 180,000 to between 35,000 and 40,000.* Thousands were killed by smallpox in British Columbia in 1862 alone.

With time, new waves of immigrants brought epidemics of other diseases to which the Indigenous people had no previous exposure and no resistance: tuberculosis, trachoma, diabetes, influenza and polio. Entire villages were abandoned and left forever empty because of disease.

---

* Robert T. Boyd in *The Coming of the Spirit of Pestilence.*

Dr. W.W. Walkem described in *Stories of Early British Columbia* what it was like to enter the ravaged community of Williams Creek, in the Cariboo goldfields north of Lytton, in February 1863. Walkem saw ninety snow graves of Indigenous people who had recently died from smallpox there. Keeping their remains beneath the snow meant they were out of sight and, hopefully, out of harm's way until the spring thaw, when soil could again be broken and they could receive permanent burial. "There was only one adult Indian from the Beaver Lake tribe living. All the rest had succumbed to the dreaded fever."

The scene was equally horrific when Walkem arrived near Lillooet, sixty-three kilometres northwest of Lytton. "The flaps of these tents were raised sufficiently to let us see Indians lying thereunder in all stages of the disease," he wrote. "Some of them were actually black with confluent smallpox, and the stench peculiar to the disease was simply awful."

As Indigenous people died of smallpox, authorities tried to take away their communities' large land base by setting up reserves along the Fraser River. New land laws allowed settlers to appropriate up to 320 acres in the Interior, often with adjacent water rights. There was an effort to push Indigenous people onto reserves, even though they hadn't ceded their traditional land.

The smallpox plague of 1862 has been blamed in part on the arrival of the steamer *Brother Jonathan* in Victoria from San Francisco on March 12 of that year. Most of its 350 passengers were bound for the goldfields of the Fraser Canyon. The Victoria *British Colonist* editorialized that, since at least one of the American passengers was quarantined for smallpox, "we fear that a serious evil will be entailed on the country."

Some considered it an act of genocide to let the infected passengers carry on up the canyon into Indigenous communities. The *British Colonist* reported on April 26, 1862, that Indigenous people were worried that

Governor James Douglas was sending smallpox into their communities
to kill them off and get their land:

> On Thursday several Nettinett Indians (who live near Cape Flattery)
> called on the Governor and said that they had been deputized by their
> tribe to ascertain whether there was any truth in a story told them by
> some white scamps that Gov. Douglas was about to send the small pox
> among them for the purpose of killing off the tribe and getting their
> land. They were assured that they had been hoaxed, and left the next
> day for their home.

Certainly, weakened First Nations meant more opportunities for newly
arrived whites to acquire land. Historian Robert Boyd argues that the
avoidable epidemic "paved the way for the colonization of their lands by
peoples of European descent."

The massive loss was later recorded by James Teit, a friend of the
Nlaka'pamux who had settled in nearby Spences Bridge, at the confluence of the Thompson and Nicola Rivers, about fifty kilometres north
of Lytton. Teit heard that there had recently been about two thousand
Nlaka'pamux people along the Fraser River between Spuzzum and
Lytton, and that this dropped to just seven hundred in a generation. He
wrote that the smallpox epidemic sent "panic-striken" people fleeing
to the mountains for safety, "drop[ping] dead along the train . . . their
bodies . . . buried or their bones gathered up, a considerable time after-
ward." Some of them made their way to a sweathouse, "expecting to cure
the disease by sweating, and died there." Particularly hard hit was the
community of Spences Bridge, where Teit lived.

In 1863, Cariboo Road construction supervisor Walter Moberly told
of riding on horseback just east of Lytton and seeing a Nlaka'pamux
man with a veil on his "badly smitten" face, travelling with a second

man. Moberly said he told them they should go back to Lytton, where they could get a vaccination from a doctor. He sounds painfully optimistic, as Lytton didn't have a hospital or doctors, and it's doubtful it had much, if any, vaccine either. Many at the time were against mandatory vaccinations, as early anti-vaxxers feared they were dangerously unsanitary and a violation of their individual rights.

The sad party continued on their journey instead. Moberly travelled that same road later in the year and heard "the dismal wailing of Indian women . . . a certain indication of death having visited their community." He saw a pack of horses around a cluster of tents. Inside the tents were "putrefying bodies." Farther down the road, by the Nicola River, he saw "the same melancholy and disgusting sight."

By this time, improved transportation meant the incoming white population was expanding rapidly just as the Indigenous people were dying off in droves. Indigenous hopes of moving back onto fertile farm sites were lost when settlers moved onto them instead. Land commissioner Joseph Trutch refused in 1864 to recognize Indigenous title to land, which was given away to settlers, miners and loggers. The attitude seemed to be that Indigenous people were a dying race, so why bother with treaty-making? Instead, whites simply moved onto unceded lands.

> One of my first summer jobs was in the genealogy department at the Nlaka'pamux Nation Tribal Council. I spent the summer surveying, mapping, documenting and creating spreadsheets of all the Nlaka'pamux graveyards and burial sites from Boothroyd to Lytton along the Fraser Canyon. There were many sites that were just mass graves, large mounds with a single large cross marking the site. It was incredibly humbling and disturbing. But what was even more chilling was knowing that these sites were from

the later epidemics that passed through the canyon and
that there were many more unmarked mass graves, whole
extended families and village sites throughout the territory
that were wiped out, forgotten about, and their locations
and stories lost to the passage of time.

Kevin Loring

CHAPTER 9

ARRIVALS

He realized that it was much easier to supply the
miners with fresh meat than to look for gold.

LIFELONG LYTTON-AREA RESIDENT DONNY GLASGOW
DESCRIBES 19TH-CENTURY ANCESTOR

LORENZO DELOSE LORING arrived in the Lytton area in 1863, at the tail
end of the gold rush. His family had left Virginia sometime in the 1810s
or early 1820s and drifted west across the continent in hopes of striking
gold. His granddaughter, Isabelle Anne Loring, lived from 1917 to 2014.
The Lorings settled in Botanie (sometimes spelled Botany) Valley outside Lytton. With Isabelle's life spanning so much of Lytton's history,
the Loring family story, and with it memories of the time that followed the
gold rush–era wave of settlers to Lytton, enters living memory.

"Mom was born in the valley, as was her father," says Donny Glasgow,
Isabelle's son, a cousin of co-author Kevin and a childhood friend of co-
author Peter. "And my uncle Ford Glasgow married Mom's sister Hazel
Loring." For a time, Donny's father, Ernest Glasgow, dated Isabelle's sister Hazel, while Ernest's brother Ford Glasgow dated Isabelle. Then they
mutually decided it would be better if the couples were reversed. It

wasn't particularly awkward when the families would get together after the reversal, Donny says. "Dad didn't really care for Hazel, and vice versa." Switching partners was the obvious thing to do, and so they did it. There were only so many potential couplings in Lytton.

Back in the nineteenth century, Lorenzo Loring and his friends mined up and down the Fraser River between Lytton and Lillooet, on both sides of the river, by sluice box and by hand. They didn't get rich and they didn't starve. "They never made a lot of money, but they had enough to eat," Donny says. Then Lorenzo got the idea of settling down in Botanie Valley, after a friend let them know they could get land there cheap. According to Donny, "He realized that it was much easier to supply the miners with fresh meat than to look for gold. There were lots of deer in the valley at the time."

Lorenzo started the Loring Family Ranch in Botanie Valley as the family fell in love with the land. "At the time, land was more or less free, so he claimed that land and built a home and started a ranch there," Donny said.

Thomas Gardiner Earl took a winding route to get to the junction of the Fraser and Thompson Rivers back in 1860, settling on the site of a traditional Indigenous village and grandly calling his new home Earlscourt. Earl brought an old six-shooter and plenty of stories that seemed torn from the works of Bret Harte, a popular writer of the times who immortalized miners and gamblers and other romantic figures of the early West.

Earl's family had roots in Newark, New Jersey, that dated back as far as 1630. He said he left Newark on January 27, 1847, at age nineteen, "alone and ignorant in the world," on the barque *Mara*, destined for Veracruz in eastern Mexico. There he hooked up with fellow adventurers and purchased horses and pack mules for the journey across

Mexico. The Mexican war had just ended and the country teemed with guerrillas. Earl's stories of Mexico included one about a bear and a bull fighting for the entertainment of the rough men there. There was also an account of the murders of fourteen Chinese workers, and another of the rescue of sixty men from New York from Mexican guerrillas.

Earl took a boat to California for the gold rush of 1849. He would later tell stories of being reduced to a diet of mule meat and salty water en route to San Diego. From there, he made his way up the coast to San Francisco on an old whaling ship. He worked as a bartender, collecting stories filled with desperadoes and monte dealers and a gold miner who was treed by a grizzly bear in Nevada. And then he heard about another chance to get rich, far up north.

The Fraser Canyon was becoming known as the next El Dorado, and Earl got swept up in the excitement. At the end of another long journey, he settled on the west side of the Fraser River, across from the village of Lytton. There he grew fruit and tended cattle. He didn't find gold, but he won some, for the quality of his produce and steers.

Earl quickly cast himself as the area's version of landed gentry. With many of the locals too busy living out fantasies of their own, nobody bothered to contradict him. He loved to describe how he chatted with the Earl of Aberdeen, then Governor General of Canada, when he visited Earlscourt. The Earl asked Earl if he spelled his last name with an *e*. Earl said no, and the Governor General replied, "Then we are all Earls together, Mr. Earl."

He also told of taking a trip to Washington sometime around 1911 and meeting American president Theodore Roosevelt. As Earl described it, he simply showed up at the White House and asked to say hello. "A Chinese deputation was waiting to see him, but he courteously gave me twenty minutes first," he told a reporter. "And when I left him, after thanking him for giving an old forty-niner so much time, he said,

'Mr. Earl, I would not be a good American if I didn't love up the old forty-niners who opened up the Pacific coast for us.'"

Earl was in his mid-seventies in 1921 when he finally retired from his ranch and orchards. He moved to English Bay in Vancouver, taking his honours with him, including four gold medals awarded to him for his apples from the Royal Horticultural Society in 1908, the Olympics of agriculture.

The gold rush around Lytton had started in 1858, but with time, the focus of frontier mining shifted up the Fraser River towards Barkerville and the Cariboo goldfields. After ten years of economic prosperity, the little town's fortunes began to slide. By 1870, most of the thousands of men who had arrived in Lytton during the mid-1860s had moved on or died off. The census for 1870 showed 524 whites, 5 "coloured" and 50 Chinese. No talley was kept for Indigenous people.

The town's boom time was over. The adventurers had left town. All that was left of the newcomers was the diehards, those who either loved the land or had nowhere else to go.

CHAPTER 10

PROMISE OF RAILWAY

The picturesque and rapidly growing town
of Lytton bursts upon the view.

1882–83 BC *YEAR BOOK*

THE GOLD HAD BEEN PICKED OVER, but the American threat just wouldn't go away.

After the American Civil War ended in 1865, railroad construction took off in the US, and there was enthusiastic talk of running rail lines up into Canada and annexing the land. That helped spur the British provinces to pull together on July 1, 1867, to form the Dominion of Canada, which grew on July 19, 1871, to include British Columbia. Sir John A. Macdonald, Canada's first prime minister, lured British Columbia into Confederation with the promise of a transcontinental rail link. Confederation and a railway offered the promise of money for roads and schools, and avoiding the north-south pull of the United States.

The clock was ticking in Ottawa. A coast-to-coast railway had to be built—quickly—to keep British Columbia from bolting and becoming part of the United States. The US had purchased Alaska from Russia in 1867. It seemed only natural that the Americans would want British

Columbia to link the lower continental states with their new northern acquisition.

The Canadian Pacific Railway Company was incorporated on February 16, 1881. The arrival of the railway threatened to tear open the land of the Nlaka'pamux and other First Nations, ensuring that they would forever lose their buffer against the outside world. Nowhere was this more apparent than 10.5 kilometres below Lytton in tiny Siska, whose name comes from the word *si'ska*, meaning "uncle" in N'lakapamux'stn but also "unpredictable" in reference to the flow of water in nearby Siska Creek. It was also called Cisco by the settlers. There were plans to build a steel cantilever bridge across the Fraser River at Siska. That would involve tunnelling into the granite of the canyon wall, cutting through the heart of the homeland of the local band.

The Fraser was at its most dangerous in this area. At Hells Gate, about forty-five kilometres south of Lytton, the little road that existed traversed a landscape so rugged that rail workers had to be lowered by rope to chisel and blast a route through the mountain.

The industrial revolution had come to the Lytton area. Chicago engineer and contractor Andrew Onderdonk had the task of supervising construction of 544 kilometres of the transcontinental railway. That included another bridge across the Fraser River, this one just south of Lytton. It was a challenge just to get building materials to this isolated location. The bridge was prefabricated in Newcastle, England. From there, it was shipped around the Horn to San Francisco, and then north to British Columbia via Port Moody.

Onderdonk was under considerable pressure from the government to work quickly and keep costs low. He needed ten thousand men to wield picks, shovels, wheelbarrows and dynamite along the Fraser Canyon through Lytton. The first white workers were paid two dollars a day, but many of them didn't last long or do particularly well.

Onderdonk looked next to China, where workers were more plentiful and desperate. There were arguments that Chinese workers would prove too frail for the job, but Onderdonk figured that if Chinese workers could build the Great Wall of China, they could handle the Fraser Canyon. Besides, many Chinese workers were motivated by the threat of starvation back home. Onderdonk first imported two thousand workers from Kwangtung (modern-day Guangdong) province, paying them a dollar a day, roughly half what was paid to white workers by that time. They sailed from Hong Kong to Victoria on crowded three-masted ships. They were kept below deck, where the ventilation was poor. Food and water were scarce. Once they reached Yale, they were split into groups of thirty and charged for their tools, camp equipment and camp cooks. They often also had to pay fees to labour contractors. They still agreed to the job, in hopes of sending money home.

Then Onderdonk brought in 6,500 more Chinese workers, many of them from Kwangtung and Fujian provinces in southern China. Again they were paid less than half the rate of white workers and forced to buy supplies from high-priced company stores.

White workers complained that the new arrivals would push down their wages and cost them jobs. Onderdonk told the Canadian government that he had no choice: he couldn't do the job without the low-paid Chinese workers. Governor Douglas considered the Chinese newcomers to be useful in the short term, but added they were "certainly not a desirable class of people, as a permanent population."

To keep the peace, Chinese workers were assigned to separate crews from whites and given the most dangerous jobs, such as inserting highly unstable nitroglycerine into canyon walls. Not surprisingly, workplace casualties rivalled what might be expected in a war zone, especially in places near Lytton like Alexandra Bluff and Hells Gate. An estimated four Chinese workers died for each mile of track up the canyon. Their death reports are filled with terms like "death by explosion," "killed by falling rock" and "smothered by cave-in." They also faced scurvy, which claimed two hundred lives in one year alone.

White workers resented being undercut, and anti-Chinese groups like the Workingmen's Protection League in Victoria pressed employers not to hire them. But the exploitation of Chinese workers was established practice by this point. The Americans had built some of their own railways using Chinese labour. Nonetheless, Onderdonk kept a distance, dealing with the Chinese workers through contractors and assuming no responsibility for their living conditions, which were particularly harsh during winters, when work—and pay—stopped. Fortunately, they weren't without connections in this new land.

Bonds already existed between Chinese and First Nations people in the Lytton area by the time the rail workers arrived. First Nations people had guided Chinese prospectors to goldfields during the gold rush. More than a thousand Chinese miners may have arrived between 1860 and 1863, according to Lily Chow, author of *Blossoms in the Gold Mountains*. Local place names soon included China San Flat and China-Eyed Flat.

Little Lytton soon had its own Chinatown. On April 6, 1860, Henry M. Ball, the assistant gold commissioner in Lytton, wrote: "Great numbers of Chinamen are daily arriving in these lower districts, and locating themselves as miners on the different bars, and have shown themselves a peaceful and orderly class of people." A month later, Ball wrote of Chinese miners on "different flats on both sides of the Fraser, principally between Boston Bar and the Fork [Lytton] . . . They are yielding $6.00 per head [per day] . . . Most of the best claims are at present worked by Chinamen." And on July 4, 1860, he wrote: "The town of Lytton is increasing in size and in importance; many influential storekeepers from Hope and Yale [are] about to locate in Lytton, and establish wholesale stores . . . The town has been surveyed and laid out into blocks and town lots."

Though Chinese prospectors competed with Americans and others to find gold, only they and the Nlaka'pamux sought jade as well. Indigenous people used it for ceremonial knives, scrapers and utensils before they had access to iron. It was found at Skihist Mountain, about twenty kilometres west of Lytton by the Stein Valley, and along the Fraser River. Some twenty-six tons of jade was sent to Shanghai in the 1850s and 1860s, at a value of $6 to $30 a pound.

The closeness between many of the Nlaka'pamux and Chinese stretched back to the summer of 1858, when American miners had accused Chinese miners of supplying arms and ammunition to the Nlaka'pamux. A group of Chinese miners near Lytton were even warned of the coming hostilities and allowed to leave the area unharmed before the onset of violence during the Fraser Canyon War. There was some intermarriage, too, such as between Ah Lock and Josephine Alexander, and Ah Lum and Ester Joseph. Ah Lock and Ah Lum returned to Guangdong province after their Indigenous wives died. There was also the marriage between Ah Ching and the daughter of Chief Pelek of Spuzzum. Ah Ching's remains were buried in the Indigenous cemetery in Spuzzum.

There were families—and children—from the unions of First Nations women and Chinese men. There was also some plurality of wives, as in the case of Yip Sang, who had five spouses. The passage of the Indian Act in 1876 meant that such unions involved major sacrifices for Indigenous women. The Act stated that "When an Indian woman married a non-status man, even if she was born with status [she] would lose it, unable to regain it even if she subsequently was divorced or widowed. Along with her status, the woman lost her band membership and with it, her property, inheritance, residency, burial, medical, educational and voting rights on the reserve." On January 1, 1880, the Indian Act dug even deeper into Indigenous rights. An amendment stated that Indigenous women "cease to be an Indian in any respect" if they marry "any other than an Indian, or a non-treaty Indian."

When thousands more Chinese workers were brought in as cheap labour for the most dangerous segments of the Canadian Pacific Railway, between 1880 and 1885, they arrived as little Lytton was becoming a hub of sorts. Stagecoach lines and major freight outfits like the Hudson's Bay Company, Uriah Nelson and Co., Oppenheimer and Co., Western Union and Barnard's Express were all passing through town. Lytton had swelled to become home to some four thousand people, many of whom lived in tents and hastily erected shacks.

The Williams *British Columbia Directory* reported on Lytton's new Chinatown: "As we entered we passed the locality, where numerous Celestials* employed on the railway find their particular wants abundantly met with the unique establishments that are being constantly multiplied by enterprising firms . . ." That included a building on Main Street—called a "joss house," a non-Chinese term for a Chinese temple or community hall—that was built in 1881. (*Joss* referred to the burning of incense, so the name literally translates to "incense-burning house.") It was a place to give thanks and to pray for good health and fortune. The Lytton centre had altars for Chinese Buddhist deities such as Kwan Yin, the goddess of compassion and mercy, Shen Nong, the god of agriculture and herbal medicine, and Zhu Rong, the god of fire.

On May 4, 1881, a boat christened *Skuzzy* was launched downriver at Spuzzum. It was nearly impossible to run the Fraser at Hells Gate, but Onderdonk hired Captain Ashbury Insley to give it a try. Insley

---

* The term *Celestials* was a common way to refer to Chinese, derived from literal translation of the Chinese name for China, Tian Chao, as "Celestial Empire."

succeeded only after he got 125 Chinese workers to climb the cliffs of Hells Gate and help pull the boat along. If the Chinese workers had let go of their rope, they would have plunged to near-certain death. It took ten days to get the *Skuzzy* through Hells Gate and another seven hours for it to reach Lytton—the only steamboat ever to do so.

The 1882–83 edition of the BC *Year Book* gave an optimistic view of the conditions in Lytton for whites and Chinese:

> Descending a long winding hill by the high road which skirts a creek beautifully diversified with shrubs and evergreens and evading a prominent bluff overhanging the way, the picturesque and rapidly growing town of Lytton bursts upon the view with a charming peep at the Fraser Valley behind at the Junction of the Thompson and the Fraser Rivers fifty-seven miles above Yale.
>
> The town named after Lord Lytton former Colonial Secretary is built upon a flat, a succession of which rise like so many terraces from the river and is indebted for much of its prosperity and importance to its central position at the meeting of the rivers so named.
>
> The annual sale of flour and dry goods owing mainly to the concen-tration of Indians here is simply enormous and since the commencement of the railway construction which crosses the heights overlooking the town, the business of the place has been largely increased.
>
> We pass through the Chinese locality . . . The European portion has also the look of thriving prosperity . . .

Life for Lytton's Chinese looked fine enough from town, but their workday presented a different perspective. To Chinese workers, the Fraser Canyon became known as the Valley of Death. Some simply quit the railway and went to pan for gold, no longer willing to put up with the beriberi, a wasting illness caused by vitamin deficiency, and the poor health conditions. There were also the bullying bosses and life-threatening work assignments.

Some Chinese fought back. Twenty-nine kilometres north of Yale, workers attacked a construction boss with sticks and stones after a premature dynamite blast. And a foreman was chased into the river after a Chinese workman was killed in a dynamite explosion. Chinese workers rioted near Lytton, in Hautier's Station, Camp 37, on May 13, 1883. There were twenty-eight Chinese labourers at the site, and foreman J. Gray wanted two of them fired. A dispute began about back pay for the dismissed workers. Whites would later say that in the resulting melee the foreman was assaulted. One of the white bosses hit several Chinese workers with a pick handle, badly injuring one of them.

That night, when the Chinese workers were asleep in a shanty, twenty whites set fire to the building, then clubbed the workers with poles as they fled. A Chinese worker named Yee Fook was killed. Another worker, named Ah Fook, died a week later from injuries suffered that night. Seven or eight more were seriously injured. The injured and deceased were taken to the Lytton joss house.

None of the whites were charged, and the Victoria *Colonist* reported that "every effort has been made by white laborers along the line to screen their guilty comrades." The newspaper also wasn't impressed by the attitude of white rail workers towards the police investigation. "Supt. Todd, who is conducting the inquest, is using every endeavor to discover the perpetrators of this the most unmanly and cowardly affair that has occurred in the country."

Here we return to a familiar and frequent vistor to Lytton, Justice Matthew Baillie Begbie. The judge sounded a similar tone in the newspaper about what he called "the terrible outrages against Chinamen" in the Fraser Canyon, saying, "The perpetrators have escaped Scot free."

Despite the labour tensions—and murders, arguably—the cantilever bridge was completed in 1882: the first of its kind in North America. Designed by C.C. Schneider of New York, it was hailed as "one of the great wonders of the C.P. Railway." Once the railway construction was done, the CPR laid off thousands of Chinese workers, leaving them stranded and far from home. Some moved into caves near neighbouring Spences Bridge. Others went to Chinatowns in Vancouver, Victoria and New Westminster, where white charities took pity on them and paid the way home for some. The 1891 census recorded only twelve Chinese names left in Lytton.

The Chinese era in Lytton was over. They had finished their dangerous job. Now they were being kicked out.

CHAPTER 11

BISHOP ARRIVES

The second day out from Yale we reached Lytton,
the dreariest, dullest, and driest place in the country.

BISHOP SILLITOE ISN'T SMITTEN WITH LYTTON

YALE WASN'T A PLACE for the faint-hearted in the summer of 1881, when Anglican bishop Acton Windeyer Sillitoe, the first Bishop of New Westminster, arrived in town. It was a far cry from his old alma mater of Cambridge University, and he later wrote that he was far from impressed:

> Yale bore at this time a most unenviable reputation. Pay day was signalized by the most fearful riots, with which the all too slender police force was powerless to contend. Drunkenness and disorder filled the place day and night. Fires kindled by lights held in hands unsteady with drink were of almost daily occurrence, the jails were overflowing, and the justices weary. Tattered, dirt-bespattered drunkards rolled about the streets, wallowing in the mud, cursing and fighting, and driving all respectable people into the recesses of their homes, while saloon after saloon was added to the number, already terribly in excess of the needs of the community.

Sillitoe's wife, Violet, recorded a similar impression. Even a massive fire during their visit didn't seem enough to cleanse the place. The fire was believed to have been caused by a drunken railway worker who had just been paid. The Sillitoes managed to save the church and vestry with wet blankets and buckets of water. Violet wrote: "Yale was a pretty rough place, and for three days after pay-day it was as well to keep away from the Front street."

The Sillitoes soldiered on upriver to Lytton, where the Bishop struck a different note, perhaps pining for the excitement he'd just left behind downriver:

> The second day out from Yale we reached Lytton, the dreariest, dullest, and driest place in the country. A great scarcity of water prevails, and there's consequently but little cultivation. Five days out of six a strong wind prevails, and the sand gets into one's eyes, and into one's throat, and down one's neck, and plays havoc with one's temper, and since the hotels are the worst managed houses on the road, one has comfort neither indoors nor out.

If the town was dull, getting there was anything but.

> Here and there bluffs formed by spurs of the mountains have proved impassable by excavation, and then the road is built out from the face of the cliff and supported by struts. There are two such places between Yale and Lytton—China Bluff and Jackass Mountain—and after driving four times over them last year, I don't mind acknowledging that nothing could induce me to do it again but the call of duty. The risk is too great to run except of necessity.

Despite their misgivings, Violet kept close watch as her husband travelled the area, "visiting the farming settlements, gathering the settlers
together to see what support could be given for church work, and finding the best centres for churches; and wherever he went I went, too."

At least there were churches for the Bishop and Violet. That included
a chapel on the hillside across from where the Trans-Canada Highway
and Kumsheen Secondary School would be built generations later.
There was also a mission on the Lytton Reserve.

Decades earlier, Bishop George Hills had written often in his diary of
the negative impact on Indigenous people of whites settling in the area,
highlighting the treatment of Indigenous women and the introduction
of alcohol. After visiting one Indigenous village in 1860, Hills wrote
in his diary: "Here was misery. This misery the Indian knew not til the
white man came." Hills was born into Britain's upper crust. He bemoaned
the lack of servants provided for him, and was tough on the helpers who
were at his disposal. Author Joan Weir notes that he was troubled to
hear men who travelled with him whistling or singing and made them
stop when in his presence. "It did not show sufficient respect for his
ecclesiastical office," Weir writes.

Hills wasn't shy about sharing whatever was on his mind, without
waiting to be asked. He reasoned that the Indigenous people around
Fort Simpson were often sick because their feet got wet, and so he
devised wooden moccasin soles, which didn't really catch on. "George
Hills was a strange mixture—autocratic, snobbish and dictatorial on the
one hand, sensitive and insecure on the other," Weir writes. "The problem of trying to preach religion to a people who understood no English
and no French was not the only factor hampering the efforts of the early
Roman Catholic and Protestant missionaries," she explains. "They were
also hampered by their conviction that they must convert the native

people not only to Christianity, but also to a lifestyle and value system that matched the missionaries' own."

Hills's solution was to hit Indigenous people with even more white culture: "Christianization" and assimilation. On April 19, 1884, the government bowed to pressure from missionaries and passed an amendment banning Potlatch ceremonies, which were central to the traditions of many northwest coast Indigenous Nations. Potlatches were central to spirituality and to governance. They redistributed wealth and acknowledged hunting and fishing territories. Chiefs gifted valuable items like firearms, blankets and canoes. They also bestowed and affirmed status of individuals and groups. They were important, joyful events that pulled people together with feasting, dancing, singing and ceremony. The Potlatch was condemned by the newcomers as anti-Christian and wasteful, and remained banned until 1951.

If the Nlaka'pamux of the Lytton area had been seeing control of their home territory decline, as of August 1, 1885, they saw less of their territory, period. Ottawa had instituted what was known as the pass system. It meant Indigenous people no longer had the freedom of unrestricted travel. Instead, they needed to ask permission from the Indian agent overseeing their reserve for a travel pass to leave and return to their home. Any Canadian citizen had the right to ask an Indigenous person for their papers, and if an Indigenous person was caught off reserve without a pass, they could be arrested and thrown in jail. That move came two months after the end of the Northwest Rebellion (or Northwest Resistance) of Louis Riel and Poundmaker on the prairies. The goal was to curb large Indigenous gatherings that could lead to armed uprisings. In practice, even in the faraway BC Interior, it meant that Indigenous farmers needed passes to sell their produce off reserve. Nlaka'pamux farms around Lytton competed directly with the settler farms in the area, but once the pass system was enforced, the First

Nations farmers stopped producing, as they could no longer easily travel off reserve to sell their produce.

Needless to say, the pass system was conceived without the agreement of status Indians, who were not allowed to vote federally. And in fact the system was entirely illegal, as it was not enacted by legislation. Despite not being codified in law, the system was strictly enforced by the RCMP across Canada until 1951, effectively making Indigenous people in Canada prisoners on their own lands on the basis of a wholly illegal and racist regime.

For his part, Anglican bishop Acton Windeyer Sillitoe eventually softened his initial negative impression of Lytton after a bout of ill health. By 1894, the Bishop considered the Lytton climate healthy, as Anglican missionary Herbert H. Gowen wrote in 1899: "as soon as he was the least bit stronger he moved up to Lytton, believing that the bracing air, which he had always found so beneficial before, would suffice to restore him. Lytton had always been a favorite resting-place for him."

The Bishop died in Vancouver in 1894 at age fifty-four, shortly after presiding over his final service in Lytton.

> Growing up I heard stories from my elders of the Nlaka'pamux strawberry farms, potato farms and orchards that once enabled the people to be more self-sufficient. But as more Nlaka'pamux farmers began competing with white farmers, the white farmers complained to the Indian Agent, who then stopped allowing the Nlaka'pamux farmers to sell their produce off reserve. The Nlaka'pamux farms eventually stopped producing, as they couldn't sell enough to make a living, but the memory and resentment of those times still live on in the community.
>
> *Kevin Loring*

CHAPTER 12

ANTHROPOLOGIST FRIEND

*We condemn the whole policy of the BC government
towards the Indian tribes of this country as utterly
unjust, shameful and blundering in every way.*

THE LAURIER MEMORIAL

JAMES ALEXANDER TEIT had good reasons to leave the seaport town
of Lerwick in February 1884 for a place he had never seen, halfway
around the world. He had a guaranteed job, for starters, something life
on the Shetland Islands of Scotland could not reliably provide. He would
be going to the hamlet of Spences Bridge, thirty-six kilometres northeast of Lytton on the Thompson River, to provide much-needed help at
the business of his uncle John Murray. Uncle John had been a prospector in the California gold rush of 1849, and then joined the stampede
into the Fraser Valley. He hadn't made his fortune in either gold rush,
but he was doing quite well running a grocery store and orchards. He
could use the help of his smart, strong young nephew, James, who had
experience working in his family's store back home.

BC offered James other opportunities as well. Land ownership was
reserved for the gentry back in Lerwick, where his father was keeping

his head above water but was by no means rich. Perhaps James could make enough money in Canada to send some back. And then there was also the messy matter of a thirty-five-year-old woman in Lerwick, considered of "notoriously bad character" by the parents of nineteen-year-old James. She had accused James of fathering a child with her. Teit's parents felt their son was being entrapped, but he still had a hand, or some other body part, in the messy matter. "Read your Bible my Dear Boy and you will find that the sin of fornication is peculiarly heinous in God's sight," Teit's father wrote to him. "May he give you grace to repent of this great sin."

James travelled to North America with newlyweds Jessie Ann Smith of Gartly, Aberdeenshire, and her husband, John Smith, who was a neighbour of Teit's uncle and also running orchards. They sailed from Liverpool in February 1884, on the steamer *Wisconsin* of the Guion Line, on a rough fourteen-day ocean passage. They landed in New York City on February 23 and got to stretch their legs a little in Manhattan before boarding a cross-country train. "I thought we would never get there, but at last we reached Tacoma, Washington, where we boarded a steamer to Victoria, the capital of British Columbia," Jessie Ann Smith later recalled. "The Canadian Pacific Railways was in the course of construction and traffic into the Interior was somewhat confused." Despite his misgivings about welcoming paying customers on a train meant for work crews travelling through dangerous terrain, the engineer allowed them to board. It took them as far as Cisco, south of Lytton. "The ride ended on a lonely mountainside, where we waited in the cold," Smith recalled.

> After a while we saw a man driving a horse which was pulling a large basket hung on a cable across the river . . . The man who drove the horse asked us to come and take our seats in the basket. When I was

seated the operator came and asked me to close my eyes when he let go of the rope. I remember looking up at him and smiling bravely to hide my fear. I said, "No! If that rope breaks I would like to see where I am going."

The man let go of the rope, and the basket with Mr. Teit, Mr. Burr, John and me in it, slid down a cable and landed us safely in a pile of hay on the other side of the raging Fraser River. I dusted the hay off my clothing at the end of the briefest but most thrilling part of our journey from Scotland to Spence's [sic] Bridge.

James Alexander Teit was born on April 15, 1864, in Lerwick, 120 kilometres northeast of the northernmost tip of Scotland. This was far into the North Sea, and Nordic influences were easy to find. Lerwick was a fishing port where street, place and family names were often Scandinavian. It was a sturdy, enduring place with stone houses on picturesque, narrow, winding, often steep streets. Shetland ponies were bred in the area to work in British coal mines.

James's father, John, ran a grocery store licensed to sell liquor. His mother, Elizabeth, was born in Aberdeen, Scotland, and moved to Shetland as a governess, caring for orphans. James was the eldest of twelve children. Eight of them lived beyond infancy, which was considered good and a sign of relative prosperity.

James stayed in school until he was sixteen, which was exceptional; most children on the islands were twelve or thirteen when they ended their formal studies and began to work. Both of his parents were strong, independent thinkers. His father helped start the Anderson Educational Institute, which offered an elementary education for children of the poor, as well as greater education opportunities for students whose parents had the money to pay school fees. John Tait had a sympathetic nature, donating his time as a volunteer teacher for the poor.

Young James took his family history seriously. Around 1891, after he made the move across the ocean, he changed the spelling of his surname from "Tait" to "Teit," which he considered its original and proper—and Scandinavian—spelling. His daughter Inga later said: "He was always studying up about things like that; he was always very interested in anyone's family name. He was always looking for roots to different words and different names." The Shetland Islands were part of Norway until the fifteenth century, and Teit traced his history back to Jan Teit, a Norwegian who settled the Shetland Islands in the twelfth century. (In a 1901 British Columbia census, James Teit described his nationality as Norse and not British. He said he spoke Shetlandic and not English, and that his religion was that of a freethinker.)

James was quiet and friendly, and he loved dancing. His uncle John Murray hadn't married and had no children, but young James found friends easily—and though he didn't know it yet, in making many of those friends he'd also found a cause on which to expend his great energy and enthusiasm for his new home. Teit quickly became close to local Nlaka'pamux people and recorded things about their culture, such as the significance of baskets. He noted their patterns, including Arrowhead, Root, Butterfly, Star, Packing Strap, Zigzag, Box and Eagle. He learned to talk with the Nlaka'pamux in their own tongue. He became very fluent, and a native speaker is remembered as saying words to the effect of "If Jimmy Teit was in a dark room with other Indians, it would be impossible to tell that it wasn't an Indian speaking."

Teit's biographer, anthropologist Wendy Wickwire, perceptively notes that the young man saw parallels between residents of the Shetland Islands and the Nlaka'pamux people, as a "collective struggle of dis-enfranchised local peoples against imperial elites." The Shetland Islands had also suffered under colonization: "It seemed more than coinci-dental that, on the other side of the Atlantic, Teit's Shetland friends and colleagues were deploying ancient Norse land rights as a way to detach themselves from Britain and reclaim their rights to their island land base." Teit didn't accept Christianity, and Wickwire notes that this too helped him bond with the local Nlaka'pamux: "Because Teit had rejected Christianity—a heretical act in most settler-society spheres at the time—he was able to appreciate the Nlha7kápmx concept of the soul or anima of the earth and its beings in ways that many of his anthropological peers did not."

Teit wrote of his bond with the Nlaka'pamux in *The Thompson Indians of British Columbia*:

> As with every other people there are both bad and good among them; but on the whole they are more honest and industrious, intelligent and receptive than other Indian tribes. They are quiet, sociable, and hospitable; yet—combined with the last two qualities are often pride and suspicion. Some are of a jocular, humorous temperament; and some are courageous, determined, and persevering, although the last named quality is not characteristic of the tribe as a whole. Some show it, however, to a marked degree when hunting or fishing. Being proud, they are easily offended, but seldom allow their wrath to get the mastery of them. As a rule they are not vindictive. They admire a man who is athletic, active, energetic, industrious, strong to endure, brave, hospitable, neighbourly, sociable, and kind. They are fond of the wonderful, of oratory, gambling, story-telling, hunting, and horseback-riding.

Teit wrote that the Nlaka'pamux were not as sports-minded as they once had been. Colonization and disease had taken their toll. They were in a state of transition, and whiskey had become more popular. He noted that liquor was all too easy to obtain, with often sad results, and is the cause of ruin, both moral and physical, of many of the young people, as well as of brawls, and sometimes loss of life. Be it said to their honour, however, many of the tribe have little or no desire for liquor, and, though it is easily procurable, never avail themselves of the opportunities so fragrantly brought to their notice. Those Indians who indulge in whiskey almost always do so to excess, and they are generally those members of the tribe who most closely copy the whites in other particulars.

Teit's natural curiosity led him to roam the Stein Valley, which stretches west from the Fraser River just north of Lytton. There, he interviewed local Nlaka'pamux people and explored caves. He saw evidence of how the valley was a long-standing spiritual refuge and he sketched pit houses sunk into the ground, where people stayed warm during cold winters and cool in the scorching summers.

Just as James was fascinated by old Shetland myths, he showed great interest in the mythology of the Nlaka'pamux. He spoke with Elders, who told him stories they'd heard from their grandparents about the arrival of Simon Fraser back in 1808. "Those stories spoke to the fears and anxieties that arose as people tried to figure out who these strangers were and where they were headed," Wickwire writes.

Teit was twenty-eight years old when he married Antko, a Nlaka'pamux woman with the anglicized name Susannah Lucy, in her village of Nkaitu'sus, just north of Spences Bridge, on September 12, 1892. The ceremony was conducted by Archdeacon Richard Small of Lytton, who overlooked the fact that the couple were not practising Christians. The Spences Bridge community was at its peak in 1892, with five general stores, a school, three hotels and an Anglican church. It was home to 130 Nlaka'pamux people and 32 residents with European ancestry.

German-born American anthropologist Franz Boas was considered at the top of his profession in 1894 when he stopped by Spences Bridge. He and Teit quickly impressed each other after they met by chance. Boas was six years older and considered the father of American anthropology. He was widely educated, with a PhD in physics from the University of Kiel in Germany, having minored in philosophy and geography. By the time he arrived at Spences Bridge for a visit on September 19 and 20, 1894, Boas was considered a pioneer in cultural anthropology and had spent a year with the Inuit of the eastern Arctic Archipelago. He was also editor of the respected journal *Science* and one of the founders of the American Anthropological Association. Boas strove to be a dispassionate social scientist who observed a "studied neutrality" with his subjects, "uncontaminated by personal bias, political goals, or moral judgements." He didn't enjoy an easy bond with Indigenous peoples. Teit advised the esteemed scholar on the virtues of patience.

Boas quickly saw Teit's value. He wrote to his family on September 21, 1894, describing Teit as "a treasure! He knows a great deal about the tribes. I engaged him right away." Boas wrote to his wife from Lytton on December 15, 1894:

> My informant is a very nice man. He comes from the Shetland Islands and has bummed around here a lot in all kinds of capacities. He is very much interested in the Indians and is writing a report for me about this tribe which will be very good, I hope. He will also make a collection for me. His name is James Teit.

Boas returned to British Columbia in June 1897. This expedition was funded by Morris Ketchum Jesup, a banker and philanthropist and president of the American Museum of Natural History in New York, who had earlier helped fund the Arctic expeditions of Robert Peary. Jesup's money underwrote an ongoing relationship between Boas and Teit for five years.

Teit was thirty-four when his wife Antko died on March 2, 1899, of pneumonia or tuberculosis. He wrote to Boas that, "as she was a good wife to me and we had lived happily together for over twelve years, I naturally took her demise as a great blow." Death was still on Teit's mind in 1900, when he published *The Thompson Indians of British Columbia*, as he noted a profound decrease in the Lytton-area Indigenous population. Mortality was particularly high among Indigenous children. The overall death rate was pushed up as whites introduced measles, influenza, TB and, for young people, venereal disease and whiskey.

Five years later, on March 15, 1904, Teit married twenty-three-year-old Leonie Josephine Morens, whose parents had immigrated from the Savoie region of France. She had turned him down the first time he asked, and he made a trip back to the Shetland Islands after his rejection. At this stage of his life, Teit was a socialist, which he underscored by his decision to wear work clothes to a fancy dress party in his honour in his hometown. In the Lytton area, he was known as "Comrade Teit." Josephine had far more conservative views but finally agreed to marry him anyway. To reach the wedding festivities, both the minister and the wedding party guests were paddled across a creek in a canoe by Teit and an Indigenous friend. It was a Catholic ceremony, officiated over by an Oblate missionary, although Teit's family was Presbyterian and he had minimal connection to any organized religion.

The Teits had five children, and each was given a Norse name—Erik, Inga, Magnus, Sigurd and Thorald. Inga later recalled to University of British Columbia graduate student Judith Banks that her parents had a very different approach to life:

He was always at the last minute catching trains. Mother wanted
to be early but he would say, "Oh, we have lots of time!" Then they
would get there just as the train was pulling out.

He was very easy going. Loved to tease and joke and laugh. His
favorite expression was, "First rate!" What upset mother was that, he
never criticized. She wanted criticism. She would cover a chair or make
a new dish for dinner. He wouldn't even notice until she showed him.

This easygoing nature extended to local celebrations, Inga recalled to
Banks:

He loved to dance. I remember him at dances because in the days
when I was a child you took all your family to the dances. And you
know, even if you were six or seven years old, you got up and danced
with the adults and they'd dance with you. He loved dancing. They
had a big dance hall, a fabulous place, great big! . . . There weren't
many people there, but everyone was full of life and they'd go for
miles to gather at these dances. I think the people from Lytton
used to come to the dances at Spence's [sic] Bridge because they
had a beautiful hall there.

After their wedding ceremony, Teit nominally adopted Catholicism,
but Inga told Banks he retained a connection with Indigenous spiritual beliefs:

Once when he was out hunting he had a dream—about a hole in a
mountain. He was leading a hunting party and he knew the valley
where the game should be but there was no game for the three days of
searching. He had a dream one night that he came to a mountain and
looked through it and saw a lot of sheep. The Indians considered him

psychic; some took his name, Teit, because of this, they told him
to act out the dream. He did and actually came to a tunnel through
the mountain and on the other side there were lots of game.

This was fascinating stuff, but it didn't pay his bills. Teit still worked
as a guide for American and European big-game hunters. On those
excursions, he shared a tent with Indigenous people rather than bunk
down with the white hunters. One of those expeditions was in September
1894 for wealthy Chicago engineer Homer E. Sargeant. This started a
work relationship with Sargeant, who funded Teit's research until Teit's
death in 1922.

Teit became increasingly involved with helping First Nations leaders protect their land. The Allied Interior Tribes of the Secwepmc
(Shuswap), Sylix (Okanagan) and Nlaka'pamux (Couteau/Thompson)
met for two weeks at Spences Bridge to discuss a petition they wanted
to present to the prime minister, who was travelling across the country
by rail on a campaign trip. Teit distilled the intentions, grievances and
concerns of the gathered Indigenous leaders into a document now
known as the Laurier Memorial. This message was hand-delivered to
Prime Minister Wilfrid Laurier at a campaign stop in Kamloops in
August 1910. It captured the turmoil and decline of Indigenous life
over the past half-century.

Gradually as the whites of this country became more and more
powerful and we less and less powerful, they little by little changed
their policy towards us and commenced to put restrictions on us.
  At first they looked only for gold. We . . . did not use it much.
We did not object to their search for it. They told us "your country
is rich and you will be made wealthy by our coming. We wish just
to pass over your lands in quest of gold."

Soon they saw the country was good and made up their mind
to settle it. They took up pieces of land here and there. They told
us they wanted only the use of these pieces of land for a few years
and then would hand them back to us in an improved condition.

Earlier, Teit had written to Laurier in May 1910 on behalf of "the
Chiefs of the Shuswap, Okanagan, and Couteau or Thompson tribes—Per
their secretary, J.A. Teit." Their letter didn't hold back in its conclusions:

We condemn the whole policy of the B.C. government towards the
Indian tribes of this country as utterly unjust, shameful and blundering
in every way. We denounce same as being the main cause of the
unsatisfactory condition of Indian affairs in this country and of
animosity and friction with the whites. So long as what we consider
justice is withheld from us, so long will dissatisfaction and unrest exist
among us, and we will continue to struggle to better ourselves. For the
accomplishment of this end, we and other Indian tribes of this country
are now uniting and we ask the help of yourself and government in this
fight for our rights. We believe it is not the desire nor policy of your
government that these conditions should exist. We demand that our
land question be settled, and ask that treaties be made between the
government and each of our tribes, in the same manner as accom-
plished with the Indian tribes of the other provinces of Canada, and
in the neighbouring parts of the United States. We desire that every
matter of importance to each tribe be a subject of treaty, so we may
have a definite understanding with the government on all questions
of moment between us and them. In a declaration made last month,
and signed by twenty-four of our chiefs (a copy of which has been
sent to your Indian department) we have stated our position on these
matters. Now we sincerely hope you will carefully consider everything

we have herewith brought before you and that you will recognize the
disadvantages we labor under, and the darkness of the outlook for us
if these questions are not speedily settled.

The Chiefs' sensitivity to recent change was considerable, as their letter
made clear. Here, Teit writes in his own voice, but no less on their behalf:

> The sudden changes in their methods of living forced upon them by
> new conditions, resulted in the breaking down of almost all their laws
> and customs and in the loss of authority by their elders and chiefs.
> The removal of the old restraints undermined their power of resistance
> and left them practically without protection against the evils of the
> white man's civilization. They had no guidance or protection from
> the white men who had forced new conditions upon them, and the
> change of life was too abrupt and far-reaching for them to adapt
> themselves to it with readiness.

Teit was making multiple trips to Ottawa with Chiefs, trying to
protect against further losses. He served on these missions as a secretary and translator, someone who could ensure the Nlaka'pamux
emissaries understood and were understood in the unfamiliar halls of
power. Whatever the effect of these trips to the capital, ultimately, the
Nlaka'pamux did find an audience. One visit, in January 1912, included
a meeting with recently elected Prime Minister Robert Laird Borden
and several cabinet ministers. When Teit returned from his trips, he
would bring back little gifts for his children, usually fancy-shaped
maple sugar. Once he brought Inga a doll, which she named Ottawa.

Teit's complexion was darkly tanned and ruddy. His beard was
reddish and his hair dark brown. When he acted as the Indigenous
spokesperson, he wore moccasins and dressed as they did. On one

trip to Ottawa, someone told him he hadn't known there were any blue-eyed Indians. Teit replied—maybe with tongue in cheek, given the pride he took in his Norse ancestry—that he was from a "different tribe."

Through his work with Chief Tetlinitsa from tiny Spences Bridge outside Lytton, Teit's adopted home had become a political meeting place for Indigenous leaders. On behalf of the Allied Interior Tribes, Teit arranged a meeting of roughly 450 Chiefs in Spences Bridge in July 1912, which helped lead to the establishment in April 1913 of the Royal Commission on Indian Affairs for the Province of British Columbia, also known as the McKenna–McBride Commission. Although the Chiefs were hopeful their concerns regarding their land base would finally be addressed, they were ultimately greatly disappointed with the results.

The McKennaa–McBride Commission was an inter-governmental commission of the federal and provincial governments set up to address the Indian land question in a province where the vast majority of the First Nations didn't have a treaty with the government. Their role was "to adjust the acreage of Indian Reserves in British Columbia." The Commission travelled throughout the province for three years gathering evidence from Indigenous and settler communities on the adequacy of reserves. They visited nearly every band and asked what little lands that remained of their traditional territories they would like to keep as their reserves. They held hearings throughout British Columbia from 1913 to 1916 and were tasked with adding and removing lands to and from the bands. The lands that were removed were usually in prime locations near urban settlements or of high agricultural value; these were called the Cut-Off Lands. By the time the Commission was done they had removed 47,000 acres of land with a contemporarily assessed (as of 1916) value of over $1.5 million from 54 reserves, and added about 87,000 acres of land with a contemporarily assessed value of less than $450,000. In many instances, prime ranch and agricultural lands were removed from the reserves and replaced with inhospitable and nonarable land with little to no irrigation or even potable water. In the case of Lytton, prime ranch land was replaced with unusable or inaccessible rocky side hills or lands where the water had a high alkaline content. Although on paper more land was added to the reserve, the value of those lands was less than a third of the contemporary valuation of lands removed from the reserve base across the province.

In his later years, James Teit remained an activist and friend of the Nlaka'pamux. He worked on Indigenous campaigns against land grabs, conscription and the ban on Potlatch ceremonies. He spoke three Indigenous languages fluently. He recorded songs, stories, customs and history, putting songs onto four hundred wax cylinders. He appeared relaxed when photographed with the Nlaka'pamux, who gave him the name Knaksht, which means "the Helping Hand."

Teit told a Senate committee in Ottawa in 1920 that the Interior Tribes of British Columbia, an alliance of Thompson, Shuswap and Okanagan leaders, "insisted [in 1909] upon my attending their meetings and helping with their writing. Thus I commenced to act as their secretary and treasurer." Teit was drafting a report for yet another lobbying effort with government, in 1922, when he became sick with bowel cancer. When he was hospitalized and receiving treatments and tests for his disease at St. Pauls Hospital in Vancouver, a group of about fifty Indigenous people from the many First Nations he had helped made the trip down to Vancouver and occupied the hospital, holding ceremonies over their friend in the hopes of aiding in his healing. This must have been quite a spectacle in a Catholic hospital, at a time when First Nations culture and spiritual practices were forbidden. He died in October 1922 at the age of fifty-eight. Letters of sympathy from around the world were sent to tiny Spences Bridge. His wife Josephine died in 1948, and they are buried alongside each other in Merritt, BC.

When I was a teenager and hungry for knowledge about
my culture, I stumbled upon Teit's extensive ethnographic
field notes about the Nlaka'pamux. These field notes were
instrumental in my journey to understanding our cultural
practices and history. Given the loss of traditional knowledge due to the residential schools, his richly detailed notes
remain some of the most important insights to our past
that we have. Years later, his work informs my community-
based artistic practice. *Asht-eetlm-a-timxw*, The Songs of
the Land, is a project I developed to retell Nlaka'pamux
creation stories as plays, with an ensemble of community
members from Lytton, Spences Bridge and the Nicola
Valley, using his wax cylinder recordings and the translations of those ancient stories that he made over a
hundred years ago as source material. The first of these
plays was a retelling of the Laurier Memorial, performed
on the one-hundredth anniversary of the writing and
presentation of the petition to Laurier.

Another huge influence for this work was the late
Nlaka'pamux Elder čálamancut (*cell-men-chut*), Jimmy
Toodlican, from the Shackan reserve in the Nicola Valley,
not far from Spences Bridge. Jimmy was a traditional
knowledge keeper and oral historian who as a child was
hidden from the authorities during the residential school
era. When he was five years old, rather than turn him
over to be taken to a residential school, his family brought
him to an uncle's cabin in the mountains. There, his uncle
instructed young Jimmy on the traditional ways of the
Nlaka'pamux. He didn't learn English until he was much
older and remained illiterate throughout his life. However,

his knowledge of the Nlaka'pamux culture was encyclope-
dic. Knowledge keepers, medicine people and storytellers
would visit Jimmy and his uncle and teach the songs,
stories and traditions of the Nlaka'pamux to Jimmy,
who was trained to be the repository of this knowledge,
at a time when the government was actively repressing
our culture.

Kevin Loring

CHAPTER 13

VIVA LYTTON

*. . . several large stores, hotels, shops, livery stables
and warehouses, a sawmill, grist mill, post office,
telegraph office, railway station, public school,
court houses and many neat residences.*

BUGGY DRIVER DESCRIBES LYTTON IN 1882

BERNARDO REBAGLIATI NEEDED a change—and a big one. Instability
had been a constant in Italy since his birth in 1857. Warfare had ended
the lives of some close relatives, and it didn't appear about to stop any
time soon as he grew to manhood. So in 1882 Bernardo sailed around
Cape Horn to San Francisco, where he found work in a store and a
bakeshop. Then, in 1885, it was on to Hastings Mills, which would later
become Vancouver. From there, he took the MV *Skuzzy* to Yale, then
travelled by horseback to Lytton.

Lytton wasn't Bernardo's original destination. He didn't even know it
existed when he got on the boat from Italy. He was just heading up the
Fraser Canyon. But when Bernardo got to tiny Lytton, he decided it was
time to stop. Perhaps he did so because it brought back memories of
his childhood among the steep mountains along the Italian coast from

Genoa to Savona. Whatever his reasons, Lytton seemed as good a place as any for his fresh start.

Lytton was still a popular stagecoach stop for horses and travellers to rest. It boasted, in the words of local buggy driver Joseph Burr, "several large stores, hotels, shops, livery stables and warehouses, a sawmill, grist mill, post office, telegraph office, railway station, public school, court houses and many neat residences."

There were still visible reminders of the gold rush, like wooden flumes and ditches along the creeks. There were also small groups of Chinese miners trying to scrape out a few last traces of gold, and Indigenous rancheries, or small farms, with log cabins, barns and pastures for cows and horses, and fenced-in vegetable gardens. There were also plenty of stumps as the land was cleared.

Bernardo opened up a store in Lytton on Main Street, with living quarters in the back and a root cellar dug into the steep slope. Soon he felt stable enough financially to send home for a wife. In 1886, Angela Rebagliati arrived in New York by ship, then took a train to Lytton. A priest from Kamloops came down to marry them. They were considered a good match by those who knew them, and after the ceremony they had a lifetime to get to know each other.

The bride and groom were both named Rebagliati before the wedding, but they were not related. Rebagliati was a particularly proud and popular surname in Italy; it could be traced back to the second century AD, when some Romans bristled at their oppression by their emperor. They moved to the north and became known as "the rebellious ones," which morphed over the years to "Rebellatus," "Ribellari" and, finally, "Rebagliati." Centuries later, the Fraser Canyon area of Lytton was chock full of non-related and loosely related Rebagliatis. Four years after Angela's arrival, in 1890 Bernardo's brother, Angelo Giovanni Rebagliati, also moved to Lytton, with his wife, Concessa, and their daughter Mary.

Concessa was the sister of Bernardo's wife. That meant a particularly tight family relationship: two Rebagliati brothers were married to the Rebagliati sisters.

Family trees got more confusing as they settled into Lytton and the two couples began to have children. They produced a combined total of seventeen, many with the same first and last names. In an effort to limit the confusion, Bernardo's wing of the family began referring to itself as "BR" and Angelo's side was called "AG," as in "Johnny BR" as opposed to "Johnny AG."

In 1892, as his family grew, Bernardo built a new store on Main Street. In time, the store morphed into a butcher shop operated by Clarence Nicolas Rebagliati. Bernard Thomas (BR) and sister Ann (BR), with the help of older brother John (BR), ran the store after Bernardo died in 1926.

Bernardo loved to tend his vegetable garden on his town property, with upwards of two types of grapes and a small orchard, at least two varieties of cooking apples, one kind of green apple and two or three varieties of red apples, plus cherry and peach trees. The local Nlaka'pamux began calling Bernardo the Apples Man, and soon others recognized his abilities too, as he exhibited his fruits and vegetables at fairs in Kamloops, at the Pacific National Exhibition in Vancouver and occasionally at the Canadian National Exhibition in Toronto. In 1913, Bernardo Rebagliati built a stately home on Main Street and a new general store, adjacent to the 1892 store. By 1913 Bernardo's brother Angelo Giovanni (AG) Rebagliati was also thriving, and opening up another store, a dance hall and the Lytton Hotel.

The Lytton Rebagliatis understood the huge potential for shipping- and transportation-related businesses in their new hometown. Angelo Giovanni's nephew Peter (Pete) drove stagecoaches from Lytton to Lillooet. Later, he owned the Shell garage and gas station in Lytton.

Johnny BR trained as a blacksmith in the horse-and-buggy days. For years John AG operated the Esso garage and gas station across the street from Pete's Shell station. That was back in the days when axles and other parts broke down regularly. At that time, Lytton had three garages, and there was another one ten kilometres south, at Cisco, and yet another six kilometres east, at Gladwin. The roads were rough enough that there were plenty of auto breakdowns to go around.

CHAPTER 14

SETTLER GROWTH

My informant told me that the Lytton chiefs were,
as a rule, peace-loving men, always more anxious
to prevent wars than to bring them about.

19TH-CENTURY ANTHROPOLOGIST CHARLES HILL-TOUT

THE REPORTER FOR the *Vancouver Daily World* sounded like a
starry-eyed tourist in a report published on September 27, 1892. The
journalist, who didn't get a byline, had arrived in Lytton via the
CPR and checked immediately into the Baillie Hotel, managed by
J. McKnight. "The hotel has recently undergone extensive repairs
in the way of new floors, partitions, painting, papering, carpeting,
etc.," the reporter wrote. "The accommodation is first class, and I am
bespeak for all good meals and the attention paid by the proprietor
to every want."

He took a tour of the town the next morning, which amounted to
walking past the forty or so buildings on Main Street. Along the way,
he spoke with Thomas O'Dwyer, who had come up the canyon from
Victoria back in 1858. O'Dwyer described how he had slept in nine feet
of snow with only one blanket while heading to the mining camps in

cheerfully named Richfield, by 1892 a ghost town in the Cariboo near Williams Creek. O'Dwyer told of how one chunk of gold he saw was worth eight thousand dollars, and how it took three animals to carry his gold out to Yale, protected by ten guards, each paid ten dollars a day. "There are undoubtedly many millions of gold in Cariboo yet," the *Daily World* reporter gushed, blissfully unaware that he was the latest in a long line of deeply disappointed people to believe that same claim.

Next he spoke with A.J. Hautier, who had run the Globe Hotel for the past six years, taking over from his parents. "He does a good business and has a very commodious hotel, well furnished, and adapted for the convenience and comfort of guests," the reporter enthused.

Then came A.B. Buis, who doubled as postmaster and general store owner. Buis made it clear he planned on staying in Lytton, prompting the reporter to write: "Such is the expression of most of the inhabitants, and it is not to be wondered at, for Lytton is really a pretty place."

Butcher Paddy Kilroy told of how he had come to town in 1858. In addition to his shop, he also owned a ranch and a herd of cattle. He had rebounded from his brush with Judge Begbie and the law, after he fired upon but did not kill Alphonse Hautier. "He is a moneyed man but makes no boast of it whatsoever and is quite satisfied to live quietly but he could sport a special car on the railways in the continent if he so desired," the reporter wrote.

Lytton then enjoyed what the reporter considered a good water system, with underground pipes. There were Anglican and Roman Catholic churches, with Rev. Richard Small preaching to a mixed congregation of an unstated number of whites and sixty to seventy Indigenous worshippers.

Near where the rivers came together, the reporter commented on a notable site linked to the local Indigenous community. The Nlaka'pamux played dumb when asked about it, not seeing the need to share their sacred stories with an outsider but not wanting to offend him either. The reporter speculated that the site was a graveyard "or battlefield, where there are thousands of skulls, bones, mortars, flint arrow heads, etc. The Indians at Lytton know nothing about it whatsoever. The place at one time must have been a fortification. On one side it is very steep and the other low. Close by is a very level place where the Indians had races and other sports." It's hard to be sure what place the reporter is describing. If the location really was just above the confluence, there used to be a large number of pit houses there. When the smallpox outbreaks came through in the late 1800s, it became common practice to bury the bodies of those who died in their homes by collapsing the pit house on top of them. This helped avoid further contagion but left the dead in something little better than a mass grave. Alternatively, the place where he was finding all those remnants really could be the site of an old graveyard. Or a battlefield. As we've pointed out, the Nlaka'pamux have lived in Lytton for millennia. After a few thousand years, people start to leave some things behind.

Much credit for the overall pleasant state of affairs encountered by the unnamed reporter went to new arrival Martin Beattie. He was described as a "provincial officer" who was originally from Ireland, and who had arrived in town the previous July. Beattie's achievements in that short amount of time included organizing a two-day sports competition in September, cleaning the streets, whitening the courthouse and finishing construction on the town hall.

Like the early Rebagliatis, Beattie was stepping away from deeply rooted European conflicts when he arrived in Lytton in 1892. He was born in County Cavan, in the province of Ulster, Ireland, in 1850. He was a farm owner who had moved to Dublin to become a manager for the Defence Association and then an officer with the Cork Defence Union. The Cork Defence Union aimed to "unite together all friends of law and order of all classes in this country in a body for their mutual defence and protection," which meant opposing Home Rule—the movement for Irish self-government—and boycotting the Northern Irish National League.

There seemed no end in sight to Irish conflict and violence. Instead of joining in, Martin moved to Canada, landing first in Victoria in 1892 and then moving on to Lytton as the provincial constable and tax collector. His family joined him the next year, after he moved to Kamloops, where he worked as a tax collector, registrar and mining recorder. Beattie's grandson, J.R. Beattie, became a deputy governor of the Bank of Canada, and one day his name would appear on all the country's paper money.

During that 1892 visit to Lytton, the *Daily World* reporter next took a look at life just outside town, noting that on the east side of the Fraser, four kilometres north of town, was the farm of T. Sewart, a justice of the peace. Sewart controlled 360 acres of land, about 100 acres of which was cultivated, including a 5½-acre orchard. The reporter wrote that Sewart grew tons of apples, pears and plums as well as an impressive crop of potatoes and tomatoes.

Sewart was most notable, however, as the area's undisputed watermelon king. "In water-melons Mr. Sewart takes the cake and the whole bakery," the reporter wrote. "Last year at the Royal exhibition at New Westminster, he carried away all the prizes in melons." Some of those melons tipped the scales at 40 to 45 pounds, with the average being an impressive 25 pounds. "Mr. Sewart is one of, if not the oldest Cariboo pioneers in the Province," the reporter noted. "He is still a hale, hearty well preserved man, and it does one good to come across a person as stored with knowledge of his country as he is."

Of course, Sewart wasn't the only Lytton area local with a flourishing agricultural enterprise. The reporter fawned over the efforts of Thomas

Gardiner Earl, still thriving as a legend of sorts in the fruit-growing world: "Mr. Earl's orchard is by far the best I have yet seen, and the quality of the fruit is A1 . . . the apple crop is simply immense, nearly all the trees in his large orchard being laden to the ground."

Next to Earl's property was a reminder that not everyone around Lytton had given up hope of striking gold and had moved on to apples and watermelons. The reporter noted that the Van Winkle Bar Hydraulic Mining Co. had a claim next door. "They have purchased their water privileges from [Earl] for the handsome sum of $10,000," he wrote, no doubt still starry-eyed with the possibility of riches. "This alone will show what faith the promoters have in their property." The new miners had drilled test shafts and installed hydraulic pipes, and optimism seemed high:

> The only drawback is the crossing of the Fraser river, which is a great nuisance. If the government would erect a cable so that a ferry could cross over with a team of horses, it would be great convenience to all concerned. After crossing the river the road is in a bad state of repair to the mines. Mr. Earl has done all the work so far himself with only $100 from the Government as its quota towards the expenditure. It is believed, however, that the administration will do something for the settlers here next year.

The article's unrelenting optimism turned next to the growing presence of the church in Lytton, which had benefited from the village's proximity to the railway:

> The new Native church was consecrated in 1886. A month later, the Marquis of Lansdown, Henry Charles Petty Fitzmaurice, who was then the Governor-General of Canada, stopped in Lytton. He heard

a deputation of Indians and then promised to send them an organ for their newly completed St. Paul's Indian church on the newly-completed Canadian Pacific Railway. He was good to his word and it arrived the next year. The Churchman's Gazette in February 1887 gushed that it was "A handsome cabinet organ . . . a powerful and very sweet-tone instrument . . ."

By the spring of 1890, Anglican archdeacon Richard Small had been in Lytton for six years, and he was getting results. As he wrote in his diary,

During the quarter of 1890, there have been 52 celebrations of Holy Communion. Twenty-nine at Lytton and twenty-three in various districts. The number of communions made has been 419, of which 228 were made at Lytton, this is exclusive of the celebrants and occasional other White Communicants. On Easter Day, the communicants at Lytton numbered fifty-eight, on Easter Monday, rounding districts went to Lytton or Kumcheen for Whitsuntie, as used to be the practice in former days.

Small went to Korea for more missionary work in November 1890, but was back in Lytton a year later. The archdeacon was certainly energetic. He rode his horse Jupiter out to visit Indigenous people who lived outside town. In one diary entry he seems to lament that he possessed a more industrious spirit than his horse:

It was a slow, weary jog over deep, slippery mud. Jupiter insisted that he had enough of it, and persistently turned off the road to an Indian's place that he knew of, instead of keeping on up the hill to a proper stopping place. The consequence to me was a bed on the floor in the corner of the Indian's house, where Jupiter had to fend for himself.

White contact brought more medicine, and also more disease. St. Bartholomew's Hospital was built in August 1893 by Anglican missionaries, at a time when the Anglican Church held a particularly negative view of traditional Indigenous medicine. Missionaries discouraged its use. But the new white medicine couldn't check the increasing infant mortality, a flu epidemic in 1889 and an influenza epidemic in 1918.

For all the beauty of this dramatic landscape, it held great danger, too. And not all of it was the fault of human activity. The dry, dusty Interior heat led to no end of fires, but the mountainous terrain held other threats. An Indigenous village near Spences Bridge on the shore of the Thompson River was hit with a landslide on Sunday, August 13, 1905, that took the lives of eighteen men, women and children. It also destroyed the church of St. Philip and St. James and other village buildings.

CHAPTER 15

ENTERING THE TWENTIETH CENTURY

*Inspectors, students, and parents all raised issues about
the quality of education, overwork, poor health, inadequate diet,
sanitation, building maintenance, fire safety, discipline, truancy,
sexual impropriety, and conflicts between staff members.*

MURRAY SINCLAIR, CHAIR OF INDIAN RESIDENTIAL SCHOOLS
TRUTH AND RECONCILIATION COMMISSION

WITH THE NEW CENTURY came new worries, ones that found their way deep inland to Lytton, where outsiders were still flowing into town, many seeking the peace of mind and body that the isolated village and its surroundings could offer. And some of those worries came from outsiders who weren't exactly new to the area by the time the calendar flipped over to the twentieth century, but who were still new enough to further upset the delicate balance of life in ltKumcheen.

No group that had arrived in the past century was having more impact than the New England Company. It had been granted a charter from England's King Charles II back in 1662 to promote "the Gospel of Christ unto and amongst the heathen natives in or near New England, and the parts adjacent, in America." In time, Anglican missionaries from the New England Company set their sights on the centre of the Nlaka'pamux world, in tiny Lytton, when they set up the Lytton Indian Boys' Industrial School, soon to be known as St. George's Indian Boys' School.

Amendments to the Indian Act were passed on April 19, 1884, that created residential schools across the country. They were funded by the federal government and the Roman Catholic, Anglican, Methodist, Presbyterian and United Churches. St. George's was set on 696 acres of farmland four kilometres outside town off the Lillooet Road in a rural, isolated setting. A main building that served as both a residence and a school featured an imposing white stone cross over the entranceway, at the peak of the roof. There was also a stone chapel with stained glass windows and a barn and other outbuildings. The chapel had once stood in England and was dismantled and shipped across the Atlantic and then by rail to Lytton, where it was rebuilt, stone by stone.

At St. George's, there were academic courses for students up to grade four, and after that the boys spent half their days learning about things like wheat, corn and cattle as they provided cheap labour to cultivate and harvest produce that was sold locally. There was also instruction in trades like carpentry.

Construction of the Anglican St. George's residential boys' school began on June 7, 1901, with the dedication "Erected to the glory of God, and in honour of St. George, for the education of Indian boys." St. George's was part of the broader cross-country residential school program that took more than 150,000 First Nations, Métis and Inuit children from their families, beginning in the 1870s and continuing for more than a century, through to the 1990s.

The school opened for the 1902–3 school year with forty-two students in residence. Attendance and residency were mandatory for the children, and parents faced the threat of jail or fines if they didn't send their children. They were told their children would be hunted down and forced to attend anyway, so they might as well just send them. A boy arriving there was first greeted by the principal, dressed in religious garb. All activity from that point on was regimented. He was given a uniform to wear and immediately pulled into a routine of daily prayer. There were prayers in the morning and at night and on Sundays, alongside staff. He underwent a ceremony to confirm that he was a member of the Anglican faith, regardless of how he and his parents might feel. This was a momentous event, attended by the bishop. The boy spent his time outside class doing mandatory chores, surrounded by pictures of white religious figures and white British royalty. If he had siblings at the school, he was discouraged from speaking with them. He was treated like a stranger in his own land, every minute of every day.

Not surprisingly, results for the boys were routinely disastrous. More than four thousand residential school students across Canada died of disease and neglect, according to a twenty-first-century federal commission of inquiry. Even as this book was in its final editing stages, ninety-three more potential unmarked graves were identified at the former Beauval residential school in northern Saskatchewan. Exactly how many students died overall in Canada or how many died at St. George's isn't clear. What is clear is that students at St. George's and other schools were physically and sexually abused by people responsible for their well-being in what the federal investigative commission called "cultural genocide."

Education didn't just mean science, mathematics and literature. It also meant attacking Nlaka'pamux culture from within. "The result of these instructions, the Company hoped, would be a number of young people trained to act as missionaries and catechists among their own people," Cyril E.H. Williams and Pixie McGeachie write in *Archbishop*

on Horseback, a biography of Archbishop Richard Small, chaplain at
St. Bartholomew's Hospital in Lytton and Archdeacon of Yale.

The Lytton residential school was meant to be a new home for little
boys who were often far from their family home. They were drawn
from the Lytton area as well as a host of equally tiny communities,
eventually including—and it's important to list them all—Aiyanish,
Ashcroft, Bella Bella, Boothroyd, Boston Bar, Canyon City, Cape
Mudge, Cardston, Carmacka, Cheam, Cisco, Coldwater, Cook's Ferry,
Deadman's Creek, Fountain, Gitlakdamix, Glen Vowell, Greenville,
Hazelton, Hope, Kanaka Bar, Kincolith, Kispiox, Kitamaat, Kitasoo,
Kitkatla, Kitsumkaylum, Kitwancool, Kitwanga, Lakalsap, Lower
Nicola, Matsqui, Merritt, Moricetown, Musqueam, Nicoamen, Nicola,
Nooaitch, Nooatch, Oregon Jack, Port Simpson, Prince Rupert, Seabird
Island, Shacken, Shulus, Siska, Skuppah, Spences Bridge, Spuzzum,
Squamish, Styne, Telegraph Creek, Union Bar and Upper Nicola.

The principal when St. George's opened in the fall of 1902 was
Rev. George Ditchman, an Anglican clergyman who knew the area. In
early 1893 he had been sent by Anglican bishop Acton Windeyer Sillitoe,
the first Bishop of New Westminster, on an inspection tour around the
Lytton area. Ditchman reported then that conditions for Indigenous
people were worst in areas closest to railway construction, as there were
more licensed drinking establishments there.

At St. George's, Indigenous children who had been removed from
their families were trained to become as white as they could be. They
were punished for speaking traditional languages or even listening to
them, and for eating traditional foods. Their hair was cut. They were
outfitted in military-style uniforms. "For school administrators, school
uniforms were especially significant—countering what had always
been seen by Europeans as the dangerous, excessive individuality of

Aboriginal society," J.S. Milloy writes in *"Suffer the Little Children": The Aboriginal Residential School System, 1830–1992*:

> Unbridled individualism, manifest in boisterous, decorative display,
> which broke the bounds of decorum and thus signalled the potentiality
> of lawlessness, was the core of savagery. In the schools, it could be
> moderated by uniforms which reduced the children to sameness,
> to regularity, to order and were, therefore, agents of discipline and
> thus of civilization.

Students were numbered and kept from their parents during the school year. They were taught English history while their own culture was attacked. They were taught to play white, British sports and did school work under portraits of the King.

Principal Ditchman's methods didn't impress William Ditchburn, the Inspector of Indian Agencies in British Columbia, who reported that "apparently robust children weaken shortly after admission and eventually become so sick that they have to be sent home on sick leave." Among other things, Inspector Ditchburn said that Ditchman neglected the health of some pupils and delayed for too long before sending them to hospital. He also accused the principal of losing the respect of students and believing more in the lash than in moral suasion.

Local Indigenous people didn't want to send their children to the new school, which could accommodate forty boys but had only twelve in 1903. Ditchman's attitude towards Indigenous people didn't help convince them. His annual report nearly drips with condescension, even when he appears to be trying to pay the boys in his care a compliment: "There has been no serious trouble with the morality of the school and the conduct has been excellent when one considers the natural deformities of these Indians." He later wrote, "Some improvement is noticeable in truthfulness and honesty, and the boys are fairly well-behaved and obedient, though they need constant supervision." When one considers how Judge Begbie had learned to favour Nlaka'pamux defendants in his court, it appears that honesty had not previously been an issue with the Indigenous residents of ltKumcheen.

After a few years, the instinct to avoid offence lost out to the instinct to protect. Fifty parents and band representatives met in 1910 with Ditchburn, who afterwards reported that the parents felt students were overworked, didn't get enough academic training and were beaten regularly by Ditchman, who couldn't control his temper. The children also didn't receive proper, prompt medical attention. The inspector concluded that Ditchman was "not the proper person to act as Principal of an institution for the education and moral training of Indians." He added that students became more vicious the longer they stayed in the school. Justice Murray Sinclair, who served as chair of the Indian Residential Schools Truth and Reconciliation Commission from 2009 to 2015, would quote Ditchburn's conclusion that "it is a well known fact amongst those who have a good deal to do with Indians that as soon as a person loses his temper with them so does he lose their respect and confidence."

Enrolment dipped to just ten students in residence. The school also had a hard time retaining teachers, having lost five in the first eight years. The state of the school became so grim that the principal of the nearby girls' Anglican residential school, downriver at Yale, complained that St. George's bad reputation made it difficult for them to recruit students.

Inspector Ditchburn urged the New England Company to replace Ditchman, and a month later it was announced that he would be gone. There had been warning signs that something was going horribly wrong, and that Indigenous people were leery of the imposing institution just outside town. Sinclair wrote in 2015, in the final report on residential schools for the federal Truth and Reconciliation Commission, that attendance had dipped to a new low at the time of Ditchman's ouster. Ditchburn wrote to the Indian Affairs department that it was time to replace Ditchham as principal. Ditchman sounded like he had already given up the fight, writing to Indian Affairs in his final report: "There are only five small boys at school—some finished and others absconded, some from the school, some from Lytton hospital—one followed the other like cattle, and as the expense was too great for constables to bring them back and hold them at school, they are still away."

It seemed as though the new school, for all its lofty ambitions, had hit an early low point with the Ditchman era. Tragically, though, the worst was yet to come.

CHAPTER 16

THE MYSTERY OF THE THREE DEITIES

Taverna did remove the gods and goddesses to his own woodshed. He then took over the Chinese joss house and converted it into a fine chicken house.

LILLOOET BRIDGE RIVER NEWS REPORTS ON
LYTTON RESIDENT BUYING AN OLD TEMPLE

CPR TRACK PATROLMAN Giuseppe Taverna lived on Main Street in Lytton at the turn of the twentieth century, next to the Chinese "joss house," or temple. He saw that Chinese sometimes visited the neighbouring building, leaving steamed chickens, fruits, incense, candles and burned paper money. He also saw how the site—and the food donations—attracted vagabonds who travelled into the village on the CPR.

Taverna wanted to buy the joss house and temple land so that his property could expand. He had visions of a chicken coop, neatly installed where the temple now sat. Taverna wrote to the Dominion land agent at Kamloops in 1901, stating that the joss house was on federal property and that the Chinese who worshipped there had no deed to the land. The land agent investigated. He was told by the rancher Thomas Gardiner Earl that the Chinese had taken over the property before 1881.

In 1901, Lytton residents Hong Wo, Wo Pin, Foo Sang, Lee Seen and Lou Alaak decided to apply to buy Lot 2, Block 13, Lytton, where the joss house stood. This attracted the interest of journalist George M. Murray, who ran the *Lillooet Bridge River News* with his outspoken wife, Margaret "Ma" Murray. George Murray read through inches of correspondence in the land office in Kamloops about Giuseppe Taverna's fight for the land where the joss house sat, and wrote:

> He [Taverna] had a small lot. His family was growing. He looked across the fence and dreamed of the day when he would be able to extend his boundaries and annex the joss house properties.
>
> What was a joss house more or less? Taverna thought to himself. The Chinese pay little attention to it. Some days they come, bring a fat pig or chicken or imitation money and place it before one of the idols there. They light a taper, burn some incense and go away. Then the tramps come from the main line freight trains, smell the cooked pork or chicken, enter stealthily, and then help the spirits hovering about the gods and goddesses to consume the sacrificial offerings.
>
> This went on year after year. The fruit trees in Taverna's yard spread their branches over the fence above the ground of the Chinese joss house. The Taverna grapevine was as anxious as its owner to get possession of the adjoining land.

Taverna wouldn't quit. He kept writing letters arguing that he should be allowed to buy the property. He called the lot an eyesore and predicted that the joss house would likely collapse under its own weight. He saw no value in the temple's furnishings, including statues of deities representing mercy, cereal and medicine. George Murray wrote:

Kwan Yen, goddess of mercy, gives courage to her worshippers. She is the taking-away-fear goddess. Her powers must have passed to Taverna, because he went ahead fearlessly to gain control of the joss house property. The god of medicine must have had a beneficent influence on Taverna's household. At any rate his family continued to increase and his need for more land continued more imperative.

Taverna was aided by lawyer James Murphy of Ashcroft, whose brother was a judge in Vancouver. Taverna and Murphy bombarded the federal government with letters saying that Taverna should own the land, including one in 1918 from Taverna that warned: "It is a fire trap. Tramps go there to sleep and eat. They throw matches and cigarettes about. If it burns, my own house will burn as well and maybe all of Lytton. There will be loss of life."

Murray wrote in 1918 that "forty years ago hundreds of Chinese washed gold in that locality. The building was of value to them then, but had recently been more or less forsaken." The government was not compelled to act.

In 1919, the Kamloops office was asked for a further report. The report went to Ottawa that the Chinese residents then in Lytton believed that while the joss house was not much use, that if it was destroyed the Chinese believe that they might all get sick again as they or their people had in 1881. The government of Sir Robert Borden apparently felt that it was no time, with the war being on, to arouse the anger of the Chinese gods in British Columbia. They left the Lytton joss house alone.

World War I gave Ottawa bigger concerns than a rundown building on Lytton's Main Street. Lytton's Chinese community had bigger concerns than Taverna too. Not only was Canada's head tax still in effect for arriving Chinese labourers, after World War I they faced a tide of anti-Asian sentiment, as veterans and trade union members worried about losing their jobs to workers who would accept less money and worse conditions than they would. The Chinese Immigration Act (as opposed to, say, the legislation of higher employment standards) was passed in 1923, spelling an end to the head tax but virtually halting immigration from China.

The political tide seemed to have finally turned in Taverna's favour. By 1927, he had even learned to read and write. He used his new skills to step up his campaign for the property. It had taken twenty-six years, but the time was finally ripe for Taverna to really press his case. Murray noted that he "wrote in a bold script to Ottawa a letter, in which he said: 'Children play in the joss house. Tramps sleep there. I offer $35 for the property.'" Murray continued: "Then J.W. Benzie, homestead inspector, was ordered to report on the matter. He did so, declaring that the joss house itself was but 18 by 27 feet of frame. It would make a good chicken house. He suggested a valuation of $50."

Taverna was able to buy it for a reduced price of $42. "No sooner had the sale been held than Chinese began to appear from all parts of the West to visit the joss house, to offer sacrifices before the idols which continued as tenants," Murray wrote. Mr. Chenhow H. Pao, consul general for the Republic of China in Vancouver, wrote to the government of Canada, alleging that the contents of the joss house were valued at three thousand dollars and that the building and contents belonged to the Chinese Benevolent Association.

In another 1928 letter, the consul general wrote: "It is true the building was very old and dilapidated, but has been repaired by the Chinese occasionally from time to time. It is unreasonably unfair to state the building has not been in use for twenty years. It is well decorated and the furniture is worth $1,000." The matter was reported back to China by Pao, and the Chinese republic protested to Ottawa and London. Little Lytton found itself at the centre of an international incident.

Taverna tore down the joss house anyway. He ignored objections from the Chinese about touching the statues of the gods and goddesses, and stuffed them in a woodshed. At long last he was free to realize his decades-old dream of a chicken coop.

Taverna did remove the gods and goddesses to his own woodshed. He then took over the Chinese joss house and converted it into a fine chicken house. Where the God of cereals, Shen Nung, once sat and received offerings, Taverna now throws scratch feed to his numerous fowls. A rooster crows where the god of anger once leered and winked. On land where Chinese of other days brought offerings of imitation money for the gods, Taverna now, by his energy and thrift, derives an income of real money. Tramps can no longer plunder the premises because the doors are well locked.

Murray continued:

The latest development in this strange case is that the Chinese continue to claim ownership of all that pertains to this certain joss house at Lytton. They are not unduly loud in their protests about it. They are not going to court about it. But officially the matter is not yet disposed of as between the consul-general's office at Vancouver and the land office at Kamloops.

As the Great Depression deepened in the 1930s, many Chinese people in Interior communities like Lytton moved to larger centres, where there was the hope of jobs and community.

Murray mocked the notion of any dangerous spiritual powers the building might have. He wrote in 1933 that Taverna hadn't suffered in the six years since he destroyed the joss house. If there was a curse on him, it was an exceptionally slow-acting one. "Taverna has not come under any blight as a result of disturbing the peace of the gods and goddesses," Murray wrote. "He and his family have flourished to the full."

Eventually, the chicken shed was torn down too. The whereabouts of the three deities remains a mystery.

CHAPTER 17

ALL HALLOWS' WEST

No bloody way are my grandkids going to go
to that Government Indian School!

LYTTON AREA RESIDENT FREDERICK JOSEPH (JOE) WATKINSON

THERE WERE AT LEAST twenty-eight elementary school students in the Little Red Schoolhouse in Lytton, and fourteen of them were Rebagliatis. At least one of those was rebellious, as befitted the family name. A student named Bill Rebagliati once survived jumping out a window to avoid a strapping. It helped that it was a one-storey building.

Down the road, on the Lytton-to-Lillooet roadway, another school was getting set to open in 1905, next to Foster's Bar Ranch. The location was flanked by ranches on both sides. Many of the children on nearby properties had mixed white–Indigenous blood, including the Watkinsons. Frederick Joseph Watkinson, the patriarch of the Watkinson family and Foster's Bar Ranch, wanted the best for his descendants, and he was well aware of the other option those kids had for formal education. Perhaps troubling rumours had already started to waft out of the imposing St. George's building on the farmland by the Fraser River, as Watkinson declared: "No bloody way are my grandkids going to go to that Government Indian School!"

Joe Watkinson set out to build his own school, with the help of neighbours Charles McGillivray and William Kane. The government was willing to pay the salaries of teachers, but communities were responsible for building the actual schoolhouses. So the neighbours built a one-room schoolhouse with timber that cost roughly two hundred dollars. It was called Foster's Bar School, and it would double as a community hall. It sat just eight hundred metres north of Joe Watkinson's homestead.

Foster's Bar School took on fifteen students when it opened in September 1905—twelve of whom were boys, and none of whom now had to go to St. George's. The school seemed to be well run, as an October 13, 1905, inspection report stated that "careful, thorough, systematic work is being done and good results obtained."

Over the years, all fourteen children of Frederick and Lucy Watkinson attended Foster's Bar School. Their son Thomas was enrolled in 1920 and left in 1926 at the age of twelve to help on the family ranch. He had the equivalent of a grade four education, which meant he knew the basics of reading and writing. Their youngest child, Robert, left school in 1934 at the age of thirteen. Thomas's son, Tommy, would go on to become a principal.

Some of the supposed upper crust of Lytton sent their daughters to finishing school in Yale, which seemed a particularly challenging spot for learning refinement. For two decades, Yale had been the starting point for prospectors venturing to the goldfields. The nuns had begun offering studies at the All Hallows' West boarding school in 1884. They'd long refused to be intimidated by their neighbours, which was important after having set up on the same street as bars, gambling houses and brothels. The brothels were easy to spot, as they had red curtains in the windows and a steady traffic of men through the front doors.

The girls at All Hallows' West studied pianoforte and violin close to where locals engaged in more earthly pursuits. Some of the All Hallows' West girls even went off to university, and the school boasted a Maltese princess and some nuns amongst its alumnae. All Hallows' West eventually took over "Brookside," the grand former family home of American railroad builder Andrew Onderdonk, which was visited in 1901 by the Duke and Duchess of York, the grandparents of the future Queen Elizabeth II.

The school housed between fifty and ninety girls at a time, but they didn't all study together. Indigenous students were separated from the "Canadian school." Students in the two sides of All Hallows' West received very different educations. White students wore a violet sash over their white dress, in honour of Violet Emily Sillitoe, the widow of Bishop Acton Windeyer Sillitoe, who had travelled the area in 1881 and declared Lytton the "dreariest, dullest, and driest place in the country." Students were trained with an eye towards passing the McGill University matriculation exams, the Royal Academy of Music exams and the Royal Drawing School exams. Indigenous students, on the other hand, could be forgiven if they felt like servants. They were taught domestic work like cooking and cleaning. To this end, they had to get up an hour earlier than the white girls to do chores before morning chapel. The Indigenous and "Canadian" girls were also segregated in chapel. They were not to acknowledge each other, not even with a smile or a nod.

Money was tight during World War I, and the "Canadian School" at All Hallows' West was shut down in September 1915. The Indigenous girls' side of All Hallows' West was relocated in 1917. There was space for them up the river at St. George's Residential School.

CHAPTER 18

BOOM TOWN AGAIN

*The statements in substance were that young women
had been seen entering Hughes' hotel and after remaining
there for some time left in an intoxicated condition.*

THE PROVINCE NEWSPAPER REPORTS LYTTON SCANDAL

LYTTON GOT ITSELF a tourist attraction in 1912. The town built a fire hall on Main Street. It was widely said to be the smallest fire hall in the province, resembling a slightly puffed-up phone booth. The bell at the tiny fire hall had an interesting backstory, as relayed by hotelier Louis Hautier, who claimed it was taken off an old rum-running boat in San Francisco and brought to Westminster, BC. It was used there as a fire bell. Some people say it had a crack dating to when it fell in the massive Westminster fire of 1898.

Fire was a constant worry in Lytton. A major blaze had damaged St. Bartholomew's Hospital on July 4, 1904. Fortunately, few people were inside and no one was injured.

Like so much in Lytton, Archdeacon Richard Small's life ended in fire. Small was the Lytton official who had married James Teit and his Nlaka'pamux bride Antko, or Susannah Lucy, despite neither being exactly Christian, let alone Anglican. He was often on the reserve, tending to his parishioners. When a fire broke out on February 5, 1909, he found an elderly Indigenous woman distraught outside her burning home. She cried that all her earthly possessions were in a canister in her bedroom. Small, who was sixty, entered the blaze and retrieved the canister for the woman. But he did not escape unscathed. He travelled by train to hospital in Vancouver the next day. He seemed to be recovering, but one night he told a nun, "I think I will go to sleep now." He never awoke. Small was buried in Lytton that May.

A memorial pamphlet was published by his friends and colleagues that stated:

> The work of his life was Christianizing the Indians . . . and no pains were too great, no journeys too arduous, no sacrifice too costly, to achieve this purpose. He followed them in their migrations, lived with them in their houses, and even in the curious underground pits, in which they sheltered themselves from the bitter winter's cold—instructing them, preparing them for the Communion at the Great Festivals, hearing their complaints, settling their disputes, pushing their interests, and identifying himself with them in every way . . .

Lytton became a boom town again in the first years of the twentieth century, as the CNR railway and the rail bridge over the Thompson River were completed. The non-Indigenous population soared to between four thousand and five thousand, with many of the residents living in tents and shacks in and around the town. Much of the growth came from a surge in construction activity connected to the CNR and a second railway that would pass Lytton, the PGE, or Pacific Great Eastern (nicknamed "Prince George Eventually"). That included freight wagons and teams needed to carry supplies from the CPR station in Lytton to the gangs of PGE workers in Lillooet.

Fifty freight teams were working the road between Lytton and Lillooet in 1912. Lytton was then home to two billiards halls, one of which was the poolroom run by Blackie Edwards (no relation to co-author Peter). There was also a barber shop, theatre, dance hall, A.G. Rebagliati's General Store and A.G. Rebagliati's Opera House and Sample Room. The term *opera house* reflected more ambition than reality; *dance hall* would be more accurate. The anchor of Main Street was the three-storey, sixty-room Lytton Hotel, built in 1912 on the site of the old Baillie Hotel. Its swinging doors led right into a bar with a towering counter that ran fifty feet north to south. "Some of the men couldn't reach the bar, as it was that high," one of the old-timers recalled. Outside, boards were laid down on Main Street so pedestrians could navigate over the beer-soaked mud. Wily children learned to look down when they walked through town, to spot coins that occasionally poked through the planks and the muck.

Boom times brought other entertainments to turn-of-the-century Lytton, some of which didn't take place behind closed doors on Main Street. Sports Day on the Dominion Day weekend drew enthusiasts as early as a week ahead of the show. Racers came from Ashcroft, Merritt, Spences Bridge and Lillooet and trained on horseback down Main Street into the night. In one event, competitors had to ride bareback down the street and then saddle up and and race back to the starting point. The ever-popular egg and spoon race required balance as well as speed. One horse race didn't even require getting on a horse, just jumping over it.

Whether it was Sports Day or any other occasion, kids piled onto the roof of J.H. Anthony's downtown store to watch. In 1910, they cheered an epic foot race down Main Street in which neither of the athletes wore shorts or a T-shirt. Bill Kane won after John George disqualified himself by pulling Kane back by his britches. The prize? Half a dozen apple trees.

Lytton had sports of its own, including a ball game called "sukkulli-laka," which vaguely resembled soccer. Two opposing teams attempted to control a round sukkullilaka ball made from tree fungus and covered with hide. The goal was to propel the ball through two poles planted at each end of the field.

Even with all the heart-pounding action on Main Street and in the open fields surrounding Lytton, some entertainment continued indoors, and some of it led to legal action. Thomas Hughes, former proprietor of the old Lytton Hotel, launched a lawsuit in New Westminster in April 1907 against Mayor W.H. Keary for damages, for alleged defamation committed in town. The suit got messy.

Hughes's accusation wasn't explicit, as befitted the Edwardian times. It was about sex, and the details were carefully covered up, although everyone still knew what was under the wrappings. The complaint stemmed from comments made at a meeting of licence commissioners in June 1905, concerning the hotel back when Hughes still owned it. "The statements in substance were that young women had been seen entering Hughes' hotel and after remaining there for some time left in an intoxicated condition," the *Province* newspaper reported. The mayor said that an undisclosed informant had told him that young girls had been enticed into the Lytton Hotel for no good purpose. When on the witness stand, Mayor Keary refused to give the name of his informant. The jury was out less than one hour before delivering their verdict for the mayor, with costs. Young girls had indeed left the hotel in an intoxicated condition, it ruled.

Years later, even after Lytton grew to have more than one street, Main Street remained the place where so much of life in the little town was lived.

I was in grade five or six and walking down Main Street
with my friend Robert Nicholson when we crossed
paths with an older boy in a cowboy costume, who had
earlier polished his tough-guy reputation by urinating
into the popcorn of the butcher's son at the downtown
theatre. The boy in the cowboy garb wore a leather
BB gun holster as he rode his pinto horse down Main
Street. He didn't crack a smile. He didn't even smirk. He
looked like he was channelling Clint Eastwood and should
have been humming the theme song for *Hang 'Em High*.

Robert never knew when to leave well enough alone.
He exchanged harsh words with the public urinator on
the horse. Then Robert picked up a rock and the kid
on the horse drew his gun. The kid on the horse squeezed
off several shots. His pistol was silent, but Robert's scream
was loud. He now had a BB-sized bulge in a finger.

The kid on horseback warned Robert to drop his
rock, training his pistol on him.

I was speechless. It was like I was in the midst of a
real-life cowboy movie.

Robert stared at his hand and the big round object
under his skin. Then he dropped the rock and ran home
crying. Peace returned to Main Street.

Peter Edwards

One day when I was about ten, I ran into my cousins
Warren Brown, Jason Adams and Darren Adams on Main
Street, and they were flipping around on their new neon-
coloured freestyle bikes. And they were like: "We're going

to be BMXers now." And I was like: "Whoa." Apparently they had read a BMX magazine and that magazine had convinced them that BMX was the coolest thing on the planet. And for us it really was. In that moment the Lytton BMX club began. At first it was just a few of us. Some were way better than others. Warren Brown was the best freestyler in town and had all the gear. He'd wear his BMX jerseys like people wear their favourite hockey jerseys. That was just his style.

At first we were into BMX freestyle. We wore neon, rolled our pant legs up to avoid the chain and sprocket, and studied those BMX magazines to stay on top of the current trends.

And then we got into racing. And street riding. We were so fucking cool.

The unofficial clubhouse was Warren and his mom Nita's house. Nita Walkem, née Brown, was our BMX mama. At the time she was the band manager of Lytton First Nation and a single mom. With the help of some of the other parents she organized the Lytton BMX club. We toured to all the tracks we could afford to get to. Lytton didn't have a track, so we had to travel to get to a race. Which was awesome. It was a chance to get out, meet new people and see new things. Mostly we rode the Kamloops and Lillooet tracks. The Lillooet BMX club was a huge part of my childhood. We'd race there a couple times a month.

Sometimes we'd go farther to compete in the big grand national tournaments. Some of us were pretty good, too. I was a pretty average rider, but it didn't matter; it was the greatest time of my young life.

At the height of the BMX club there were about twenty-two of us kids. By the end of it there were just three of us, Warren, Mike Durant and myself—we were the diehards. Warren still rides today.

It wouldn't be uncommon to hear loud music blasting out of Nita's place and see about a dozen teenagers working on bikes, watching BMX videos or reading BMX magazines. We were fanatics. I began to see the world, the landscape of Lytton, as one giant BMX course. We rode everything we could. We'd bunny-hop onto whatever we could bunny-hop onto. We'd be flipping our bikes around at each other, wall-riding the alleyways. We even created a game we called joust where we'd try to knock each other off our bikes. No holds barred. It was kind of like The Floor Is Lava, but on BMX bikes, where ramming, kicking and tailwhip strikes were allowed.

We were a bunch of wild teenagers racing around town, so of course the RCMP harassed us. Somebody probably complained to the village council so they began to get strict about riding on the right side of the road and staying off the sidewalks. In a town the size of a city block, it felt like oppression. At one point the cops began to escalate their harassment and began confiscating our bikes and taking some of us on starlight rides out to the dump. They'd impound our bikes and drop us out there. Fortunately, the Three Mile Reserve and Snakeflat are just two kilometres from the dump. So for my cousins who lived out there, it wasn't so bad, but other kids lived outside of town down at Siska. And there are bears at the dump. Despite this, they'd have no qualms about dropping us off in the middle of the

night. Nita brought a number of complaints to the sergeant
about the strict enforcement, but they landed on deaf ears.

One day I was riding my bike on the sidewalk. There
was no one around, a cop car drove up to me, flashed
his lights, pulled me over, scared the shit out of me. I was
twelve. He confiscated my bike. When my dad got home,
I was so scared that I'd be in trouble for losing my brand-
new BMX. He had just bought it for me at the hardware
store. I'd only had it a week and I was already a criminal
in the eyes of the law. When I told him what happened,
he was pissed. But not at me. He went up to the cop shop
and laid into the sergeant about the cops having nothing
better to do than to harass us kids. The sergeant apologized
and gave my bike back. They stopped after that. Nita was
irritated that it took one white man to complain while her
multiple complaints were ignored. I think other parents
were getting pretty pissed off at having to fork over the
money to release their kids' bikes from jail, so probably the
sergeant decided the petty cash wasn't worth the trouble.
Whatever the case, we were all happy the tyranny had
ended and we could shred with impunity.

Nita would organize everybody and get us signed up
for BMX races. We'd work at bingos and do car washes
to raise money. Just enough to pay for gas and registration
fees. I was often the bingo caller. I like to think that's how
I got my start in showbiz. It was fun to try to come up
with clever things to add to the call. "Under the B, one.
Be one with the force."

After working as the band manager for Lytton First
Nation for many years, Nita would go on to found

Nlha'7Kapmx Child and Family Services Society, which is
one of the first Indigenous-led child and family welfare
organizations in the country. NCFSS was established
through a bilateral "Transfer of Authority" agreement with
the provincial Ministry of Child and Family Services and
six Nlaka'pamux communities of Lytton, Skuppah, Siska,
Nicomen, Cook's Ferry and Kanaka Bar. This means that
when an Nlaka'pamux child from one of these communities
is taken into foster care, rather than handing that child over
to the ministry the child is put into NCFSS care. This
community-based organization then has authority over the
care the child receives, ensuring access to the resources they
require and the support of their community, rather than
authority over the child being handed to the government.

Kevin Loring

CHAPTER 19

SUFFERING LITTLE CHILDREN

They used the shackles to chain runaways to the bed.
They also had stocks in the playgrounds. And they were used.

FORMER STUDENT DESCRIBES ST. GEORGE'S RESIDENTIAL SCHOOL

IN MAY 1911, ST. GEORGE'S got a new principal. But even with
Reverend George Ditchman gone, his reign of cruelty ended and
Leonard Dawson installed as the residential school's second principal,
Indigenous boys routinely fled. Indian Affairs education official Martin
Benson wrote in 1916 that

> the desertions . . . are of frequent occurrence, as many as eight or ten
> boys being absent at one time. This shows an unsatisfactory state of
> affairs, which would be prevented if proper discipline were maintained.
> A case occurred last January were [*sic*] the constable found a boy at
> the railway station waiting to steal a ride to Kamloops. He took him in
> charge and he was returned to the school. It appears that this boy was
> given permission to go to Kamloops for the purpose of enlisting for

overseas service. He was under military age and physically unfit and should not have been allowed to leave the school . . . The boy was insufficiently clad and would have most likely frozen to death if he had boarded the freight train and proceeded on his journey.

And yet, for all these concerns over the boy's state of health and the bitter temperatures, he had chosen the long, cold ride to Kamloops and the possibility of fighting in a European war over staying at St. George's. Clearly, the change in principal hadn't changed everything, or maybe anything.

Decades later, a former student told the federal government's Truth and Reconciliation Commission how Dawson treated two runaway girls. They were "chained together and driven home in front of the Principal. They used the shackles to chain runaways to the bed. They also had stocks in the playgrounds. And they were used."

The school had a dark reputation in the Indigenous community. Joe Watkinson had opted out of St. George's for his fourteen children by building an alternative, and many others wished they could have found their own way out. St. George's wasn't doing so well with staff either. Employees complained in 1921 that they hadn't been paid for six months. Making it worse, they said they were also overworked.

Student Simon Baker was born in 1911 and sent to St. George's at the age of seven. He was the grandson of a Chief, from a family that took their traditions seriously. His mother had attended residential school too. The family simply stopped sending her after a couple of years because she was repeatedly punished for speaking her Squamish tongue. Simon later recorded how it felt to arrive at St. George's, more than 250 kilometres from his home on the Capilano Reserve in North Vancouver:

I can always remember seeing this great big building. I couldn't figure
it out. We all felt a bit excited. We were taken into the building and
shown around. So we were all taken downstairs and they gave us
school clothing. They took our own clothes and then put them
away and that was the last time we saw our clothes.

Simon soon found the overall atmosphere of the school to be repressive
and regimented:

We were just told what to do all the time. In fact, we had to answer to
bells all the time like well-trained rats. A bell would ring to wake us,
another bell for chores, bell for meals, for chapel, for school, for study
time, for bedtime.

Simon was shaken to see a fellow student beaten by the farm supervisor. Other students who were working in the barn saw it too. The boy
was beaten because he decided he didn't want to walk all the way to the
outhouse to urinate, so he relieved himself in the barn loft. Urine leaked
through the floor and down onto the farm supervisor, who took out a
leather strap and beat him. "Maybe he did a naughty thing, but he never
should have gotten a licking like that," Simon later recalled.

Simon and four other boys bolted from St. George's that night, hop-
ping a train to Vancouver. They stopped in at Simon's grandmother's,
and she helped them get to Squamish. There, they hid in the bush. They
were eventually caught and returned to St. George's. They escaped a second time and took the same route to Squamish, where the same police
officer found them and sent them back again.

Simon remembered St. George's students being routinely fed too
little and worked too hard. They weren't allowed to consume the butter
they made at the creamery or eat the vegetables and fruit grown at the

farm; those items were sold. Simon threatened to lead the students on a strike if they weren't fed better. If they worked like men, why couldn't they be fed accordingly? The principal gave in.

A particularly low point came when Simon's brother, Jim, died of spinal meningitis at St. George's:

> I used to hear him crying at night. I asked the principal to take him
> to the hospital. He didn't. After about two weeks, my brother was
> in so much pain, he was going out of his mind. I pleaded with the
> principal for days to take him to a doctor. "For god's sake, you better
> do something for my brother." They finally took him to the small
> hospital in Lytton. Each day I would ask how he was doing and
> they'd say he's doing all right. On the third day, on a Sunday night,
> the principal's wife came in, spoke to her husband and they called
> me into the office. There they told me that my brother had just passed
> away. I went to the hospital with the principal. There lay my brother
> Jim in a room that was like a morgue.

The coffin for his brother was too short, so Simon said Jim's knees were broken to make him fit.

The school's attendance shot up after the transfer of girls from the recently closed All Hallows' West in Yale, and also because of the passage of the residential school policy by Ottawa in 1920, which made attendance compulsory for First Nations children aged seven to fifteen. At the time, St. George's had ninety-five students. Parents could no longer decide not to send their children to the school that was designed to unlearn them in their Indigenous ways.

Finding staff for St. George's was proving difficult by 1920, when Anglican Reverend Louis Laronde was appointed as principal. There was also a funding crisis when he took the job. Laronde was described

by Indian Affairs official Martin Benson as "a French half-breed, a
graduate of St. John's College." Murray Sinclair notes that Laronde was
experienced and qualified but that Benson had written with concerns
to Deputy Minister Duncan Campbell Scott: "I think our past experience goes to show that we would be taking great risks in putting a
school of this class in charge of a half-breed."

He got the Lytton job anyway. Sinclair notes that Laronde described
his predecessor, Leonard Dawson, as running an administration marked
by "repression, with such paraphernalia as hand-cuffs, leg-irons, stocks,
convicts' haircuts and prison cells." However, Laronde had barely settled into his new role when he started to get a bad name of his own.
"The archdeacon of Lytton dropped a bombshell in a letter of April
1921, in which he informed the Court that Laronde had been accused
of 'gross familiarity' by a number of Indian girls, that the family of one
girl had named him as father of her child, and that others had accused
him of persistent drunkenness,"* describes J.S. Milloy.

Sinclair writes that an Anglican Church official investigated the sex
charges against Laronde and noted, "Some filthy literature which I
threw in the fire in disgust should not be in any decent man's possession." Laronde confessed to everything except for the paternity of the
student's child. "The archdeacon dismissed him on the spot, but because
he thought it did not concern them, did not inform the Department of
Indian Affairs of the reason," Milloy writes. "He covered up the scandal,
as was the usual way of dealing with abuse at the time, and for the usual
reason, that it would damage the name of the school."

---

* The description of the archdeacon's letter and his dealings with Laronde comes
from J.S. Milloy's 1996 report for the Royal Commission on Aboriginal People
called "*Suffer Little Children*": *The Aboriginal Residential School System, 1830–1992.*

The turnover at St. George's continued. Enter Reverend A.R. Lett, who arrived at the school in 1923 with his wife and baby, as well as high hopes of cleaning up the ongoing mess. Indian Affairs deputy minister Duncan Campbell Scott was optimistic that Lett would finally set things right, writing: "He has had practical experience in farming. He is just now in charge of a rural parish. As far as one can judge from all the facts and recommendations, he seems to fill all the needs of the case." The local Indian agent noted that the school buildings at St. George's were in a sad state of decay, students were poorly fed and clothed, and the farm and orchards were a mess. "The agent thought that if radical action was not taken quickly, the institution should be closed," Milloy notes.

It was Lett's first time as a principal, and he tried to rise to the challenge. His wife worked in the school as a matron and soon seemed close to a nervous breakdown. "Lett, himself, was increasingly troubled," Milloy wrote. "While he struggled to get the farm and orchard back into efficient operation and cope with a fractious staff, he faced serious moral crises in the school."

Soon Lett was hearing things far worse than accounts of a bad orchard, an unhappy staff or rampant theft. "In the dormitory we have a moral problem, which owing to the arrangement of that part of the building, we are unable to combat," Lett reported in 1924.

> We had one of the boys run away two weeks ago, and questioning him on his return, find out that the bigger boys were using him to commit sodomy, hence, his getaway, afraid to come to me. I suspected this for sometimes, but myself and the supervisors had not been able to check up on it. It at least will be an impossibility to eradicate it, until we have proper accommodations where we can separate the older boys from the mediums and youngsters.

The unsatisfactory accommodations at St. George's exacerbated the strain the school was putting on the Letts. "Mrs. Lett, baby and myself occupy one bedroom, not even having a spare room for visitors," Lett reported. "The living and clinic rooms are so public that we dare [not] talk over business affairs and repair to our bedroom, but then must confine ourselves to whispers."

Forced sodomy and overcrowding weren't the only challenges in the 1920s. There were also issues with funding, sanitation and fire safety. The quality of education at the school wasn't very good and the students were visibly unhealthy. "The Children were lean and anemic and T.B. glands were running in many cases," Lett reported shortly after his arrival at St. George's. "Energy was at its lowest ebb. Five minutes leap frog was the most I could get out of the boys at once. In examining the Bill of Fare I found that here lay a great deal of the trouble in the health and welfare of the children. They were not getting enough to eat . . ." The school had tried to appeal to Indigenous parents by promising their boys would receive the "care of a mother" and be educated in a "circle of civilized conditions." But despite Lett's early optimism and efforts, conditions remained bleak. Indian agent F.J.C. Ball gave this sad assessment of conditions for one employee at the Lytton school in 1922, prior to Lett's appointment as principal:

> There is a man of sixty-three, Mr. Hooper, acting as teacher, minister, janitor and general handy man around the School. He also has charge of the boys' dormitory at night. This man is certainly overworked and is conscientiously trying to do more than his strength will stand and his work should be divided, which I expect the new Principal, when appointed, will attend to. I watched this man rather closely and am inclined to think he is heading for a nervous breakdown.

Five years later, Lett had not seemed to make life in the school any better. A doctor's report from February 1927 detailed dramatically overcrowded dorms and defective heating and ventilation and drainage systems. Toilets were often broken and water pails had to be used to flush them, spilling contents onto the floor. The laundry room was in particularly rough shape, an inspector wrote, adding that "the building is in such a state of dilapidation that the wind blows through it. The children working in the building are cold, while breathing in damp steaming air." Not surprisingly, the doctor concluded, the school saw numerous cases of tuberculosis. A May 1927 report said that thirteen children had died at St. George's from flu and mumps. The report's author blamed it on the cold buildings, adding that it wasn't fair to blame Lett: "The Principal is doing the very best he can under existing circumstances, and it is only, I think, the fact that he has hesitated in adding expense to the Department that he has carried on to this period. Furthermore he has intimated his resignation if conditions are not changed."

Six years later, Lett had not made good on his threat, and the building was still a mess. It now housed 136 students. An inspector's 1933 report identified fire escapes at the Lytton, Fraser Lake and Cranbrook residential schools in British Columbia as particularly deficient: "It is impossible for small children to make their way down such escapes at night in sub zero weather as their hands would stick to the iron rails and the skin would be torn off each time they tried to catch hold of the guiding rails." An Indian Affairs officer named H. McArthur sounded painfully naive when he wrote that he thought conditions would get far better if the students could only be encouraged to feel more pride in themselves. Milloy notes that, "on visiting St. George's classrooms, McArthur had been 'surprised to observe the absence of teaching of any kind based on Indian life,' despite a 'rich store' of 'Indian art, and Indians culture generally . . .'"

McArthur seems to have missed the entire point of St. George's and other residential schools across the country. They aimed to extinguish Indigenous culture, not build upon it. McArthur sounded as though he was swimming against the tide as he reported back to his department:

> All admit that Indians are under severe handicaps in Canada and indeed in all parts of America. One trait that is traceable to these handicaps is a sense of racial inferiority . . . To give confidence to Indian children to enable them to look others in the eye in the knowledge that they, too, are Canadians and that in natural capacity they are not inferior to white children— Those should, I think, be the primary aims I think that they must be given a pride in their racial heritage and a knowledge of their racial history and culture. To cut Indians off from their origins—to try to make whitemen of them—is I believe both futile and undesirable.

Even the cows at St. George's weren't healthy, government inspectors noted. The Department of Agriculture told Lett that the log barn had to be torn down, as it was beyond cleaning. That explained why the school had lost eighteen head of cattle in the past three years, he reported.

Problems persisted, despite a new school building opening in 1928. Lett said he was "living on nerve pills" after suffering a breakdown in the spring of 1933. He hung on, but wrote in February 1934 that he planned to resign. Lett felt he was being undermined by S.E. Higgs, a fellow Anglican missionary, whom he accused of trying to take over operation of St. George's. Lett even accused Higgs of forgery in an attempt to make him look bad in the eyes of local First Nations people, saying Higgs went so far "as to publish an article purporting to have come from the old boys of the school but which was written by himself." Lett was also frustrated that the local Indian agent, A. Strang, had recruited only two students in the past two years, while Lett had brought in twenty-two. Lett contended that the school could handle seventeen more students. Strang countered that it was tough to recruit when St. George's reputation was so bad.

A recent example of what was driving that reputation came in the form of the boys' supervisor, Alfred Batcheler, who punished a runaway boy who had been captured. The boy said that Batcheler

> blindfolded me and told me to open my mouth as he wanted to give
> me a chocolate. Instead of a chocolate he poured a spoonful of mustard
> into my mouth. He then grabbed me by the legs and held me head
> down in a pail of water (ice cold) and poured a cup of cold water down
> my back, and then he put me on a stretcher and held me up in the air
> and told me to jump.

Batcheler later confessed to the abuse, admitting "it was a very foolish thing to have done."

G.H. Barry, the district inspector of schools in British Columbia, advocated doubling down on pressuring parents to get students to attend the school. Rather than treat them better, Barry recommended that "all available Indian children should be forced to attend" the school. This might involve trumping up some offence, he continued, writing that "in a few cases it may be necessary to secure convictions which would result in the sending of certain boys" to St. George's.

The chronic deprivations suffered at the school took a deadly turn in the winter of 1936–37, when 152 students suffered measles and whooping cough. Then influenza killed thirteen students while striking 170 more, as well as eleven staff members and four nurses. Lett wrote an odd letter to the parents of the dead students, suggesting their children weren't really gone; their faith was merely being tested. "Your children are just gone before and are patiently waiting for you and as their arms were flung around your neck and shoulders here, so they will greet you in your last and everlasting home. <u>Do not fail them</u>. Remember their joys and smiles and ask God to give you grace to go to them."

Barry wrote in 1937, in one of many damning reports, that he considered poor heating "the cause of illness." He added that the local Indian agent regarded Lett as "perfectly useless," and "not popular with the Indians." Barry also didn't like the way Lett handled staff. He wrote in 1938 that older children were not getting enough classwork, and that staff didn't always tell the local Indian agent about runaways. The St. George's principal was too often absent. Barry added that Lett hired the most unsuitable candidates as supervisors. He singled out the boys' supervisor as making "too great a use of corporal punishment," adding it was "most difficult to regulate the punishment of children in a school where the Principal fails in the general administration and control of his own staff."

Lett was eventually replaced in 1942. Incoming principal C.F. Hives warned his bosses in Ottawa not to expect much, writing: "After years and years of mal-administration, please don't look for definite results too quickly from St. George's."

The site for the school had been chosen in the nineteenth century by missionary John Booth Good because it was a safe distance from the "evil influences" of the town of Lytton. Murray Sinclair later concluded that St. George's became sadly symbolic of residential schools across the country:

> The fact that the federal government was prepared to accept four
> decades of "mal-adminstration" of the Lytton school is emblematic of
> the residential school system's failings during this period. The Lytton
> school, it should be emphasized, was not a remote, hastily constructed

mission school that operated without scrutiny. It was built in the early twentieth century, and a new school was constructed in the 1920s. Senior Indian Affairs officials received regular reports on the problems with the operation of the school, which the department owned after 1928. Throughout this period, parents, with very good reason, were unwilling to send their children to this school. The government used coercion to get the children into the school—and then failed to protect them from neglect, disease, overwork, and abuse. This was the residential school system in operation.

CHAPTER 20

INROADS

David Spintlum [Cexpen'nthlEm] did not want
this loss of life and succeeded in stopping the war.

LYTTON MEMORIAL INSCRIPTION

GOOD NEWS CAME IN 1926 for tourism in general and the Lytton
Hotel in particular when an improved Cariboo Road opened, speeding
access to the Interior. It was essentially the same roadway that had been
carved out by the Royal Engineers seventy years earlier, with a coat of
modern pavement.

The Lytton Hotel was then boasting in an ad that it had "60 modern
rooms, hot and cold water, private baths, ideal climate in dry belt . . ."
But the appeal didn't lie entirely in the luxury accommodations. "Lytton
is distributing point for Lillooet and Bridge River gold fields," the ad
continued. "Splendid trout fishing in vicinity and at Britannia Lake,
12 miles distant. Beautiful scenery."

Visitors to the village could see a memorial stone cross to Chief
Cexpen'nthlEm. It was erected in Lytton by the Chief's band on April 16,
1927. The words on the memorial helped explain why visitors weren't
presently standing on American soil:

When the White Men first discovered British Columbia the Indians were using the land and this caused bloodshed. David Spintlum [Cexpen'nthlEm] did not want this loss of life and succeeded in stopping the war. He saw Queen Victoria who was visiting Canada and reported to her what he had done. Her Majesty was glad to hear this and said, "There shall be no more war in Canada." She presented him with a flag and a hunting knife and told him he should be Chief forever. David Spintlum made his posts at Spuzzum at Lillooet at Stathshone and at Sheheous and these four posts are the limits of the Thompson Tribal Territory.

This is incorrect. The Queen never visited Canada. Not that Queen. The memorial sign may have been referring to a meeting with the Marquess of Lorne, Governor General of Canada, a representative of Queen Victoria. After the peace was reached, the Chief was given a knife, flag and Bible, but not much more. The old Chief wouldn't have been happy with what happened in February 1920, when an Indian Act amendment meant Ottawa could dictate who it thought should be removed from band lists, essentially determining who held Indian status. The old Chief also wouldn't have appreciated a 1927 amendment to the Act, which made it illegal for Indigenous people and communities to hire lawyers or launch land claims against the government without the government's consent.

Consent. Now there's a thought.

CHAPTER 21

WORLD'S FASTEST MAN

You had to help the school. You were a bum if you didn't try out.

OLYMPIC CHAMPION PERCY ALFRED WILLIAMS

THE DRY HILLS AROUND LYTTON provided an escape for many people. There was a time when one of them was the fastest man on the planet. Percy Alfred Williams was "slender, even delicate," in the words of sportswriter Trent Frayne, and an extremely unlikely sports hero.

Born in Vancouver in 1908, Percy was sent to St. Michaels University School in Victoria in 1920 after his parents, Charlotte and Fred, separated. Running was expected from the students there, and Percy immediately excelled. He set a school record in the under-thirteen boys' hundred-yard dash at the school's annual athletic meet, but he didn't rejoice or brag or even seem particularly excited. "You get pushed into these things," Percy later told a reporter. "You had to help the school. You were a bum if you didn't try out."

Percy had a good excuse to skip the exercise if he had wanted to. He contracted rheumatic fever when he was fifteen and was told by doctors that he had a damaged heart. He was under orders to avoid strenuous exercise. Percy had family friends who lived on a farm outside Lytton, and made visits for a couple of weeks at a time to stay with them. The warm, dry air seemed best for his condition, so he made a habit of going three times a year. He enjoyed helping out with the haying and chopping wood and other farm chores. That manual labour built up his strength, but Percy remained on the scrawny side.

Sometimes his father, Fred, joined him. Those times were the young man's favourite. There was even a horse named Spot he enjoyed riding. For Percy, there was a mystery to his parents' split, but it was clear that his father had become sad living alone. The hills around Lytton offered a quiet kind of healing for father and son both.

Most of the time, Percy lived with his mom, Charlotte, and her parents while Fred stayed alone in a hotel. And most of the time, Percy tried to keep things simple, even though something was clearly wrong. "He tried not to think about that," Samuel Hawley wrote in his biography of Williams, *I Just Ran*.

> Being sentimental, after all, was just a form of weakness, a chink in the armour he was expected to wear as a man. That was one of the reasons why he liked it so much up here in the hills, going out riding. Complicated feelings, the uncertainties of life, that nagging vulnerability—all of it subsided and for a while everything became simple. It was just himself, his horse and his rifle.

Once, Percy was riding with his father near Lytton when they saw old human bones near the trail. They decided they must be from an Indigenous burial ground. He posed for a photo with a skull.

His parents never reunited. Charlotte took a job in the spring of 1927 as a cashier at the Capitol Theatre in downtown Vancouver just as talking motion pictures came into vogue. At King Edward High School, the teenaged Percy won awards for shooting and was a cadet corps member.

He spoke in fashionable slang, with good things called "nize" and "a beaner," and not-so-good ones written off as "crushed apples."

There was also running—sometimes. Percy's sporadic participation in school track events caught the eye of Bob Granger, who was a dozen years older and a volunteer track and field coach at the University of British Columbia. Percy was five foot six and a skinny 110 pounds, but there was something special about how he moved on a track. Granger found a poetry in running and gave his time as an unpaid track coach.

Percy continued to visit the little farm at Lytton after he left high school. On April 14, 1927, he wrote to his mother, using his habitual relaxed syntax, including the slang *jake* to mean "okay":

Lytton, B.C.
April 14/ 27

Dear Mom,
I'm having a fine time up here, and I got your letter to-day, thanks
for the money and I've got lots now so I won't need any more.

Coming up on the train, when we pulled into Lytton I was dead
asleep and just as I woke up, I saw Lytton marked on the station.
So I grabbed everything I had and jumped for it. But just as I was
about to jump the bag of fruit broke but we both landed jake.

All this week we've been to Sevilla's baling hay and that's darned
hard work. We've had good weather though and that helps a lot.
Today we packed . . . lumber so that all we have to do. I think we're
going after my horse tomorrow. Say hellos to the Allans for me as
that's about all this

As ever,
Percy

By his late teens, Percy was up to 126 pounds, which was still wispy, but more substantial than before. Granger called Williams a "child of nature." The coach had to use inventive means to keep the young star on the track. Percy was happy to say it was Granger who "egged me on." Percy later said, "He'd want to try this out or that out. So I'd enter another meet and we'd give it a whirl. He just kept me at it. He was quiet. He never ranted at me. I don't remember him ever getting angry. We never had an argument. He was the boss."

Granger later said that one of his motivational tricks was a poison pen letter. He admitted that he had forged the letter over the name of someone Williams intensely disliked, saying that Williams had no chance of victory the next day. Granger said he forged the letter "because Williams ran best on hate." Williams won easily the next morning "after stewing all night on his adrenalin," he added.

The coach pushed him all the way to the 1928 Olympics, where Percy was well under the radar of so-called sports experts. The favourite to win the hundred-metre event was Jack London of Britain, a much more powerful athlete at six foot two and two hundred pounds.

There was no government money to send Granger to the Amsterdam Games with Percy, so Granger worked his way to eastern Canada as a dining room assistant on a train. Then he crossed the ocean on a freighter with a third-class ticket, paid for in part by Williams's mother. Once at the Games, Granger shifted into full coach mode. At night, he slept outside Williams's door to make sure no pesky reporters disturbed the young athlete. Before race time, he rubbed Williams down with cocoa butter and dressed him in three track suits, four sweaters, and blankets.

Granger's curious preparations seemed to work. Percy qualified for the hundred-metre sprint final on September 14, 1928. After two false starts, he smoked the field for the gold medal. Granger wept with joy as he greeted his charge with blood-covered hands, as he had been clutching a wire fence hard as Percy sprinted to victory. "Williams said he would have given up running after high school, but Granger kept egging him on, testing one theory and then another," sportswriter Archie McDonald of the *Vancouver Sun* wrote. "When Williams proved best of 87 entries in the 100 at Amsterdam his first words were, 'Won't Granger be pleased.'"

The victory was so unexpected that the band assigned to play the champion's national anthem for the medal ceremony didn't have sheet music for "O Canada" and played "The Maple Leaf Forever" instead. There was also a delay as officials scrambled to locate a Canadian flag.

That night, Percy wrote in his diary, "Well, well, well. So I'm supposed to be the world's 100 metre champion. (Crushed apples.) No more fun in running now." But Williams did it again, winning the Olympic men's 200-metre final. Suddenly the scrawny, shy kid who loved to ride horses alone outside Lytton was internationally famous, dubbed the "BC Bullet," "Canadian Cheetah" and the "World's Fastest Man."

American humorist Will Rogers evoked ghosts of Lytton's past, saying that the US should annex Canada so that Williams would become an American citizen. Rogers may not have realized that in the early days of the sprinter's favourite getaway, his joke might have seemed more like a threat. But in the wake of Percy's victories, hyperbole was the order of the day. "[No achievement] has so thrilled the Canadian people—and held the centre of the world's attention—as did Williams' incredible sweep at Amsterdam in the fading Twenties," wrote Ray Gardner in *Maclean's* magazine. Percy's hometown *Vancouver Sun* ran front-page headlines on him for four days straight while newspapers everywhere anointed him "The Fastest Man on Earth." Crowds waiting for his return were so enthusiastic that Premier Simon Tolmie said they represented "perhaps the most remarkable homecoming in the history of British Columbia."

The shy athlete addressed fans waiting for him at the train station. "This is the best of all," Williams said. "I am glad to get back home . . . I have seen a lot of Europe, but if you put it all beside Vancouver, I would choose Vancouver." Then there was a tickertape parade down Granville Street, and some of those without confetti tore up newspapers and tossed the pieces in the air. Vancouver mayor L.D. Taylor presented Percy with a shiny new robin's-egg blue Graham-Paige coupe. There was also a $15,893.25 trust fund and $500 in gold, to match his medals.

Some scientists studied Percy in an attempt to make sense of his speed. Dr. Charles Best, the man who discovered insulin with Dr. Frederick Banting, co-authored a paper for the Royal Society of London that concluded that Williams's scrawny stature meant his muscles had less friction to cope with than was the case with his more muscular competitors. Dutch doctors took it even further, calling him the only "perfect athlete" of the 3,600 Olympians competing in the 1928 Amsterdam Olympics.

For all the praise, Williams's heart still wasn't in it. He was out of track and field by his mid-twenties—but not forgotten. A Canadian Press poll in 1950 called his double gold at the Olympics the most dramatic sporting event of the previous half-century. None of it seemed entirely real to Percy. "Sometimes I look at the clippings and ask myself: was that really me or some other guy?" he later said.

Things quieted down as more Olympic Games came and went. Percy settled into a basement apartment in Vancouver's west end with his mother and never married. When Charlotte died, he carried on there. He gave his two Olympic gold medals to the BC Sports Hall of Fame, where they were stolen and not recovered. He supported himself in the insurance business and golfed whenever possible. Golf offered him peace, but he wasn't nearly as talented on the links as he was on the track.

Lytton retained its quiet, soothing charms for Percy, who particularly loved the company of golden retrievers there. He sometimes hunted and was an excellent shot. "I never did like running," the aging double Olympic champion told a reporter a quarter-century after his glory years, adding that all his accomplishments were "because of the dedication of Bob Granger, my coach." Before Granger faded from the public eye, he told a reporter in 1964 how it felt to watch Percy run: "It was fascination in the flesh. I wanted to feast my eyes on the sight. I wanted that finish line to run before him to the ends of the earth. He was thistledown before the summer breeze."

Sometimes Percy stayed with the McKay family in Botanie Valley outside Lytton during those quiet later visits. He was also friends with Jimmy Johnson, who had a small farm just south of the ferry on the west side of the Fraser River and was popular with the west bank Indigenous people. Johnson had moved to Lytton from North Dakota around the turn of the twentieth century and married an Indigenous woman. He got the ferry job when the previous ferryman, Dutch Charlie, drowned. Percy was an old man with a cane by then, sometimes staying at the Totem Motel.

Lytton had no golf course, so it wasn't heaven in Percy's world, but it remained a particularly nice place to visit, even if it had rattlesnakes instead of fans. He told Ray Gardner of *Maclean's* magazine, almost thirty years after his Olympic victories, that he had been uncomfortable with his sudden celebrity status. "I was simply bewildered by it all. I didn't like running. Oh, I was glad to get out of it all."

Percy had an extremely low profile in Lytton, which he still visited in his final years, when possible. His health was in decline, and he had become somewhat of a recluse. He was the only Canadian Olympic gold medallist to decline to take part in a ceremony at the 1976 Montreal Olympics. His days of riding Spot and hunting around Lytton were long gone, though he still collected guns. A stroke in October 1982 was followed by another one in mid-November. He had been suffering from severe arthritis in his ankles and knees and had a doctor's appointment scheduled for the end of the month. He was seventy-four and paunchy. Whatever peace he'd gained throughout his life from his escapes to Lytton, it seemed unlikely he'd ever taste it again.

Instead of keeping the November appointment, the double Olympic champion drew a bath. He sat back in his tub and pulled up a twelve-gauge shotgun. It was one of his favourites, a gift for his 1928 victories. He put a toe to the trigger, pressed down, and shot himself in the head.

CHAPTER 22

DOWNTOWN FIRES

*Lytton occupies a beautiful site at the junction
of the Thompson and the Fraser Rivers. Perhaps
rebuilt Lytton will be worthier than ever of
that glorious natural environment.*

VANCOUVER *PROVINCE* COMMENTS ON 1931 FIRE

THE HARSH ECONOMIC TIMES of the Great Depression explained
why F.J. Thibodeau showed up alone in Lytton in September 1931. The
forty-two-year-old from Vancouver planned to sell Christmas cards to
stores in the Fraser Canyon for the Arts-Point Card Company and send
his earnings back home to his wife and four kids. Jobs were not easy to
come by and it had taken several months to land even that one, which
paid by commission. It was far from ideal, but Thibodeau was a survivor. He had fought overseas with the 14th Battalion of Edmonton in
World War I. He could handle this too.

Desperation drove others to Lytton during the Great Depression.
More than six hundred men came to try their hand at panning for gold.
They didn't get much gold, but at least here they could hold on to a sliver
of hope.

Thibodeau sent home a dollar to his wife immediately after he arrived. It wasn't much, but there should be more to follow soon. Then he went to sleep in his room on the second floor of the Lytton Hotel, on the evening of Wednesday, September 10, 1931.

The ringing of a bell jolted Thibodeau awake early Thursday morning. Fellow guest George Finlay later described the scene in the hallway outside. "It was like a horrible nightmare of 'Dante's Inferno,'" he told a reporter.

> My room was on the second floor. I was awakened by a bell. It was
> the fire bell, I afterwards learned. Then I heard the roar of flames
> and my throat burned from the smoke that was rapidly filling my
> room. I heard women screaming, the shouts of men.
>
> Men and women were pouring out of their rooms, still in their
> nightclothes. Flames blocked their panicked rush to the stairs. If
> they were to avoid being trapped in their rooms, where they would
> surely burn to death, the only option left was the second-floor balcony,
> such as it was.
>
> We started jumping. Some of the people were even jumping
> from the third floor. I don't know how many took the leap. Some
> waited, afraid to leap out. They were scorched by the fire along
> the window sills.

P.L. Englefield, the assistant manager of the Lytton Hotel, suffered a broken hip from his jump. He was taken to Vancouver General Hospital, also needing treatment for burns to his face and body. Hotel cook Jueng Kwo was also listed in fair condition. Forty-year-old Frederick Arthur Richardson of Edmonton died in hospital in Kamloops.

Canon Stanley Higgs was in his pyjamas at home, saying his prayers, when he heard the town fire bell. That was about the same time he heard footsteps rushing onto his front porch and an excited shaking of his screen door. "I could see a great bank of flame," he later recalled. "I hastened to answer the door." It was a friend warning him, "Get your car out. Your garage is on fire." Higgs recalled, "It was obvious that the Lytton Hotel was on fire and burning violently. My garage and four houses a block away had caught fire from some burning debris carried on the wind . . . I ran to the garage and rescued the car. The hospital was directly in the path of the fire and would have to be evacuated."

Wind was sweeping the fire through Lytton's entire business district. "The fire was growing rapidly," said Higgs.

> It had spread across a narrow lane to the annex of the hotel which occupied the rest of the block, and already the annex was ablaze from end to end. The roar of the flames generated a sense of urgency. But what was to be done? One had to assume that the occupants of homes already engulfed had escaped to safety. Their homes were out of reach already.

Higgs rushed to the hospital to try to help. "The doctor had arrived, and as I was leaving for the hospital again, he asked me to fetch some ether. The first serious victim had been brought in. He was a travelling salesman, named Thibodeau." Thibodeau had also leapt from the hotel balcony. He'd suffered a broken ankle, severe burns and shock. Dr. Ellis asked Higgs to urge the CNR to hold the first eastbound train so that Thibodeau and any other seriously injured people could be rushed to Kamloops Royal Inland Hospital. "The trip down to the CNR was a case of running the gauntlet of fire," Higgs recalled.

> On the left of the road the hotel and annex were totally ablaze. Opposite, the office of the Indian agent was already beyond recognition. Behind it and fronting onto the hotel street the agent's house was a mass of flame . . .

All the landmarks down to the CNR station had either gone or were a blinding mass of flame.

I drove to where I thought the corner of the main street was, and saw a hose being played on a building quite beyond saving. I persuaded the user to move down to the hospital and help keep the roof wet.

A group of Nlaka'pamux people used shovels and soil to stem the fire's spread. One man, referred to as "Jumbo," helped move patients, equipment and hospital records to a safe location.

Losses would eventually be estimated at more than $100,000. Twenty-eight buildings were destroyed, including the old Globe Hotel, the old general store bought in 1893 by A.G. Rebagliati, and the old Rebagliati Opera House. Thibodeau's car was parked outside the hotel and also destroyed by the blaze. It had taken just half an hour for the village's business section to be destroyed.

The next day, September 11, Thibodeau's wife received the dollar he had sent in the mail. The day after that, Thibodeau died alone in Kamloops.

Higgs wasn't impressed with the hotel management when he visited Englefield in Vancouver General Hospital a week later. "He was suffering greatly as he had been required to jump some eighteen feet and lay beside the burning building waiting to be carted to safety," Higgs said. "Already he had been approached, on behalf of the management, while in an extremely weakened state, and asked to sign a release whereby he would be deprived of any claim upon the owners for any injury or loss occasioned by the fire."

The Vancouver *Province* tried to sound upbeat about Lytton's fate on its editorial page:

History was made in Lytton in the days of the Cariboo gold rush. Lytton was then the chief town of the interior. Since the re-opening of the Cariboo Trail as a scenic motor highway Lytton has been making a remarkable come-back from its long dormant period.

The fire will be a temporary setback. It may ultimately be a blessing. Lytton occupies a beautiful site at the junction of the Thompson and the Fraser Rivers. Perhaps rebuilt Lytton will be worthier than ever of that glorious natural environment.

A coroner's jury in Kamloops praised the efforts of CNR employee James R. Knight in sounding the alarm and saving lives. Meanwhile, however, Thibodeau's widow was reduced to an even lower rung of poverty. She told the *Province* how deeply she appreciated readers for raising $185 in about a week. "Please say for me, that words cannot express my appreciation of the great kindness shown to us, and I shall always remember it," she said.

In the wake of the fire, Antonio Madori of Lytton bought the hotel property. The fire had destroyed the home he shared with his wife, Nita Medori (née Rebagliati). Antonio was born in Pietracamela, Italy, in 1894 and had fallen in love with Nita while he was the night clerk and part-time electrician at the Globe Hotel, which was spared the fire. He bought the Lytton Hotel property with financing from Colonel Joseph Victor Norman Spencer, who was now the owner of Earlscourt Ranch, across the Fraser River from Lytton. Spencer's father, gold-rush participant David Spencer, had gone on to found Spencer's department store, which would later be bought out by the Eaton's chain in 1948 for $14 million.

The Colonel's title came from his time fighting in the Boer War. He'd come home to take up ranching, buying five properties: the Douglas Ranch Lake in Nicola Valley, the Pavilion Ranch on Pavilion Mountain, the Bryson Ranch in Pavilion Valley, the Circle S Ranch at Dog Creek and Earlscourt Ranch. He now lived part-time at Earlscourt, where he owned two thousand acres and ran about 250 head of Herefords, raised for breeding only. He also became the first person in British Columbia to grow fruit commercially, after buying his first trees from a Frenchman in Oregon. The Colonel helped Antonio Madori build the New Lytton Hotel, with a garden to provide vegetables for the dining room.

The Globe Hotel, where the Madoris had met and fallen in love, survived the fire of 1931, but its reprieve was short. Fire struck Lytton again on January 29, 1938, after a blaze had broken out at the Globe. As in 1931, Lytton's persistently strong winds fanned the flames, and the entire rebuilt business district of Lytton was threatened. Firefighters—realizing they could not save the Globe—concentrated on preventing the fire's spread. They succeeded, but a mere three months later another fire destroyed two cafés and a barber shop in town. And three months after that, yet another fire took a bakery shop and two cafés.

Fire struck again in July 1939, but this time the dryness of the surrounding area was more appealing to the blaze than the town itself. The fire left several Nlaka'pamux ranches in smoking ruins and killed a local firefighter named J.H. Brown. Indigenous people, railway work crews and village residents rallied to fight that blaze across the Fraser from Lytton, which burned 12.8 kilometres along the river. Once again, winds fanned the flames as some two hundred tons of hay were lost, as well as orchard trees and livestock. The flames also threatened—but eventually spared—Earlscourt.

After each fire, residents simply rebuilt and soldiered on. It was part of the price to pay for living at the Centre of the Universe.

CHAPTER 23

GLASGOWS ARRIVE— WATKINSONS SURVIVE

I think they just headed for the Fraser—the goldfields.

DONNY GLASGOW DESCRIBES WHY HIS
FATHER AND UNCLES WENT TO LYTTON

FORD GLASGOW WAS JUST TWENTY when he rolled into Lytton during the depths of the Great Depression, driving an old Model A Ford, a step up from the Model T with its top speed of sixty miles per hour. With Ford were his younger brothers Ernest Johnson, who was eighteen, and John, who was sixteen. Ernest, who was born on August 11, 1916, in Winchester, Ontario, south of Ottawa, was named after his uncle, a World War I hero.

Their family had fallen on hard times in Ontario after a promising few years. They owned a telephone exchange in the Winchester area, which they used as collateral to buy a brick factory. "They were relatively well off for the time," Ernest's son Donny later said. But then the Great Depression hit in 1929. Bricks weren't the commodity they'd been during the Roaring Twenties. "Nothing happened with selling bricks," Donny said. "Nobody's building anything."

Determined, the Glasgow brothers ventured west. They looped through the US, staying for a time with relatives who owned a ranch outside Thermopolis, the county seat and largest town in Hot Springs County, Wyoming. The town's name is Greek for "hot city," but it wasn't as hot as their next stop. They hit the road again and kept going until they wheeled the Model A into Lytton in September 1934.

They'd seen across half the continent that times were desperate, but the Glasgow brothers hadn't given up hope. "I think they just headed for the Fraser—the goldfields," Donny said. "They wanted to mine for gold." The brothers and some companions spent their first winter outside Lytton at 14 Mile, bunkered inside a spinoff of a form of housing that had been used by the Nlaka'pamux for millennia. "They dug a hole in the ground and put a tent over it and that's how they spent the winter," Donny said. "In this tent in the ground."

As a young man, Donny got a taste of his father's goldfield optimism: "In the spring of 1980, Dad and I went back to the 14 Mile and did some gold mining of our own," he said. "In ten days of work, five to six hours a day, with Dad's backhoe we made just over one ounce of gold, which back then was $980 per ounce." Even adjusted for inflation, that wasn't much, considering the time and equipment involved, but it was something, and it gave father and son a chance to bond. "We did expect a little more, but still a good time," Donny said. "Dad was happy just working like the old days."

The Great Depression was just ending as Canada joined the war effort in September 1939. Service meant regular food and a place to stay, as well as a righteous cause.

The three Glasgow brothers enlisted in May 1940. Ford and Ernest were accepted, while the youngest brother, John, was turned away. John was already married and worked the Rosebank Ranch by the Watkinson property. Recruiters said they needed to keep some farmers at home and on the job.

Ford and Ernest were placed together in the Rocky Mountain Rangers and then Princess Patricia's Canadian Light Infantry. After the war, they seldom spoke of their shared experience. "They were quiet," Ernest's son Donny said. "Nobody said anything . . . They just buried the whole horror of the war." When Donny was twenty-two, he finally asked his father about it. Ernest told him about being at sea, as part of the invasion of Sicily that led to the end of the war, and said, "Anywhere you looked was a ship." When asked if he ever killed anyone, Ernest replied, "I don't even want to think about that."

"It really affected him," Donny said. "He wasn't angry. He was just sad. [It was as if he thought] 'It was so horrible I don't want to think about it.' He just walked away."

Donny's uncle Ford also never fully recovered from his time overseas. Ford lost a lung from shrapnel from a German artillery .88 shell. Once back in Canada, he and his wife, Hazel, became known as the "gypsies" in the family. "They just moved from place to place," Donny said.

Two things brightened up Ernest when he reflected on the war: the occasional funny moment and the Harley-Davidson motorcycles ridden by Allied dispatch drivers. The Glasgow family has a love affair with motor-cycles. Donny was given a Yamaha 80 cc bike for his fifteenth birthday. He later got his own Harley, which came with mixed feelings. "When it ran, you felt like you owned the world. But they were just so much trouble."

His older brother Kenny would one day build an outdoor art park in Botanie Valley that featured greatly oversized sculptures of Harley-Davidsons. They were created in Kenny's shop, in which a quote was painted high on the wall: "Welcome to my debris of independence, the remaining parts of my thrown away youth, my hovel of broken accomplishments, my plans of yesterday's failures, my wreckage of shattered dreams, my promises of great returns. Yes, come in. We can cry over yours as well, for it is only human to share."

Vancouver writer Ethel Wilson visited Lytton in the fall of 1940, checking into Brophy House. A fair was under way, but Wilson reported that even this tiny community in the mountains had been hit by the war:

> If one lived surrounded by the peaceful hills of Lytton it would need a great deal of imagination to believe that the horrible bombardment of London, the city that is at once the dear possession of the Englishman, the Canadian, the Australian, of everyone of British birth the world over, was in its sixteenth terrible day and night.
>
> But in Lytton people have imagined all that. A large and lighted store window in the main street was filled with Red Cross articles as excellent as any you would see in a large centre . . . These garments represented a third shipment of completed work about to be sent to the provincial headquarters in Vancouver.
>
> There were pyjamas, surgeon's gowns, sweaters, various other garments, neatly finished and correctly folded. There were socks and more socks and more socks. There were refugee garments . . .
>
> We turned back to the Brophy House, above the river, and went to bed. At 11 o'clock the noise of the fair stopped suddenly as if it had been turned off at a switch, and the silence flowed over again, like the sage-brush into the orchards. The tattooed man, the bearded lad, the Indians, Howard the Lobster Boy and all of us one by one closed our eyes in sleep, and the soft Lytton wind blew on and on between the hills.

As tiny Lytton went onto a war footing, the Lytton Pacific Coast Militia Rangers were established. That came just after the Japanese bombed the American naval base at Pearl Harbor in Honolulu, on

Sunday, December 7, 1941, drawing the US into World War II. The militia's ranks comprised twenty unpaid volunteers who were either too young or too old for the armed forces. They did target practice at the airport site and trained at Jackass Flats, with their barracks at Hobo Hollow. Their task was to guard local railway bridges. The Rangers lasted a year in Lytton before they were sent overseas and replaced on bridge duty by WWI veterans.

The area also saw internment camps for displaced Japanese, including four camps in the nearby Lillooet area and another down the river in Spuzzum. The Lillooet camps held a combined total of nearly a thousand men, women and children. Residents of the East Lillooet internment camp built uninsulated tarpaper shacks with no indoor plumbing. They leased land, which they plowed with horses borrowed from local First Nations. Their tomato crops were so impressive they soon supported a cannery. In their free time, many internees played baseball with the locals. It wasn't until four years after the war—in 1949—that they were allowed to return home to the coast, which had been off limits to them throughout the war, as it lay within a hundred-mile "exclusion zone" ordered by the federal government.

After the war, a few of the internees settled in Spuzzum, an unincorporated settlement down the Fraser River from Lytton that's so small, both sides of a sign on the highway once read *You are now leaving Spuzzum*. The sign was a joke, but just barely. The settlement is fifty kilometres north of Hope, so it's sometimes called Beyond Hope.

The Gyoba family moved to Spuzzum after their release from a camp down the Fraser River near Hope. This was while restrictions on settlement for people with Japanese blood were still in effect. Spuzzum was outside the exclusion area. It also had plenty of jobs available in the sawmills. Among the Gyoba family's new friends was esteemed Nlaka'pamux Elder Annie York. The family often drove her to Hope to shop.

Catherine Edith (Dolly) Campbell felt rich when she was growing up on the Tollie Croft* near the Scottish medieval coastal burgh of Dingwall.

Dingwall had once been the Viking capital of Scotland. In later years, it became notable for shunning the Beatles, just before the Mop Tops recorded "Please Please Me" and ignited Beatlemania. For their Dingwall concert, the Beatles drew an audience of nineteen, and some of them reportedly left mid-show. Dolly's original hometown was small and isolated, but it didn't feel that way to the people who lived there. Sometimes beggars came to Dolly's door, and they didn't go away empty-handed. "Everybody was poor—although we didn't think we were," she recalled. "We worked hard and just survived. Everyone was in the same boat. I had a great life as a kid. I thought we had everything!"

Music and dancing filled Dolly's childhood, especially on Saturday nights, as she listened to accordion, mouth organ and harp music, as well as the skirl of bagpipes, played by her father. Dolly grew up in a happy home, always redolent with the aroma of freshly baked scones and oatcakes. "The other families always came to our place," she recalled.

After completing grade nine, Dolly was expected to find a job, and by sixteen she was working in Edinburgh as a maid. There, in October 1942, she met soldier Tom Watkinson of Foster's Bar Ranch when he was on leave. He struck her as quiet and interesting. "He was a good guy! . . . He was quiet! . . . He was different." As the couple fell in love, Edinburgh was being targeted by Luftwaffe bombers, since it was home to factories, engineering works and shipyards. The thousand-year-old fortress had been converted into a military hospital. The crown of

---

* A croft is a small, rented agricultural unit that is part of a larger estate.

Scotland was hidden under a medieval latrine at the castle, just in case the city fell to the Nazis.

Whenever Tom had a pass, he visited Edith in Edinburgh, where they would go to movies like *Gone with the Wind* or just walk and talk and enjoy each other's company. Late one day, during one of their strolls, they watched an aerial battle as the Luftwaffe tried to bomb the George IV Bridge. Allied aircraft defended the bridge as enemy planes darted in and out, trying to drop their bombs. If the bridge had been destroyed, it would have cut off supplies heading in and out of Edinburgh.

Edith was called up for training as a Women's Royal Naval Service worker. She worked in communications in a naval office in London, adjacent to the office of British prime minister Winston Churchill. It was getting harder for her and her intriguing Canadian beau to get together, so, only four months after their first meeting, shy Tom tried something bold. "He asked me if I would like to come back to Canada with him," Edith recalled. "I just said, 'No!' He said, 'I mean get married first.'"

Two months later, on August 21, 1943, Tom and Edith were married in the village of Maryburgh. Tom was twenty-eight and Edith twenty-two. Plenty of Canadian soldiers attended the wedding, along with the villagers. "We had dancing and piping and all kinds of things," Edith recalled. "The Canadians just loved it!"

Edith became pregnant during a leave and her commanding officer indelicately told her to return to duty in London "when empty." She gave birth to Fredrick Donald Campbell Watkinson on the morning of June 20, 1944, in Dingwall Memorial Hospital. "Tom was pretty fortunate to be able to leave the barracks to spend 10 minutes with me and the newborn baby," Edith said. "Major Crabtree was good to Tom, knowing that I had just given birth and that Dad was shipping out so he may never get to see Fred. This was war time!"

Tom wasn't preparing for any ordinary manoeuvres. On August 5, 1944, he became part of the Allied invasion on the Normandy beaches that clinched them the war, at the terrible cost of 209,000 Allied casualties, including more than 18,700 Canadians. Later, Tom was among the Allied soldiers pushing north through Belgium and into Holland, amidst often horrific fighting.

There was relief—however temporary—on Christmas Day, 1944, near Antwerp in Belgium. Tom was still away from his bride and baby Fred, who were both on the family croft in Scotland. The couple had never imagined the war would go on so long. Amidst what was surely a mutual sense of unreality, the Allies and the Germans in the area agreed to a twenty-four-hour truce. Cooks did their best to make the meal memorable, with turkey, pork, dressing, mashed potatoes, creamed carrots, pudding with sauce, tea, bread and butter, and a few other trimmings. Then it was back to the killing and dying.

Tom didn't see his bride or baby son for almost a year following the Allied victory, and then only briefly. By then, he had spent some 1,301 days overseas, 470 of them in the bloody theatres of France, Belgium and Holland. When finally discharged in January 1946, he headed home, where he would wait for Edith and Fred. He found no hero's welcome at the Lytton train station. He walked alone in the night down the old stagecoach trail, followed part of the way by a coyote. When he reached 18 Mile Ranch, he stayed over. Millie and Jake Foster drove him the rest of the way home in the morning.

It was six more months before his war bride and baby set out for their new Canadian home. Edith had sent her most precious worldly possessions ahead to the Watkinson farm, packed into one small trunk. Her brother Alex had painted her name on it. It arrived at the Watkinson ranch without a key. Before she left, Edith's father advised her, "Keep writing and don't let anybody sit on you!" That was his way of saying she should stay in touch with him and stick up for herself.

Edith and baby Fred arrived at Pier 21 in Halifax on July 3, 1946, after four and a half days at sea. They'd crossed an ocean but weren't even halfway to Tom. The pier was connected to a railway station, where they boarded a train for another journey, this time 5,624 kilometres across Canada. Other war brides on the train were also getting their first look at their new country. "There were many little old stations across the prairies, that brides got off at," Edith recalled. "I remember the endless wheat, and when we arrived at Calgary, lots got off there. I remember that one woman got off and no one was there."

Excitement picked up when they neared Spences Bridge, at the confluence of the Thompson and Nicola Rivers, about fifty kilometres north of Lytton. There, the gold-rush-era rope ferry across the Thompson River had been replaced with a more solid structure by a road contractor named Thomas Spence, and so the community's name changed too, the inspiration being pretty obvious. As her train reached the tiny community, Edith prepared to see her husband again. "I had a little kilt for Fred," she recalled. Tom was waiting at the Lytton CN stop. "It was very hot and dry with lots of sage brush and large trees (ponderosa pine)," she recalled. "It was very bumpy and dusty but good to be experiencing something different."

Different wasn't going to be easy, though. It would take the Scottish war bride time to adjust to the climate, and to married life too. "The first month was difficult and I was sick most of the time from the heat. There was no respite from the heat or the family . . . I cried for a year when I first came out here. I was homesick! Fred cried a lot too!"

They first lived in the town of Lillooet, upriver from Lytton, renting modest quarters at the back of a bakery as Tom worked for the highways. They moved onto the farm in October 1949, just after their eldest daughter, Mary, was born. Another child, Rosslyn, followed. In time, Fred and Rosslyn would help the family finances by delivering the *Province* newspaper.

The old family ranch was no longer thriving, and there was real danger it would soon fall out of family hands. Several of Fred and Lucy's children had struggled to keep it afloat during the Depression and then the war, with negligible success. The men became indebted to a store in Lillooet that sold them seed for their crops.

Alcoholism took its toll on the family, as it did on many others in the area. Tom's younger brother Jeffery Davidson Watkinson was killed in a work-related accident in Williams Lake on November 16, 1947, when he was crushed by a train. The death certificate stated the cause of death as "struck by a train due to being intoxicated." Further, it stated "severed legs off—one at the knee and one at the ankle." Jeffery was buried at the ranch alongside earlier family members.

The area was full of readjustments after the horrors of war.

My grandmother Doris Loring was known affectionately by many Lyttonites as "Gramma Love." She would always greet folks with her signature enthusiastic "Hello, love." She was a fiery redhead from Lancashire. She worked in the office of the Royal Air Force in London during the Second World War. She met my grandfather, James Noel Loring, who had been injured and was back in London, healing up. They fell in love and were promptly married. When Noel was sent back to Canada, Doris followed a few months later. She took a boat across the Atlantic and then a train across Canada alone. When she finally arrived, my grandfather's two sisters, Isabelle and Hazel, the same Isabelle and Hazel who would a few years later marry the

Glasgow brothers, met her at the train station in Lytton. What had she gotten herself into?! She was shocked to see that people were still using horses and buggies to get around! Needless to say this London girl was not immediately impressed with her new surroundings. She insisted that they move to Vancouver. Noel agreed and they lived in Vancouver around the Commercial Drive area and had five children: James, Virginia, my father Bryan, Marie and Susan. When Noel had an opportunity to move back home to Lytton to be a weather station operator with a salary, he jumped at the chance to get out of the city and move home. They moved the family back to Botanie Valley, where Noel was raised. Noel built a house beside his sister Isabelle and her husband, Ernest "Ernie" Glasgow, a few kilometres up the Botanie road. It was a handsome little house on the side of the mountain. He even built a swimming pool for the kids.

Noel was not well, and my grandmother always said he succumbed to the lasting effects of his injuries from the war. He passed away in 1967 at the age of 51. Doris was now widowed in her thirties and left to raise her three younger children alone. My uncle James, the eldest, had left home and eventually joined the air force, and my aunt Gina was going to nursing school, leaving Doris to raise my dad, Aunt Marie and Susan. My aunt Susan was just ten years old at the time of my grandfather's death. Someone had decided that she was too young, and she wasn't allowed to attend his funeral. She was the baby of the family, a daddy's girl for sure, so the trauma of his loss and not being able to properly have closure over it haunted Sue her whole life.

Eventually, my grandmother got a job working at the bank in town, where she worked for thirty-eight years. Once, she and the bank manager were nearly robbed on Jackass Mountain at gunpoint when they were making a cash delivery to Boston Bar. They were in the bank manager's Jeep driving down the canyon when someone brandishing a pistol tried to get them to pull over. The bank manager outmanoeuvred the bandits and they got away.

Being a World War II veteran, my grandmother was often asked to speak to students about the war and her experiences in the office of the top brass of the Royal Air Force during the Battle of Britain. Every year at the Remembrance Day powwow she would lead the grand entry in her uniform. She was given the status of honorary Elder of Lytton First Nation. When she passed, the family donated her uniform to the Lytton Museum, which was destroyed in the Lytton Fire of 2021.

Kevin Loring

For all the adjusting going on after the war, Lytton offered some the promise of quiet.

Between our yard and Dominic Pasquale's home was a little one-bedroom shack where old Jimmy Dodge lived. Jimmy was a war vet like most of the older men in town,

and he still had shrapnel in his leg from his time overseas.
He walked with a cane and drank Dominic's homemade
wine, and every couple of days he would pay my mom to
go pick him up some groceries and a case of beer. I had
this little red wagon that she'd pull me around in. She'd
load it up at the store and we'd deliver him his newspaper
and groceries. Despite our vast age difference, I thought of
him as one of my friends and would visit him regularly. He
slept on a simple cot and would sit in his shack and drink.
He'd feed me cheese and crackers, grapes from Dominic's
vines, and tell me stories. He called me his little mouse.
The one story I remember, I asked him why he walked with
a cane. He said a mortar shell had exploded next to him
and killed two of his friends, and the shrapnel went into
his knee and was still there. I recall my dad talking about
how the war had affected old Jimmy Dodge. One day my
mom went to go bring him his mail and discovered that he
had passed. That was the day I learned what death was.

Kevin Loring

CHAPTER 24

ESCAPE TO LYTTON

Kinda lonely, but kinda nice there.

CHARACTER IN ETHEL WILSON'S
1954 NOVEL *SWAMP ANGEL* DESCRIBES LYTTON

NOBODY HAD BETTER DOGS than the Watkinsons. Nobody had tougher ones either. They were Heinz 57 mixtures, including Lucky, who was part border collie, German shepherd and a few other breeds. Lucky's name was inevitable, considering his fondness for shaking poisonous rattlesnakes to death. One rattler managed to get a bite into Lucky's cheek on its way to snake heaven. The dog's face swelled up and he crawled under the porch, as if to die. Tommy and Harvey occasionally crawled under the porch to check up on him and leave him food and water in what seemed to be his final hours. Three days later, Lucky crawled out from under the porch and, not long after that, was healthy enough to resume shaking rattlesnakes. Despite his lifestyle choices, he lived to be seventeen years old.

Nothing felt cooler when I was growing up than a trip to Watkinsons' ranch, at the old stagecoach stop on the Fraser

Canyon halfway between Lytton and Lillooet. I would shine up my black cowboy boots for these visits. I got to hang out around a corral with real horses, and ride some of the gentler ones.

I went totally into cowboy mode for those bus rides to the ranch. Once I said to a kid sitting near me, "Gimme chew." He wordlessly complied by taking his round tin of snuff out of his back pocket and opening it up for me. I tucked a thick wad under my lower lip and nodded in manful appreciation. For some reason, snuff transactions were best conducted wordlessly. A little farther down the road, I accidentally swallowed the entire wad. I couldn't scream or cry or beg for someone to shoot me, but I wanted to do all of those things. I was ready to give my soul to any god from any religion—or atheists if they had a better offer—for relief. There was no great spiritual reckoning, just massive nausea. I was wobbly on my boots like I had drunk too much firewater when we finally got off at the ranch.

Everyone worked hard on the ranch. If you had time to sit around, you were expected to at least chop wood for the kitchen stove. They could always use more wood. No one but me was comfortable with me swinging a sharp axe, but I helped stack the kindling by the house. We weren't ordered to work, but it somehow felt good to help out. I could rest up when I got back home and started dodging chores again.

The Watkinsons were extremely self-sufficient. Fresh-caught salmon from the Fraser River was preserved in jars. It tasted great heated in a white sauce on toast. The eggs on their table were fresh from the henhouse. If we ate chicken

for dinner, it was from the henhouse too, freshly killed
and plucked. If I wanted a drumstick from that chicken,
I had the task of holding the bird over a wooden block
while Tommy or Harvey chopped off the head. I don't
remember anyone ever even considering trusting me with
the chopping. I didn't want that job anyway. I might have
closed my eyes while swinging the axe.

Tommy and Harvey were the second- and third-youngest
of the seven Watkinson children. Their childhoods were a
combination of creative play and hard work. They explored
the hills and gullies of the ranch and took care of the hard
chores like tending gardens, mucking out stalls, chopping
wood, moving irrigation pipes and stacking bales.
Occasionally, they were expected to help out when their
father had to butcher a steer or pig. There was never any
joy in those jobs, and things went quiet when their father
took his Savage rifle off the rack. He had weathered the
heavy combat of Normandy in World War II but never
looked comfortable when he loaded up his high-powered
rifle and walked towards the livestock. Did it bring back
thoughts of the battlefields of Europe? Was it just ugly
enough on its own? Whatever the case, I just hid behind
the barn until the shooting and squealing were over.

Peter Edwards

Lytton was finally incorporated as a municipality in 1945, when it
had a population of 1,073, including the outlying area. It wasn't a rich
place. Lytton's annual revenue then was $2,000 and its total land was
assessed at $48,488. The new municipality had no power plant of its

own, drawing power from generators across the Fraser River at the Earlscourt Ranch. Long gone were the days when it was considered a candidate for provincial capital.

Lytton did offer undeniable beauty and solitude. It's a five-hour drive from Vancouver, making it remote but still accessible for people yearning to escape the city, as sprinter Percy Williams used to do back in the 1920s. There was something memorable and yet remote about the place, as Bruce Hutchison wrote in his book *The Fraser* in 1950: "No one will forget Lytton . . . Where the two rivers meet at the north edge of the town the greenish waters of the Thompson, cutting a sharp and solid line across the brown of the Fraser, present an unforgettable conflict of color and force." Hutchison liked to drive to Lytton while it was still dark and await dawn in the canyon, just outside town:

> The dawn here is stark and violent. It is pungent with the exudation of sagebrush and pine, with the heavy sweetness of syringa and alfalfa in the spring, with the alkali dust of summer, and the smell of dried poplar leaves in autumn. The colors of this dawn are too vivid for the painter. The snow of the peaks turns to orange. The bulk of the mountain floats in blue haze. The walls of the valley glow deep red where the rust of iron has smeared them. Safe from sight, nature can squeeze out the paint tubes, load her brush, and let herself go.

Hutchison was aware of our community's history as he wrote:

> Lytton, 71 miles from Hope, is an ancient town, more ancient than any built by white men in America. Here, it will be recalled, Fraser found a thriving Indian community, centuries old. The confluence of two great rivers and the natural trails of men's travel made this one of the crossways of the continent.

Vancouver writer Ethel Wilson also found inspiration here. She spent three weeks at Brophy House, later known as the Totem Motel, to write her novel *Hetty Dorval*. It was published in 1947 and centred around a mysterious, beautiful woman who seeks refuge in Lytton. The novel makes much of the area's scenery, depicting the emerald Thompson and muddy Fraser coming together much like a blending of innocence and experience:

> Long before the Fraser reaches Lytton it has cut its way through different soils and rocks and has taken to itself tons of silt, and now moves on, a wide deceptive flow of sullen opaque and fawn-coloured water. Evidence of boil and whirlpool show the river to be dangerous. At Lytton it is refreshed and enlarged by the blue-green racing urgent Thompson River. This river in the course of its double journey from north and east spreads itself into lakes and gathers itself together again into a river, until it approaches Lytton it manifests all its special beauty and brilliance.

Wilson described what we saw daily from our Fraser Street homes: "Though there was nothing around you but the hills and sage, all very still except for the sound of the river, you felt life in everything and in the moon too." Her narrator lived on a farm on the road to Lillooet, which we travelled on our much-welcomed trips to the Watkinson ranch, or rode Saturdays on bicycles. We didn't need books to tell us it was magical.

The mysterious newcomer Hetty in Wilson's novel arrives in Lytton via Shanghai and Vancouver, in much the same way real-life non-Nlaka'pamux residents of the community arrived there by singular, often exotic routes. In Wilson's 1954 novel *Swamp Angel*, Lytton is again a place of escape. A man riding a bus up the Fraser Canyon with her

main character calls the Lytton area "kinda lonely, but kinda nice there."
He goes on to affectionately describe the confluence of the silty Fraser
and the emerald-coloured Thompson: "People tell me there's two great
rivers in Europe act like that but I'll bet they're not prettier than the
Thompson and the Fraser flowing in together . . ."

Wilson's work seems simple, like the land it's describing, but it's not,
and neither is the land or the water. She writes that "all fly-fishermen are
bound closely together by the strong desire to be apart, solitary on the
lake, the stream." Her character is drawn there by some force beyond
words, she writes. "So, like a fish, she goes upstream to stay. She seems
in the darkness to recognize."

> A large part of my writing practice before the fire was that
> I would go home to Lytton and stay at the Totem Motel.
> There were these little bungalows that you could rent, and
> bungalow number three was a self-contained cabin that
> wasn't attached to anything else. I would stay there and
> isolate myself with a couple bags of good coffee and sit and
> write. My mom's house was just across the street, so it was
> super convient. I have written seven plays and a documen-
> tary out of bungalow number three at the Totem Motel.
>
> *Kevin Loring*

CHAPTER 25

THE PRINCIPAL

We cannot get away from the fact that this country was once their home before we took it over. And I doubt if the good we have done them outweighs in the balance the evils and disease of body and mind we have given to them.

ST. GEORGE'S PRINCIPAL CHARLES F. HIVES

CHARLES F. HIVES SAID he was immediately tested by a student when he arrived in Lytton in 1941 to become the principal of St. George's Residential School. The student boasted that Hives would never strap him, Hives later told a gathering of principals. Strapping any body part other than the hands was officially prohibited. Still, he and others felt free to break their rules. Hives told a 1955 conference of residential school principals, called "The Psychology of the Indian Residential School Pupil," that he felt sorely tested during his first year as St. George's principal. He recalled a group of captured runaway boys that he ordered to face a mass assembly at the school. Amongst the group onstage was the student who had boasted that Hives would never dare strap him, Hives told the principals. "I told them to take down their pants, which they did, and I strapped them."

Hives came to Lytton as the voice of experience, having begun his residential school career in 1908 as the farm instructor at the Red Deer, Alberta, school. He rose to become principal of the Anglican schools at Lac La Ronge, Saskatchewan; Fort Stanley, on the Churchill River in Saskatchewan; and the Shingwauk Home in Sault Ste. Marie, Ontario. When he became principal of St. George's in 1941, Indian Affairs official R.A. Hoey said his department was "very fortunate in securing the services of an experienced man such as Mr. Hives."

Things had taken a harsh turn from the days of Lett and McArthur. Soon after his arrival in Lytton, there were complaints about Hives as he called for a stronger push towards assimilation. He assumed that traditional Indigenous family units could not be good homes. "During the time in residence we endeavor to create in them the true meaning and love of home life," he added. Often there were problems after students returned to their real homes, he added. "Up to that point we are proud of them but after they leave the school, in the majority of cases, their lives become a hopeless mess with no objective vision or aim."

> The wonderful world of opportunity about which we have so often preached to them, and of which they have dreamed is, in most cases, far beyond their reach.
>
> In their efforts at making a living and partaking of some of the attractions in the world, they as Emerson said, "pluck at the lowest fruit in the whole Garden of God," and become victim to the exploitation and contumely of the lowest class of humanity.
>
> We cannot get away from the fact that this country was once their home before we took it over. And I doubt if the good we have done them outweighs in the balance the evils and disease of body and mind we have given to them.

That said, Hives reasoned that they needed more white influences.

> I have found from personal experience, that perhaps the greatest asset
> in the development of proper deportment and poise of character in
> these Indian young people, is the daily mingling in the classroom with
> other Canadian children. Such an influence, at that time of life, fosters
> in them confidence and courage to face the world, and which they
> otherwise would never receive or develop living in isolation on the
> reserve or in an Indian school.

As Hives pushed for assimilation, rumours bubbled up that things
weren't going so well at his school, including an April 1948 story in the
Vancouver Sun headlined CHURCH INDIAN SCHOOLS FOUND INFERIOR.
Hives attempted to counter this in a letter to the *Sun*. He wrote to the
newspaper that a young Indigenous man who was quoted in the article
criticizing St. George's was from a large family, "all of whom owe far
more to Church Indian school education than they can ever hope to
repay. Not very often does the church receive recognition or even
appreciation for anything she has done for them." Hives sounded hurt
that the students weren't grateful for his efforts, as they were not being
forced to pay for an education from a church whose "one aim has been
to give to them that which shall eventually lead them to equality of citi-
zenship with all other peoples of this country."

He also sounded a little martyred as he pressed on. "More frequently
than not, her efforts to educate have received vigorous protest from the
pupil, and have required on the part of the teachers much patience,
faith, and a very careful manipulation of the very limited financial
resources with which to carry on the work." Hives wrote that he was
proud of the job being done with the school's 198 students. "While
they are here they are looked after as a family and are no cost to their

parents. Last year we admitted 58 new pupils, all between the age of seven and eleven years. Most of these had never had a chance to attend school."

There was more bad press in January 1949, when it became public that 150 of the students at St. George's had come down with influenza. Too many kids were ill to admit them all to the local hospital, and classrooms had to be converted into sick wards. But any misgivings occasioned by the outbreak had disappeared by November of that year, when the *Vancouver Sun* magazine supplement made the school sound like a well-run, even fun place:

> Three miles out of Lytton on the Lillooet Road is St. George's Indian Residential School, recently rated by government officials as one of the best run Indian schools in Canada. It occupies a beautifully developed tract of land with lawns, orchards and meadows sloping to the Fraser. The school recently celebrated the 300th anniversary of the New England Company, a Church of England auxiliary which established the school in 1901.
>
> Here two hundred Indian children, some from as far away as Prince Rupert, are boarded from September to June. Under affectionate supervision of Canon C.F. Hives and his wife they are educated along both cultural and practical lines. Up to grade four their work is purely academic, but from then on the girls spend half the day in kitchen, laundry or sewing room, while boys assist in the dairy and fields, learning modern agriculture. The school raises purebred stock.
>
> This year an attractive swimming pool has been added to the school's recreational facilities.

Hives told the 1955 principals' conference that he had used the strap only about twice a year, but Helen Clafton, an ex–dormitory supervisor, counted differently. She told the government in 1957 that "the 'strap' is altogether too much in evidence" and that there didn't appear to be any limit on who could administer it: "The child can be punished, nagged, pounced upon or threatened by anybody and this is carried to fantastic lengths."

Social-welfare worker Betty-Marie Barber also complained in 1957 after hearing troubling stories from six teachers at the Lytton high school.* The stories included allegations by three students who came to school tired and in rough shape, without their homework completed. "Two said their teacher hit them in the face and strapped them," Sinclair later reported. "A third said that although she liked her teacher, she could hear children being strapped in another classroom." An economics teacher in Lytton asked Barber if she could do anything "about children who were being beaten" at St. George's.

Barber met with two St. George's boys at the Lytton high school on November 28, 1957, each of whom had "severely swollen black eyes," which they could barely open. One of the boys said the beating had come from other boys at St. George's. Barber suspected his beating wasn't from students, but the boy wasn't about to point at staff.

Also on November 28, 1957, Barber met with a teacher identified as "Miss Cameron," who had been hospitalized for a severe rash she developed while working at St. George's. "She has verified the fact that the children are continually called dirty Indians and told that they are not respected by the rest of the country, nor are their parents any good," Barber reported. The teacher with the rash also said that Hives had told students in chapel that he would punish anyone caught speaking to any student who became pregnant while studying there. "Miss Cameron

* By this time, older students still living at St. George's took classes at the Lytton high school.

also states that the older boys and girls who step out of line or make any remarks to their teachers while walking down the halls are usually struck or slapped in the face as they do so." Barber was also told that three St. George's teachers planned to quit their jobs by the end of the year. Some students didn't wait for their chance to escape, like thirteen-year-old Ruby Dunstan, who ran to freedom after being struck for speaking her native language.

Hives was still principal in 1958, when Ellen Fairclough, the federal minister responsible for Indian Affairs, heard complaints about him from her own staff, provincial staff, school staff and students. They all said that Hives displayed what a report called "an inability to handle the staff of the school, an unwholesome attitude towards Indians, improper treatment of the children, and failure to co-operate with Provincial school authorities."

Hives was well into his seventies when he was finally dismissed at the end of the 1958–59 school year. None of the allegations about behaviour during his reign led to reports to police, police investigations, charges or convictions.

CHAPTER 26

ROOTS

You can't burn out roots that go down more than a hundred years.

THE FOSTER'S BAR SCHOOL by the Watkinson ranch closed in 1940 when a new school opened near Halfway, just across McGillivray Creek. Sometimes kids played in the old schoolhouse, until it was finally bought by Tom Watkinson's parents from Ashcroft School District #30 on August 22, 1949. There was still a blackboard on the north wall, chalk on the ledge and two outhouses off to the side. Young men from Lillooet burned down the schoolhouse in the 1950s, to the dismay of the Watkinson parents.

Fire also destroyed half of Lytton's downtown in the summer of 1949. The blaze started at 7 a.m. on July 12. Soon the Copper Kettle café, owned by Mr. and Mrs. Sid Baker, was consumed. The flames spread to Lloyd Miller's B.R. Store; Maurice Floyd's Lytton Meat Market; Alexander Gammie's Store; Sitko's bakery; J.E. Dowie's drugstore and living quarters; and the grocery store that had been established by B.T. Rebagliati and recently purchased by Wilson Miller, a

World War II veteran. Volunteer firefighters couldn't do much as the fire took on a life of its own, burning out of control for hours and destroying all these establishments.

Telephone operators Muriel Floyd, Ethel Ferguson and Mary Reid stayed at their switchboards through the fire, even though the flames were uncomfortably close to them. As they worked, water was sprayed on the side of the phone building, where there was a pile of telephone poles. For all that was lost, people were relieved. Much more could have burned down if the winds hadn't suddenly shifted. There was no question of whether the community should rebuild. Elsie Marsh of the *Vancouver Sun* magazine supplement surveyed the damage four months after the fire and reported that all would be well—again. Lytton had a reputation as a place for survivors.

> You can't burn out roots that go down more than a hundred years. And the fire couldn't touch such things as natural geographic advantage. Lytton served the up-country traffick in the last century and folks are still at it, in a bigger way than ever. And in some new fireproof buildings.
>
> Tourist traffic is so heavy that the town's hotel, two guest houses and three auto camps cannot always cope with it, and occasionally weary tourists sleep in their cars.
>
> A few miles west of Lytton the forests thrive in generous rain.

CHAPTER 27

ENTERTAINMENT OPTIONS

Swimming in the back eddies of the Fraser River—a dangerous
fun enjoyed by youngsters of the area for years—no longer
is necessary. Lytton has a new swimming pool.

THE PROVINCE

EVERY KID WHO SPENT a summer in Lytton from the 1950s onwards
owed a debt to a man they likely never met—Colonel Victor Spencer.
There already was a swimming pool at Earlscourt, where he lived,
tucked away from town on the west side of the Fraser River. After a local
youth drowned in the Fraser during a heat wave in the early 1950s,
Spencer donated money for materials to build a pool in town too.
Volunteers did the actual construction.

One of the pool's early lifeguards was James Baker, who had done
much of his early swimming at the junction of the Fraser and Thompson
Rivers, where the currents were something that had to be respected. "You
soon learned you didn't try to swim against the current," he said.

By the mid-1950s, Earlscourt was being run by Colonel Spencer, the
son of David Spencer. The Spencers had a reputation for being community-
minded, and the Colonel presented medals at a local boxing meet, which

he helped finance. He had been a boxer himself at Upper Canada College in Toronto and felt comfortable telling the athletes that boxing was a clean sport that taught young people self-reliance and sportsmanship. The Colonel also promoted rugby, rowing and horse racing. He even donated the racing shells used by University of British Columbia rowers at the 1956 Summer Olympics.

His son Victor Vance Spencer was a co-founder of the BC Lions football team in the Canadian Football League and successfully lobbied to bring the British Empire and Commonwealth Games to Vancouver in 1954. Curiously, Victor Vance sometimes posed for photos holding a lamb, with no apparent explanation. He loved to claim he had walked into a bar with a lamb dyed in the Lions' team colours of orange and black. The lamb was propped up on a bar stool by Victor Vance, who then ordered a double whisky for himself and said the lamb would like a double mint. He said the bartender instead threw them out. "Well," Victor Vance continued, "I guess they only serve lamb in the dining room."

When Lytton's new outdoor pool opened in June 1953, it immediately became a gathering spot—as wildly popular with the kids as the bars at the Lytton Hotel and the Legion were with their parents. It was named the Bert Erickson Pool after Earlscourt foreman Carl Bertil (Bert) Erickson, as the Colonel set out to honour a particularly valuable member of his team. It was such a big deal locally that the Vancouver *Province* reported on July 29, 1953: "Swimming in the back eddies of the Fraser River—a dangerous fun enjoyed by youngsters of the area for years—no longer is necessary. Lytton has a new swimming pool, donated to the town by Col. Victor Spencer . . ."

The good press kept coming for the Colonel. Earlscourt's blue ribbons at the prestigious Royal Agricultural Winter Fair in Toronto made the news, along with the story of a financial win for the rancher. He had imported the Hereford bull Atok Tiberius earlier that July from

Herefordshire, England, and then, after Atok won the grand champion-
ship at the Pacific National Exhibition, resold him to a California buyer
for the princely sum of $15,000.

The Colonel's head stockman was Robert Roshard, who worked for
him from 1949 to 1957, travelling all over North America to show
Earlscourt's prized Hereford bulls. Like many others in the area,
Roshard had found, at the junction of the Fraser and Thompson Rivers,
a place to reinvent himself. He had emigrated from Switzerland in
1948, spending his first Canadian winter in the Lillooet area, cutting
wood with two Indigenous men known as Strawberry Sam and Charlie
Narcisse. He had known his future wife, Esther, back in Switzerland. By
the time the war broke out, Roshard was in Canada, learning to raise
purebred cattle, while Esther was a German national living in London,
England. She spent the war in an internment camp on the Isle of Man.
In 1950, Esther boarded the *Queen Elizabeth* bound for America and
the long journey across the continent, where she could finally rejoin—
and marry—Robert.

In October 1956, when Esther was ready to give birth to her daughter,
Christ'l, she walked a few miles across the railway trestle over the Thompson River into Lytton, and then up the hill to tiny St. Bartholomew's
Hospital, where Dr. Kenneth Edwards was the only doctor. "Your father
probably delivered me," Christ'l would later tell his son Peter.

Christ'l grew up to become editor of the *Bridge River Lillooet News*
and eventually serve as mayor of Lillooet, Lytton's sister community. She
recalls of her childhood the pleasure of simple entertainment, which was
what so many of us remember fondly about growing up in the Fraser
Valley. She would be sent off each morning by her mother with the
expectation that she would return around suppertime. "She'd give us a
chunk of cheese and a chunk of bread and a bottle of water and send us
off," she recalled. "We'd just go off in the hills. All summer we were out."

There was a flurry of excitement in town in the spring of 1958 with news that the new owners of the Totem Motel would soon be arriving in town. Several local kids waited on the motel's veranda for the new family to drive up. They had heard there were six boys in the Manders family, which would dramatically change the downtown social landscape. Locals Mike Rebagliati, Ron Sharp, Doug Dodge, Ken Roberts, Jackie Millar and others made the trip to the motel porch to see the new arrivals.

The Manderses' appearance lived up to their billing. The boys were, in order of age, David, Douglas, Philip, Terry, Patrick and Keith. They and their parents, Elspeth and David, had been living in North Vancouver, where David was an engineer with CAE, a company that made flight simulators for airlines and the military. David was promoted to a job in Montreal, but Elspeth didn't want to make the move. She had spent the war years in Halifax and didn't care for what she called "eastern" weather. So they bought a motel, even though they had no experience or knowledge of that business. They settled on Lytton after scoping out several communities in the Interior. At the time, with the old highway, it was about a day's drive from Vancouver and an obvious waypoint for travellers.

"All of us have very fond memories of growing up in Lytton," Patrick Manders recalled. "And all of us went on to do okay in the big world outside. I was a dentist. There were three dentists from Lytton. [The others were] Ken Roberts and Al Floyd. Ken and Al graduated the year before I started."

It was a shared belief among the boys as they got older that growing up in a small town offered definite advantages: "Getting to try anything you want as there are never enough players for the team, thinking you are a big fish (not realizing it is a tiny pond), knowing everyone personally from the police chief to the undertaker, and because you know everything about everybody, you live many lives vicariously," Patrick said.

The Manderses' arrival meant more than a half-dozen new kids to hang out with. They built a tree house, and quickly. It took the combined efforts of the six Manders boys to construct and maintain such a structure, a getaway perched high above the adults, where boys could do what boys did back then.

> It was like a penthouse in the sky. *Penthouse* was the operative word. During my initial visit, I was shown a wall of centrefolds from *Playboy* and *Penthouse* magazines, hidden behind a wall of what seemed to be just newspapers used as wallpaper.
>
> The newspapers were fastened onto a blind, and pulling the blind's string revealed the wall of centrefolds, a shock for nine-year-old eyes.
>
> I suspected that the centrefolds were stolen from an adult's stash. How any kid would have had the nerve to buy them under the eyes of neighbours was a mystery to me.
>
> *Peter Edwards*

The tree house was also a place for eating forbidden food. Patrick Manders sometimes bought candy from The View convenience store by the reserve and snuck up to the tree house to eat it where his mother couldn't catch him. "As the years went by, it was added onto by Keith and I," Patrick said in an email interview. "As you might remember, it was a favourite meeting place for many local kids."

And then one day, as with so many great things in Lytton, the tree house went up in flames. It was an event of Biblical proportions for us boys. "The fire was caused by my brother Keith smoking," Patrick divulged more than half a century later. "Something, to the best of my knowledge, he has never done since."

It seemed the whole village went down to the train station on Tuesday, July 14, 1959, when Queen Elizabeth II and Prince Philip rolled into town.

Already that day, the royal couple had made a stop in even smaller Spences Bridge. The Prince had clearly done his homework. While in Spences Bridge, the Prince had promised to make a return visit someday to get fresh eggs at Vaughan Hammond's chicken ranch. There was also a stop in Ashcroft, where a wet cocker spaniel puppy brushed against the Queen's leg, causing the Prince to laugh. Her Majesty's reaction was not recorded in print.

It was Lytton's first royal visit since the Queen Consort of Siam, Sirikit, came to town back in 1931, during a cross-Canada trip on a specially outfitted train. The Queen of Siam, known for her exquisite collection of Parisian outfits, was handed a bouquet by schoolgirl Dorothy Arnold during a stopover of a few minutes.

The British royals seemed approachable as they got out of the train at the Lytton CN station, just under Fraser Street. MP Davy Fulton was close to the Queen's lady-in-waiting and Mayor Tommy Taverna stood nearby as officials shooed away a curious unleashed mongrel. "That dog was at the last place we visited," the Prince quipped.

The Queen was presented with a two-inch imperial jade brooch in the shape of a tomahawk by Doris Elizabeth Phillips, a student at St. George's Residential School and the daughter of Dunstan (Rattlesnake Dan) Raphael. The brooch was the work of St. George's student Cliff Bolton, of the Tsimshian First Nation from Prince George, a champion marksman who missed winning the national title by just a point.

Also on the platform that day were cadets from St. George's, Chief Dunstan Raphael and band councillor Tommy Lick. While the royals smiled, others in the party refilled the train's supply of drinking water, noted Charles Melanson, a high school student and babysitter of future author Peter Edwards. "I remember that they took on water in Lytton because Lytton had the best-tasting water in the province," he said.

CHAPTER 28

BIG ON SPORTS

He was a phenomenal rider. He yahooed all the way down.

DESCRIPTION OF CHAMPION DOWNHILL
HORSE RACER RATTLESNAKE DAN RAPHAEL

My parents weren't big on sports. My father particularly hated a form of horse racing that seemed unique to Lytton. We called them "suicide races," but the more proper local name was point-to-point races. Point-to-point riders raced in a pack down a steep, sandy hill. To stay on top and not flip, riders had to slalom, like a skier going through the gates. Races were done in heats of three, and riders could only see between the horse's ears as they headed down. At the bottom of the hill, riders turned sharply left for a hundred yards to sprint to the finish line.

As the area's only doctor, my father definitely wasn't a fan. There were enough health problems already. It was no fun treating the broken bones of your friends, or watching horses get put down.

Peter Edwards

Aficionados of the downhill "suicide" races couldn't agree whether anyone in recent memory had been killed when his or her horse flipped and rolled. It certainly was possible, given the frequent spills. Some of those aficionados were tough critics. Charles Melanson recalled a spectator laying into a losing rider, telling him: "You fell off your horse. You old woman. You were winning and you fell off like an old woman."

The best rider in memory during the 1960s was Rattlesnake Dan Raphael. "He was a phenomenal rider," local James Baker recalls. "He yahooed all the way down." Floyd Adams was another notable racer, as well as a talented runner, and also Jerry Tom, an Indigenous man who played pro baseball for a short time and then returned to Lytton, where he joined a local band that played "Hot Rod Lincoln" repeatedly.

Around this time, a new soccer and gymnastics coach showed up at the Lytton high school, a mysterious man named Alex Kerestes. It turned out Kerestes was a world-class gymnast from Hungary. He wowed locals with the ease with which he could perform an iron cross on the rings. Rumour got around that Kerestes was a double defector. First, he defected to the West from Hungary when he was supposed to be competing in the Olympics for the Communist country. Then he returned for a visit and flipped against the Communists again when they attempted to turn him into a spy. That story was unverifiable, but it held up locally. What wasn't up for debate was the fact that he was an out-of-this-world athlete. "Was he ever fit," recalls Baker, a teenager at the time.

Sports gave Lytton's kids a way to stay out of trouble at a time when teenagers getting into trouble was all the rage. David Manders, the eldest of the six Manders boys of Totem Motel fame, was easily Lytton's top boys' 100- and 200-yard sprinter. Lyle Dunstan was the champion in the half-mile and one-mile boys' event, while his close friend Mark Rebagliati specialized in shorter distances. "We both trained very hard," Mark Rebagliati recalled. Training took dedication, because there were no facilities to make sports more comfortable. "Lyle ran the three miles to and from his home on the west side of the Fraser River and the Lytton high school each day. To do so, he had to cross the CNR bridge over the Fraser River. At that time there was no enclosed walkway on the side of the bridge. To cross the bridge, you had to walk on the timbers between the rails and hope no train was coming. There was no school bus for students living west of the river."

Lyle's motivation as he ran—apart from medals—was a desire not to be hit by a train on the bridge. His training system worked. He won all his half- and one-mile races, while Rebagliati did the same in the 440. Rebagliati recalled, "I trained by running the three-mile loop from my home north through Lytton and the Indian reserve up to the Trans-Canada Highway, south to the high school beside the highway across from the cemetery at the south edge of Lytton, and back into town and my house before breakfast." His friend Harvey Dunstan made his own mark, flirting with a sub-four-minute mile, a world-class time. And Charles Melanson, when not babysitting for Dr. and Mrs. Edwards, was proving himself a talented 100- and 200-yard runner, with a scorching 10.7-second time in the 100 yards.

In the summer of 1959, Lytton runners were making history. "We didn't get beat as a school team," Melanson said, which was remarkable, given the size of Lytton relative to its South Caribou District competition. Lyle Dunstan ran an eye-popping 4.23-minute high school mile that year. He qualified for the Canadian Legion's Junior Olympics in Vancouver and came third in the mile. Mark Rebagliati qualified for the 440 but chose to go goat hunting with his friend Sonny Sitko instead. The Sitkos ran the town bakery. Walter Sitko Sr. had survived three shots in the back in World War II to head off to Lytton and become famous in the Fraser Canyon for his glazed doughnuts.

In their hunting adventure, Rebagliati and Sonny Sitko went up 18 Mile Creek, passing by the lean-to canvas-and-tarpaper shelter of the late Wasyl (Bill Bazook) Bereziuk, which held a No Trespassing sign. "At the head of the creek, we came to Devil's Lake," Rebagliati later said. "Legend had it that *snyee* [Indigenous ghosts] lived near the lake. To avoid their spell that would give you bad luck, you needed to blacken your face with charcoal so they wouldn't see you."

The boys took their chances and left their faces clean. "We kind of laughed about it," Mark later said. They shot an old goat, and Rebagliati's horse Bucky objected strongly to carrying it on the saddle. When they went to cook up their catch back in Lytton, they were profoundly disappointed. "That old goat was so tough, its hamburger was like trying to eat a mouthful of chopped rubber bands," Rebagliati claimed.

Much of the sporting life in Lytton was improvised. Traffic on Main Street was halted in the late 1960s by a fist fight between a local swinging a belt and threatening to kick with his pointy pickle-stabber shoes and another local, who resembled heavyweight champion Joe Frazier. The resident Mountie backed off and eventually the two pugilists went home. Apparently the two combatants were so intimidating that no one had the nerve to say who won the fight.

In the summers, kids could always count on the swimming pool. As the only one in the community, it served as the unofficial town babysitter. Mothers would cringe and gaze up at the heavens on bad-weather days, when the pool was closed and kids were forced to stay home. Local swimmers had a rivalry with those from nearby Boston Bar, whose athletes were more safe than speedy, as their coach made many of them wear life jackets. Lytton swimmers got a boost from visits by Canadian age-group swimming champion Brian (Budgie) Budd, whose sister Sonya was the lifeguard and movie-star beautiful. Brian was as athletic as his sister was stunning. He swam for the elite Vancouver Dolphins, whose athletes also included world record holder and three-time Olympic medallist Elaine (Mighty Mouse) Tanner. Brian was gifted at every sport, it seemed. He went on to dominate ABC TV's made-for-television athletics competition *World Superstars*, which tested the skills of the world's best athletes, including pro athletes and Olympic gold medallists. Budd won the contest for three consecutive years, from 1977 to 1979. Then the network instituted what became known as the "Brian Budd Rule," barring repeat winners. He also played pro soccer against the likes of Pelé, even without the kind of skills foundation he might have gained if he had specialized in soccer since childhood.

That said, a young local named Robert Bolan almost won a challenge race against Brian Budd one day at the Lytton pool, even though he didn't have real training or even a Speedo. Everyone, including Brian, was good about it and went on to enjoy the rest of the day. Years later, Robert said he didn't even remember the race, although he did remember that Brian was taller and had longer arms than he did.

> Summers in Lytton consisted of hanging around the town swimming pool, riding bikes, trips to a friend's ranch and Scouts.
>
> Lytton made a valiant attempt at Scouting. The Boy Scout stetsons went over well—although the Lord Baden-Powell birdwatcher-style shorts and odd high socks were generally regarded as something best kept out of town.
>
> Our scoutmaster was a nice man named Mr. Keeble, and one hot summer's day he took us on a hike through the mountains above town. High above Lytton, a large kid announced he couldn't walk anymore and poor Mr. Keeble had to lug him home. I was impressed with Mr. Keeble's

burro-like carrying ability as well as his restraint, considering how easy it would have been to roll the kid off a cliff.

When it was too hot outside, we played Ping-Pong in
our basement on a homemade table. My older brothers,
Jim and David, and I would often retire to play a version
of Ping-Pong unofficially called "Maim Your Brother."
Nobody in Lytton called Ping-Pong "table tennis," and
certainly not when referring to MYB.

The only rule in MYB was that you had to keep running
around the table clockwise between shots and keep the
ball in play. There was no real scorekeeping. The goal was
to impale a sibling's privates on a corner of the table by
making him leap to return a well-placed drop shot.

If you did it just right, you would knock the tabletop
over too. It wasn't pretty, and my parents made a point
of not watching. Still, it was far better than when we played
floor hockey and knocked a leg off the piano.

The evening temperatures in summer brought us back
outside for fastball at a ballpark midway between town and
the reserve. This was big stuff in Lytton, and we kids never
made it onto the field in a meaningful way. This was for
adults and skilled teenagers. It seemed half the town and
reserve residents would scream, "Down in the dirt, big
chucker!" and "Chuck-chuck-chuck-chuck-chucker!" at
the same time. When I was older and moved to more
refined Ontario, I never heard anything remotely like that.
No one there even seemed to know what a big chucker
was, and I wasn't about to educate them.

Peter Edwards

Lytton has a Karate Club. Kanamaru-Ha Sho Shoh-Ryu
Karate-do was founded by Zenzaburoh Kanamaru
(1874–1936), who studied martial arts under the Nambu
clan's Sho Sho Ryu Yawara. This form is considered
to be one of the oldest martial arts styles in Japan.
Zenzaburoh passed his knowledge down to his first-born
son, Chichiroh Kanamaru (1911–93), who then passed
his knowledge down to his son Akio Kanamaru, who
departed for Canada in 1967. Akio moved to Ashcroft,
BC, where he set up his first dojo in an apartment complex
where he taught a handful of students. Soon word spread
that a karate master had moved to town, and he started
teaching at the local elementary school gymnasium.

This led to the opening of the Honbu Dojo in Ashcroft,
and later Akio opened dojos in Lillooet and Clinton. Some
years after that, he started coming to Lytton. My father
signed my brother and me up, and for the next eight years
we were committed to the club.

We competed provincially, nationally and internationally. And we did well. Unlike with my BMX habit, my
dad was really into Andrew and me taking karate, and so
as a family we would go on trips across the province to
compete. We even went to Vegas to compete at the NKA
International karate competition. And a number of us
from the club came home with medals. Aki believed that
young people who learned karate developed more self-
esteem, respect and discipline and that troubled youth,
in particular, benefitted from practicing the art. The
Chief and Council of the Lytton First Nation recognized
these benefits as well and for a time covered the cost of

LFN students to attend the classes. This greatly increased
the class size for a time but eventually the novelty wore off
for many of the students and class sizes dwindled. We
trained twice a week. Aki would come once a week and
send a black or brown belt the other nights. And then
when the club started to dwindle, he would only come
twice a month. Eventually, I started to lead the Lytton dojo
through our exercises, just to keep it going. Sometimes
I was teaching the class six nights a month, even though I
was just a teenager with an orange belt. But I really enjoyed
it and I wanted the dojo to continue. I was proud to be
Aki's student and that he entrusted me to lead his classes
for him. Aki was a kind of father figure to many of his
students, including me.

Aki's children Yoriko and Hideaki carry on the
Kanamaru martial arts legacy after Soke Aki's sudden
death in 2013. They each have their own dojos, and
Hideaki still comes to Lytton to train the small but
dedicated Lytton dojo.

Kevin Loring

CHAPTER 29

DOWN ON THE RANCH

We never turned anyone away.

EDITH WATKINSON ON VISITORS TO HER RANCH

TOM SR. AND EDITH WATKINSON had been slowly raising the money to take over the family ranch and pay off their debts to the store in Lillooet. With back taxes finally settled, they moved in during the spring of 1960. Tom Sr. was forty-eight years old, with a family of seven children, when he finally realized his dream of owning the home where he was born. "It was hard work when we moved to the ranch," Edith told her son Tom Jr. as he researched his family history. "We got everything polished up and we put in new linoleum."

The ranch had been constructed before the days of indoor plumbing. "Although there was a sink in the kitchen, it was not connected to anything," Edith recalled. "We spent much of the spring scrubbing walls and floors trying to make it liveable."

The bedroom floors were bare wood and insulation was poor. The winters were cold. Tom Sr. and Edith willed the ranch forward. They

installed indoor plumbing in 1962 and built a cesspool, which was covered with discarded railway ties. Over time, they added irrigation pipes
and modern machinery. The cattle herd and hay production increased.
Profits were reinvested in the ranch. In the spring of 1965, they upgraded
to get propane lights and a stove. It wasn't until just before Christmas
1970 that the house was finally wired for electricity.

> I was well under ten years old during my visits to the
> Watkinson ranch, too early for the electricity days. I liked
> to identify with tough cowboys, like what I saw on TV and
> in the comics. I was proud to be thrown from a horse that
> ran at full gallop under a low-hanging branch of a tree.
> I landed flat on my back and wondered, for a second, if I
> was dead. Then I opened my eyes and saw the sky, but no
> God or even angels. I tilted my head and saw the horse
> staring at me with what appeared to be pity.
>
> *Peter Edwards*

The Watkinsons' wringer washer was a step up from when they first
arrived at the ranch, when Edith and the Watkinson girls scrubbed
clothing in a round tub with a washboard and then hung the clothes on
a line outside. In the winter, frozen clothing would be brought in and
hung on a rack in front of the stove. The floor was covered with newspaper to soak up the water.

Mornings at the ranch began at five-thirty, with Edith and their
daughters making a breakfast of porridge and pancakes over the flames
of the wood stove. Tom Sr. went to work for an early shift with the
Department of Highways, based out of Lillooet, maintaining and building bridges from Squamish up to Clinton and beyond, and maintaining

ferries on the Fraser River. Then he would drive home to chores on the ranch.

While the Watkinson ranch—like so many of the ranches outside Lytton—seemed isolated, neighbours were essential to its operation. Grain was harvested with threshing bees, and machinery was continually loaned from one ranch to another.

The Watkinsons kept their doors unlocked. There was no reason not to. Edith and Tom Sr. got along with all the neighbours. "Mom was generous with food and took the time to visit with people over tea and baking and often a meal," Tom Jr. recalled. "She was able to make a meal out of anything. She was hard-working and would never think to turn someone away."

"They were all good people," Edith said of the neighbouring ranchers.

Mary Glasgow, at the neighbouring Rosebank farm, was married to John Glasgow, whose brother Ernest Glasgow lived in Botanie Valley, and he was the father of Donny Glasgow, who is the cousin of writer Kevin Loring and friend of writer Peter Edwards. Everyone seemed connected in Lytton if you looked hard enough.

The Glasgows and Watkinsons were particularly close. "John Glasgow would come looking for an eye-opener [alcohol] quite often," Edith later recalled. "Once, in his old car, you would hear a flap, flap as a tire was unravelling. He would just laugh about it. Lots of people would come out from town to visit and to have dinner." Edith was taught to drive by Mary Glasgow at Rosebank in an open field, where there was nothing to crash into. The Rosebank Glasgows weren't easily ruffled.

> There wasn't organized hockey anywhere in the area, but
> we enjoyed skating on the pond at Glasgows'. Once, I fell
> through the ice, and was quickly plucked out. It was
> bitterly cold and I was taken back to the farmhouse to

thaw. I was given a change of clothing while my jeans dried out on the stove. It felt odd to be handed a pair of pants belonging to Dorothy Glasgow, who was about a year older than me. They were warm, but the red-and-black plaid with a zipper up the side hurt the cowboy image I was trying to project.

To improve my mood as I sat by the wood stove, I was shown a large plate of freshly made mini-doughnuts and told to eat all I wanted. My mother never dared say that sort of thing to me. She knew better. Back in Lytton, I had a standing order to buy day-old doughnuts at the bakery for half-price with money from my paper route. These dough-nuts at the Rosebank Ranch were fresh out of the pan.

I ate a couple and then a couple more. I lost control, and somewhere around the dozen-doughnut mark I went into an odd, trancelike state and shifted into autopilot. I kept on stuffing doughnuts into my mouth and didn't stop until there were just crumbs on the plate. I knew the Glasgows were nice people, but now I would find out just how nice. They didn't get angry when they came in from the cold, asking about the source of that fresh-baked aroma still lingering in the kitchen. They seemed to marvel at my gluttony. Maybe they also felt sorry for me because I had fallen through the ice and was now sitting by myself, wearing red plaid girl's pants.

Peter Edwards

For sheer entertainment value, it was hard to top the Watkinsons' bull. Edith recalled to her son Tom: "Before we left for town, I'd said to your dad, 'We need to put the bull in the corral.' However, he said the bull would be okay out. When we were gone, he [the bull] must have walked on top of the old cess pool and the wooden ties must have given away." The Watkinsons needed to ask a neighbour with a particularly heavy tractor to help rescue the bull from his smelly trap. "He was stuck pretty good," Edith said. "Once Bill started pulling, the bull popped free and got his front legs over the top edge and then he fell back in. He thrashed around some more and he was quite frantic. Eventually he was able to get his front feet up again and he struggled out. He was covered with mess, and toilet paper was wrapped around his right horn. Once out, he ran down to the crabapple tree, trying to rub the crap off of himself and then he ran down to the bottom of the hayfields. Dad made the comment, 'Someone was using too much paper.'"

Life on the ranch soon became unspeakably sad for the Watkinsons. Many stories around Lytton ended in car accidents or fire. Mary Glasgow was killed in a car accident in 1968, which also severely injured her daughter Dorothy. "The summer of '68 was a difficult time," Edith Watkinson recalled. "It was awful. It was just awful! She was returning from Lillooet, after being at the 'Only in Lillooet Days' celebrations and she must have fell asleep at the wheel. She went off the road and down 400 feet just before the Big Slide."

Edith Watkinson and Mary Glasgow had shared a particularly strong bond, and her death was devastating. "Mary and I used to do lots of things together, including Weight Watchers' classes," Edith recalled. "After the meeting we would have a big piece of cake with icing on it. We would talk on the phone and she would help me and I would help her."

In 1971, three years after Mary's death, her husband, John, drowned in the pond on the Rosebank Ranch. It was the same pond Peter had fallen into while skating. "[Uncle John] really struggled after his wife

Mary died," Tom Jr. recalled. "Dorothy tried to run the ranch, but it was too hard for her, so she sold it in the mid-seventies."

Christmas 1972 was the first for the Watkinson family with hydro-electricity, Tommy Jr. recalled.

> Those of us that were living at home were thrilled! The tree was set
> up in a corner near the window looking out onto the porch. The big
> wood stove heater was located closer to the entrance of the kitchen.
> We would go up the creek to cut down a small tree and Harvey and
> I would carry it home. If there was snow on the ground we would drag
> it down the trail to the ranch. Often they were "Charlie Brown" trees!
>
> It was normally a wonderful time, although we were quite poor.
> There was a stocking in front of the tree that Mom would fill with
> candies, an orange and nuts. We would get one or two gifts. Since
> I liked sports I received a soccer ball and then the following Christmas
> a basketball. I remember getting a book each Christmas and I would
> read it late into the night.

Tommy Jr. and Harvey lost their father on August 2, 1978, to a massive heart attack, after he pulled his truck up to the front door of the home where he had been born sixty-four years earlier. His obituary reads:

THE LAST OF THREE GENERATIONS.

> The last male issue of 3 generations of Watkinsons in direct line, died
> August 3rd of a heart seizure. He stopped his truck at the front door of
> the old family home at Foster's Bar Ranch on the Lillooet-Lytton Road.
> He was Thomas, son of Fred and grandson of Joseph Watkinson who
> came from Cornwall in 1860 to work the bars on the Fraser River with
> his partner Thomas Harris. Tom's father, Fred moved from the original

home down by the cemetery and built the house in which Tom's family lives today. The Fred Watkinson family ran a stopping place at Foster's Bar for stages and freight teams plying between Lytton and Lillooet. In his youth Tom joined the Canadian Army from Squamish where he was logging.

A saddled horse with Tom Sr.'s boots placed backwards in the stirrups was part of the funeral procession to the family cemetery overlooking the Fraser River, under an old weeping willow tree. His coffin was carried to his final resting place in the back of his pickup truck. The casket rested on two wooden sawhorses before it was lowered into the ground. Tom Sr.'s black-and-white dog, Snoopy, seemed to sense what was happening and positioned himself under the coffin, as close to his lifeless master as possible.

Donny Glasgow's other aunt was Rosemary Hazel Loring, whom everyone called Hazel. She also died in a car accident. She was driving from Edmonton in 1982 when she crashed into a semi-trailer.

Life in the Interior, among the mountains and rivers, was remote and beautiful. But all that untamed beauty sometimes came at a terrible price. A good sense of humour helped.

Tom Watkinson Jr. eventually became the principal of Lillooet Secondary and then principal of an elementary school near Vernon, BC. When Edith was seventy-seven and long widowed, she moved off the ranch to Lillooet. She rented an apartment above the old newspaper office of Margaret Lally "Ma" Murray, publisher, editor and columnist of the *Bridge River Lillooet News*, which announced in every edition: "Printed in the sagebrush country of the Lillooet every Thursday, God willing. Guarantees a chuckle every week and a belly laugh once a month, or your money back. Subscription: $5 in Canada. Furriners: $6. This week's circulation 1,769, and every bloody one of them paid for."

There are now seven generations of Watkinsons in Canada, many in the Lytton and Lillooet area. Tom Jr. would recall his childhood as a happy time, despite the daily challenges:

> Even as kids we all had a love for the land. We worked hard as kids but we had lots of good fun and it was always nice to be able to have friends come and experience ranch life. For me I enjoyed all seasons and really loved late spring when the days lengthen and the alfalfa fields started growing. There was such a beautiful fragrance in the air. When you got water on the fields or the garden, you could watch the crops and vegetables grow. It was a good life!

Edith Watkinson died on June 19, 2016, at the age of ninety-five. Her ashes are buried with Tom Sr.'s grave on the ranch. By then, Dolly the Scottish war bride had fourteen grandchildren, four step-grandchildren, twenty-two great-grandchildren and six step-great-grandchildren in her adopted country. They had all been coached in her credo, which could have spoken for most people in the area: "Be good and work hard. Help each other and help other people as much as you can."

CHAPTER 30

THE CHONGS

He assured me that I was a Lytton boy at heart
and when the time came my shyee *would come back to Lytton.*

DAVID CHONG TO LOUIE PHILLIPS,

AS RECORDED BY CARSON MAK

CHONG'S GENERAL STORE on Main Street was a sanctuary for kids. All through the 1960s they could stand at the comic rack, right next to the cash register, and casually read *Archie* comics under the gentle smiles of Peter and Alice. The Chongs never pressured kids to buy. They seemed to enjoy their company and watching them chuckle at the comics. The store had a little of everything, from fashionably pointed shoes known in the era as "pickle-stabbers" to sporting goods. It always seemed they ran their store as a community service, not a money-making venture.

I remember they didn't have just the right baseball glove for me, so they picked one up in Kamloops and brought it to town for no extra cost. I could feel them watching my face light up when they handed me the glove, soaking up the joy. That was the sort of thing they always did. I heard

they also extended locals generous credit, and didn't charge
interest. That didn't surprise me.

Peter Edwards

My father always made a point of visiting with Peter Chong.
He'd go in to buy something from the hardware store and he
and Peter would end up shooting the shit for hours. Often
I'd be with my dad and I'd go into the toy section, and if I
wasn't too much of a pain I'd leave with a toy for being good.
Sometimes when Peter would go down to the coast, he
would bring back seafood and exotic fruit like pineapples
and other goodies for my dad from the market, things we
would never see in Lytton. I remember, when I was a young
child, my dad bringing home a bag of live prawns that Peter
had picked up for him in Vancouver. Dad put a couple
of the strange bugs on the kitchen table and pitted them
against each other in an involuntary race to the finish. Peter
was always friendly and warm, and the hardware store was
a vital business in a town as isolated as Lytton.

Years later, after Peter had retired and moved down
to the Lower Mainland, he came back to visit only a few
months after my father was killed at work. He hadn't
heard the news yet and came over to our house to see him.
I was the only one home at the time and had to break the
news. I'll never forget the look of shock and sadness on
his face. I felt awful to be the one to tell him, but it also
endeared him to me even more.

Kevin Loring

There was an enduring feeling about the Chongs' store. That and the village swimming pool seemed as eternal as the mountains and the rivers in those years.

> When I made an unannounced visit to Lytton in the 1980s, Peter and Alice Chong insisted that I drive their blue truck. They hadn't seen me for more than a dozen years and there had been no communication between us. I told them I couldn't drive standard shift. I had never even tried it. Peter wouldn't take no for an answer. He insisted I drive their truck and made driving it sound simple. It also seemed that he and Alice would be deeply offended if I didn't take it for a spin, and so an attempt was made.
>
> The grinding sound and oily smell started as I drove away. Peter just smiled the same smile he shared with us freeloading kids back in the 1960s, when we would read his comics for free.
>
> *Peter Edwards*

Deeply loved and respected, Peter Chong lived into his nineties. Some two hundred people showed up for his ninetieth birthday party, which is impressive considering the village's population was just 250, with maybe two thousand more in the surrounding area. Among them was his brother David Chong.

The Chongs' family history in Lytton goes back to the time of the gold rush—at least, it nearly does. David and Peter's grandfather, Lau Gow, was born in Jungesing county in Guangdong province, China, in 1862, back when British Columbia was known in China as Gum San, or the Gold Mountain. Lau Gow planned to earn money in the Gold Mountain to provide for his young wife and growing family back home. He arrived in Victoria in April 1885. He likely then went to New Westminster, where a riverboat took travellers up the Fraser River to Yale. From there, Chinese freight wagons would have been en route regularly to the Cariboo goldfields. Lau Gow arrived in Lytton the year the railway was completed, so he had gone halfway around the world and up an imposing canyon only to find there was no work. Exactly why he stayed in Lytton isn't clear. David Chong thought his grandfather simply found company. "He went there probably because he had a friend or acquaintance or maybe a distant relative there," David said. "There were other people from the same district . . . There really isn't much there to do."

At the height of the railway building boom in the late nineteenth century, Lytton had a population of more than twenty thousand, including a Chinatown, but very few remained by the time Lau Gow arrived. There was still a sprinkling of Chinese men who spent their winters there. Lytton in the early twentieth century had plenty of abandoned shacks, which became winter homes for Chinese seasonal workers. Those workers would leave in the spring with a rolled-up blanket and work for local farms. Peter and David's father was one of them. "A lot of people would come back to Lytton and winter there," David said. "Quite a number of them had relationships with the First Nations people. Probably had friends, had girlfriends and things like that. That's what brought them back to Lytton."

Despite Lau Gow's bleak circumstances in the Fraser Canyon, the Lytton area still represented hope for his family back in China, where prospects were much tougher. That's why Peter Chong's father, Lau Bing (Jack) Chong, arrived in Lytton in 1903 as a seventeen-year-old. He too had hopes of finding his fortune on the Gold Mountain.

The family's surname was Lau, but a switch was somehow made when Peter's father's immigration papers were filed. He was listed instead as "Lau Bing (Jack) Chong," as if his surname were Chong. And that was the name by which the family became known in their new land. The Chong Wah store at Main and 3rd Streets in Lytton was particularly popular with local Chinese and Nlaka'pamux people. *Wah* meant "splendid," but locals often mistakenly inferred from the name of the store that the Chongs were the Chong Wahs. However, the family had bigger concerns than correcting everyone.

Back in the 1960s, we used to hear a story whispered in Lytton of a heartbroken woman in the Chong family, generations before, who had hanged herself because of loneliness. That woman was Lau Gow's young wife, whom he had left behind in China. He had struggled to earn money to send payments home to her. His letters and money were sent to China, addressed to a store there. The store didn't pass them on, and his wife became increasingly depressed, until she ended her life.

Lau Gow returned to China around 1930 as a widower. There he married a young woman, and they had a son together. That son is alive at the time of the writing of this book, as are his three children, grandchildren and great-grandchildren. The Chong family in Canada maintains a close relationship with this Chinese arm of the family, with many members of both sides of the family frequently visiting one another.

Peter's father, Lau Bing (Jack) Chong, worked on Lytton-area farms for about four years in the 1930s—including two years on the Loring ranch and another two years on the nearby McKay ranch. Jack Chong was able to speak and understand some of the First Nations languages. New Chinese arrivals and long-standing inhabitants alike congregated at the Chong Wah store.

"I was born in that store," Peter Chong said. Peter was born in 1921, the eldest of several children, all of whom were born in Lytton. The elder siblings were expected to look out for the younger ones. Peter readily accepted the role of the dutiful son. David later said, "For me it is as if I had three parents: my mother and father, of course, and my brother Peter."

Peter began his life as an alien in his own land. "The family was poor," David recalled. "It was a very difficult time to be Chinese in Canada. The family lived in a community where most people shunned Chinese and some were openly hostile." The Chongs were legally classified as "alien"—even Peter, who was the first of the family to be born in Canada. They had no legal status, no right to vote or be employed by the government in any capacity, nor to enter most professions or hold some business licences. Many industries and businesses would not employ Chinese. They were also blocked from using some public facilities or buying property in certain areas. It was as though a message was being sent that they shouldn't get too comfortable. David recalled:

> We grew up with the awful apprehension that we might be deported at any time. The spectre of deportation was so great that I remember my sister, while giving my two- or three-year-old brother a bath, telling me to take note of the birthmark on his right shoulder blade so that, if we all became separated, I would still be able to identify him.
>
> The laws and policies of the time emboldened misguided people to inflict indignities upon Chinese and often even to physically attack them. My sister told me about [our brother] Peter coming to her rescue when other children were throwing stones at her.
>
> I guess we were the only Chinese family for many, many years . . . People were very, very poor. There was very little in Lytton. I still can't understand how they were able to run a business in Lytton.

Still, things were better in Lytton than in larger centres. "In the bigger towns it was quite discriminatory," Peter said. One of the most infamous examples of that prejudice had occurred back in September 1907, when a white mob marched through Chinese and Japanese neighbourhoods in Vancouver, breaking windows and attacking residents. Years had passed, and Lytton didn't have the critical mass of antipathy encountered in the cities, but there was much to endure just the same.

Harry Lowe, or Lowe Thiem, was a member of the Lytton Chinese community who lived with Nlaka'pamux woman Lucy Black as husband and wife. Peter Chong's father, Jack, had trouble with this, since Lowe still had a wife and children back in China. "To Chong, taking an Indigenous wife in a foreign country meant abandoning his Chinese family at home back in China," Lily Chow notes in her well-researched, thoughtful book *Blossoms in the Gold Mountains*.

Peter was a dutiful eldest son. In his early teens, he was sent by his father to Williams Lake to work in the small hotel that his father owned a share in. Peter washed dishes, did janitorial work, fuelled furnaces and went to school. "Eventually he went to UBC, working in Williams Lake between terms," David later said. "After graduating with a degree in commerce, Peter worked in Williams Lake until the hotel was sold."

Peter moved home to Lytton in 1946 to run the family store. The name of the store was changed from Chong Wah to Lytton Supplies in the 1950s. The family was gradually doing better financially. "I never wanted for anything," David recalled. "[But] I didn't go to a private school, and I didn't have braces for my teeth." Under Peter's management, the size of the general store was roughly doubled with an addition around 1960. A decade later, Peter bought out a closed store in town and began selling hardware from it while maintaining the old general store.

The family felt particularly close to their Nlaka'pamux neighbours. "We got along quite well with the First Nations families," David said. "Some . . . were very, very good to us." As time passed, the number of

Chinese in the area decreased, until there were only the Chongs and three or four other Chinese men. For a time, almost all the patrons of the store were Nlaka'pamux. "My father, who had lived in Lytton much longer than my mother, was able to speak and understand some of the local First Nation's language," David said. "My mother"—Lily, who was born in Victoria—"did not speak the language but understood much of it and knew many phrases and the names of all the items of merchandise in our store." The vocabulary came in handy. The store had scales to weigh gold, which would be packaged and shipped through the store. They also worked with Indigenous trappers. "They'd bring their skins in, animal skins," David said. "She'd wrap them up and prepare invoices for them and ship them off to buyers."

Their Nlaka'pamux friends brought the Chongs venison, garden produce, mushrooms, berries and salmon. "It may have been because of their friendship with our family or because it is natural for First Nations people to be kind to children, but I found them to be extraordinarily kind to me when I was a boy," David said. "There was a relationship that was more than just having a store."

Despite their tight financial straits, siblings Peter, David and Ron Chong all attended the University of British Columbia, obtaining degrees respectively in commerce, law and pharmacy. As the family grew, Peter broadened his responsibilities. He operated the family business in Lytton until 1987, when he retired and moved to Burnaby. He didn't stop being a dutiful son, brother and uncle. "His need to care for his siblings, and his nieces and nephews, was so great that he worried about their well-being until the very end of his life," David said at Peter's funeral in 2017.

David retired from law at the age of eighty-seven. Towards the end of his life, he recalled how one of his early friends was Louie Phillips, a Nlaka'pamux man from the Lytton area. "His visits to the store were always marked with a good deal of joking and teasing for some reason," David recalled. Louie Phillips and David remained great friends until his final days, spent at St. Bartholomew's Hospital. "We discovered many things and he assured me that I was a Lytton boy at heart, and when the time came my *shyee* [spirit] would come back to Lytton," David said. "I think my brother Peter's will as well."

HO! FOR FRAZER RIVER.

Gold rush on the Fraser River announced in the December 1860 issue of *Harper's Monthly* magazine.

RETURNED FROM FRAZER RIVER.

After the Fraser Canyon gold rush in the December 1860 *Harper's Monthly* issue.

George A.G. Rebagliati (left) with freight wagon, circa 1912. (Photo courtesy of Mark Rebagliati.)

Giuseppe Bernardo Luigi Rebagliati (BR), 34, and Angela Maria Gironima Agostina Rebagliati, 26, circa 1892, with Louisa, 3, Mary, 2, and George, 6 months. (Photo courtesy of Mark Rebagliati.)

Future Olympic snowboarding champion Ross Rebagliati atop an oversized tricycle sculpture by artist Ken Glasgow. (Photo courtesy of Mark Rebagliati.)

Ryan Rebagliati, son of Ross Rebagliati, on hill overlooking Lytton in 2020. (Photo courtesy of Mark Rebagliati.)

Frederick Joseph (Joe) Watkinson who came from Cornwall, England, in 1860 to work in the sandbars on the Fraser River during the gold rush. Photo circa 1875. (Courtesy of the Watkinson family.)

The Watkinson family in December 1990: (back row, left to right) Fred, Harvey, Tommy and Lindy; (front row, left to right) Rosslyn, Mary, Heather and Edith Watkinson. (Photo courtesy of the Watkinson family.)

The Chong Wah General Merchant grocery store on Main Street of Lytton in 1905. (Photo courtesy of the Chong family.)

The Chong Family: (Back row) Lily, Jack; (front row) Beatrice, Grandfather Lau Gow and Peter. (Photo courtesy of the Chong family.)

Kevin Loring's grandfather Andrew Adams and Kevin's maternal uncles at Snake Flat, a.k.a. Maxumptn: (left to right) Donald (Joey) Adams, Gerry (Poncho) Adams, Archie Adams, grandfather, Buster (Dakey) Adams, Ritchie Adams, Sandy Adams. The two children are uncles Albert and Marty (Dean) Adams. (Uncle Floyd Adams was not present.)

Kevin Loring with his cousin Tanya Adams in the May Day Parade.

Some members of the Lytton and Lillooet BMX bike clubs: (left to right): Kevin Loring, Mike Durant, Sandy McKay, Coralee Beaton (nee Nelson), Ken Smith, (Mad) Max Bissat, Josh Bissat, Cody McKay, Darrell Coldwell and Sheldon Swan.

Kevin Loring with spring salmon caught in the Thompson River at Thompson Siding, just past Tank Hill along the TransCanada Highway.

Combined grades two and three class photo at Lytton Elementary School in 1964. Including Peter Edwards (second row from back, far right); brother David (top row, third student from left); Shiela Adams, aunt of Kevin Loring, (second row, far left); Donny Glasgow, cousin of Kevin and friend of Peter and David (top row, second from right); Dorothy Glasgow, (third row, third student from the left, in white hair band); Patrick Manders, friend of David and Peter, whose parents ran motel where Kevin Loring did some of his writing (top row, seventh student from left).

A day by the Fraser River, 1962: (left to right) Peter, Melanie, David and Jim Edwards.

Dr. Kenneth Edwards sneaks a drink in mock jail during 1967 Centennial celebrations.

Winona Edwards in an orderly moment with her children: (left to right), David, Peter (flowered shirt), Jim and Melanie.

Winona Edwards trying to read to her children: (left to right) Melanie, Peter, Jim and David.

Queen Elizabeth and Prince Philip on the front page of the *Montreal Star* visiting Lytton in July 1959, where the prince chatted with Chief Dunstan Raphael.

J.R. Beattie's name appeared on Canada's paper currency when he was deputy governor of Bank of Canada. His grandfather Martin Beattie was a constable and tax collector in Lytton.

Yoga practitioner and bestselling author Kareen Zebroff on the cover of Germany's *Der Spiegel* magazine in January 1975. Kareen Zebroff and Winona Edwards were best friends in Lytton, and Peter Edwards was the Zebroff family's paperboy.

1955 postcard of Lytton Main Street in rush hour.

A postcard of the New Lytton Hotel circa 1940; the hotel was across the street from the future site of the Edwards' family house.

The ferry across the Fraser River, linking the east and west sides of the river. (Photo courtesy of Kevin Loring.)

Lytton Buddhist monks hold an Easter hotdog roast. (Photo courtesy of Tricia Thorpe and Don Glasgow.)

July 2022 fire on the west side of the Fraser River. (Photo courtesy of Tricia Thorpe and Don Glasgow.)

The reconstruction of Tricia Thorpe's and Don Glasgow's house. (Photo courtesy of Tricia Thorpe and Don Glasgow.)

The completed house of Tricia Thorpe and Don Glasgow. (Photo courtesy of Tricia Thorpe and Don Glasgow.)

After 2022 the fire, music festivals were a signal of the community rebuilding and recovering.

CHAPTER 31

CENTENNIAL YEAR

Kids were fine. Parents not always.
For a long time I said I was Austrian.

NEW LYTTON RESIDENT KAREEN ZEBROFF,

WHO WAS RAISED IN GERMANY

LYTTON FELT LIKE A PLACE where, if you waited long enough, the world would show up for you. Such was the case when Kareen Zebroff arrived in the village in the summer of 1966 and quickly became a close friend of Winona Edwards, the wife of Dr. Ken Edwards. She arrived with her husband, Peter Zebroff, a high school principal, and three daughters, one of whom was just three months old.

Kareen was German-born, with a backstory like something out of a novel, which was appropriate, as she was particularly literate. She brought a cosmopolitan flair to the village, something authentic and exotic at the same time.

The Zebroffs settled into a house above the highway on Snob Hill. Exactly how Snob Hill got its name isn't clear. There were no snobs up there, but it definitely sat on a hill, giving it a panoramic view of the

town, the confluence of the Fraser and Thompson Rivers, and the valley
north towards Lillooet. The Zebroffs had already lived in the small
towns of Squamish and Enderby, so tiny Lytton wasn't a culture shock
to them. Kareen later praised the great friendliness of the townspeople,
including the young Chief and his kids, who were the same age as the
Zebroff girls and used to play with them. She later called co-author
Peter's mother, Winona, "without a doubt, the greatest friend of my
life!!! . . . We were soulmates."

Kareen was born Helge-Kareen Bruggemann in Windsbach, near
Ansbach in Central Franconia, Germany. She was the daughter of a
doctor who survived two world wars, including time on the French
front during World War II. She told me he would take wounded soldiers
back from the front to Germany, and they were often strafed along the
way by Allied fighter planes.

Kareen spent most of World War II in Marienbad, now called
Mariánské Lázně, a Czech town best known today for a water spa fre-
quented by the locally famous. Her family fled Marienbad as Russian
forces approached, and lived for a time in a citadel near Donauwörth,
Germany. Next was Garmisch, where she contracted TB at age nine,
apparently from infected cow's milk. She was hospitalized in Oberam-
mergau for several months, and then was sent with her younger sister
to a children's home/orphanage in Kempten for nearly a year.

Kareen was reunited with her family and fled Germany after the war.
She arrived in Lytton, now married and the mother of three daughters,
after taking a winding route that included Edmonton, Dawson Creek,
Taylor Flats on the Peace River in northern BC, Fort Nelson, Vancouver,
and Enderbee in the Okanagan, when her husband Peter had a chance
to move up from being a vice-principal to principal. He took language
courses in an attempt to connect with Indigenous students, who out-
numbered the whites.

Kareen was in her late twenties when the family arrived in Lytton. She later said she was becoming increasingly self-confident as she arrived in town. "All this to say that a once-shy teenager became more and more self-reliant and self-aware about her own strength and ability to deal with every change and challenge," she told an interviewer from the *Yoga Journal* in Germany. "I was defensive about being German," she said of her early years in Canada, when she went to school as a teenager in Dawson Creek. "Kids were fine. Parents not always. For a long time I said I was Austrian." She said she didn't encounter anti-German discrimination while in Lytton. "We had a good time . . . I can handle anything that comes at me. Anything that happens, I adapted."

The Zebroffs left Lytton in the late 1960s, around the same time as the Edwards family, and then it became increasingly easy to follow what Kareen was doing. She took a spin at acting, appearing in episodes of the TV shows *The Beachcombers*, *Danger Bay* and *MacGyver*. She also learned from the meditation-oriented Swami Shyam Acharya and visited the ashram of teacher Indra Devi in Tecate, Mexico.

After that, Kareen wrote several internationally bestselling yoga books and hosted yoga TV shows on CTV in Canada and in Germany. Her eight yoga books included one that was published in eleven languages. Another was briefly Germany's number-two bestseller, behind only Aleksandr Solzhenitsyn's *Gulag Archipelago*. When she made the cover of *Der Spiegel* magazine in Germany in 1975, she was one of only five women to have ever done so, even though she refused their request to pose nude. The women who had appeared on the cover before her also didn't doff their clothing, although one doubts anyone popped the question to Golda Meir or Indira Ghandi. Perhaps the other two women, Marilyn Monroe and a beautiful killer, were asked, but it seems unlikely.

Lytton had seen considerable rebuilding since the disastrous fires of the 1930s and 1949 and the numerous smaller fires in the area. By the Centennial year of 1967, the local board of trade boasted that the town included a doctor, a barber shop, a drive-in theatre, and Anglican and Roman Catholic churches. As if that wasn't enough excitement, it was also noted that the area was a "rockhound's paradise," with plenty of jade, agate, garnet and onyx to be found. The board of trade didn't mention that in 1962 Lytton had the highest illegitimacy rate in BC, at 37 percent. That year, 22 of Lytton's 59 newborns were the progeny of unwed parents. The rate in Vancouver was a relatively low 9.6 percent, while the provincial average was 6.7 percent.

Life was a little less optimistic on the west side of the Fraser River, across from Lytton. It had rich soil, good timber, beautiful beaches and the old Earlscourt ranch. And a dose of misfortune.

The Colonel died in Pasadena in 1960, and in 1962 Earlscourt was bought by Dr. Raymond V. Mundall, a wealthy physician from Oakdale, California. He quickly became discouraged when a shop full of equipment burned to the ground in November 1963. He moved away in the summer of 1964 to Sedona, Arizona, and then to Belize, in Central America, where he worked as a medical missionary. In his absence, tenants ran Earlscourt. An apple-packing facility on the property burned to the ground in January 1972, suspected to be the work of a local pyromaniac.

Aside from the old Earlscourt ranch, the west side of the Fraser River was the Indigenous side. There was just one telephone in those years for the entire Nlaka'pamux community there, and some homes were sixteen kilometres from it. Nlaka'pamux dwellings also lacked electricity, gas and water, as well as visits from public health officials. The west side was connected to Lytton by a tiny ferry operating on cables. In July 1967, a car plunged off the cable ferry into the Fraser.

Neither the car nor its four passengers were seen again. In the aftermath
of the tragedy, there was a fight for stronger cables, a ramp to prevent
runaway cars, and an extension of the schedule to midnight from its old
shut-off time of 7 p.m.

> A favourite drinking spot for some people was behind
> Jim MacMillan's tin shed at the end of Fraser Street. Jim Sr.
> used to run the first Taxi in Lytton. He stored his two Ford
> Model T taxis in the shed. People would come into town and
> get their bottle or case of beer, or jug of wine and hang out
> in the shade behind the shed. The spot overlooked the river
> and you could watch the trains roll by, hide out from the
> cops and just sit and drink. The tin shed was just down the
> street from our trailer.
>
> One of my favourite things to do when I was about
> seven or eight was to smash the empty bottles. I'd line them
> up like soldiers in the sand and throw rocks at them.
>
> Years later as a young adult, I was the one sitting in the
> shade, hiding from the cops, smoking marajuana and
> drinking behind the tin shed, adding to the collection of
> empty bottles littering the sand.
>
> *Kevin Loring*

Even perched as it was between two great rivers, Lytton was in constant danger of burning. A team of a hundred firefighters worked through
the night in August 1970 as gusts of 110 kilometres per hour whipped
flames surrounding the town into an inferno so intense it blocked the
Trans-Canada Highway. Five air tankers took turns water-bombing

the area. When it was over, the fire had destroyed six thousand acres of yellow pine, open range and brush, but the town—except for four houses—and human lives had been spared. The pond water that was polluted by the smoke was called "Lytton bourbon."

> I saw Main Street burn down a couple of times in my childhood. Once was when Sandy's garage caught fire and burned the whole block down across from the Lytton Hotel on Main Street.
>
> A few years later the greatest store at the centre of the universe, Gammie's General Store on Main Street, burned down. Bill Gammie and his store were a pillar of the town, many of us older Lyttonites have fond memories of it. He seemed to have everything a Lyttonite could want that they would otherwise have to go to a city to get. That's where we got our toys and candy, our parents would buy rifles and ammunition for hunting, fishing rods, you name it.
>
> I remember watching Gammie's burn. Standing on Fraser Street and watching with my mother as my uncle Vic Loring and the Lytton Volunteer Firemen tried to put the fire out. My grandmother lived in the apartment above Gammie's with my aunt Susan and her new husband Brian. As the fire reached my grandmother's apartment, ammunition from inside the store started going off and the bullets ripped through the burning walls and penetrated the Bank of Nova Scotia windows and sign across the street. It sounded like firecrackers. I remember that awful burnt-house smell and my grandmother in her nightgown sobbing. She lost everything, all the personal treasures she had carried with her from England. Photos and heirlooms,

the material record of her life, all gone. At the time, I was too young to understand. I understand now.

Kevin Loring

Adults had bigger concerns than entertaining their kids in those days. So we were responsible for our own entertainment. That included Christmas pageants at Lytton Elementary School, when we pretended we were in Bethlehem by wearing bathrobes and putting homemade camel heads on broomsticks. It was mystifying stuff. The notion of finding three wise men in one place seemed as mysterious as any of the religious talk.

As Lytton's paper boy in the late 1960s, Christmas was a prime time for tips. I remember going to collect from two of my teachers who lived together on Snob Hill and seeing them surrounded by empty beer bottles. One of them was sprawled on the floor with his legs above him, resting on the couch. The other staggered around and slurred something incomprehensible that had nothing to do with my lessons. They apparently had just celebrated a little Christmas party of their own. I recall getting quite a generous tip of crumpled-up dollar bills from them that Yule season. They didn't seem to remember a thing when I saw them at school the next day.

Peter Edwards

I have great memories of playing kick-the-can on Fraser Street. A couple dozen of us kids running around with rosy cheeks and snotty noses. Hiding in the alleyways,

sometimes along the banks of the railroads. In Caboose
Park. On a warm summer night. "Got you, you're it." Being
tagged, captured and penned up until someone kicked the
can down the street, freeing all the captured kids. Then
we'd run giggling into that perfect evening twilight and
hide all over again.

My childhood was filled with those evenings. Dust
devils and tumbleweeds rolling down the street. The dogs
barking to each other across the yards. The coyotes across
the river teasing back.

In elementary school we'd play war along the railroad
track embankments just above town. We'd hive off into two
teams, build weapons out of our parents' broom and axe
handles. At the time, we were fascinated with movies about
ninjas and kung fu. We imagined ourselves as samurai
warriors out to destroy rival clans. We took axe handles
and broomsticks and fashioned them into weapons. We'd
wrap them in electrical tape and beat each other. The game
was to disarm your opponent and capture them. However,
once a prisoner had been taken, various forms of torture
were commonly practised. One of my cousins was accidentally almost hanged at Hobo Hollow when my other cousin
strung him up a little too enthusiastically.

As we got older, our pretend warfare escalated to BB
and pellet gun battles. One time I climbed a large tree
down at Hobo Hollow with my pellet gun. It was the one
we used to kill rats. From the safety and obscurity of my
perch high up in that huge pine tree, I sniped at my friends
and cousins all day long.

It was a fun game, but as the saying goes, we're lucky nobody lost an eye.

Kevin Loring

Television connected Lytton to worlds far, far away, like the California of the *Beverly Hillbillies* sitcom or space travel or the Toronto Maple Leafs and their 1967 Stanley Cup win. Back then, anything seemed possible. The effort to bring television to Lytton began before our time, in the early 1950s, when Bill Shaw, proprietor of Shaw Springs Auto Court and Restaurant, drove up Botanie Mountain to the forestry lookout with a group of friends in a four-wheel drive, hauling a TV set and some aerials. There, they watched *The Ed Sullivan Show*, the Sunday night variety program that had big acts like Elvis, the Beatles and the Rolling Stones, and a few less enduring acts, like Topo Gigio, the talking Italian mouse. For some of the group, that trip to Botanie was the first time they had ever watched TV.

When we got a new TV in our home in the early 1960s, it was a prime piece of furniture. It resembled a bulky china cabinet with a shiny, hypnotic screen. We didn't dare play floor hockey around it like we did around the piano, which lost one of its legs in a particularly enthusiastic game. We were happy to let the new TV control us.

Dad didn't need to read Marshall McLuhan to see its powers. He delighted in calling it the Idiot Box as we sat transfixed in front of its glowing screen. My poor mother likely saw it as a way of numbing us a little before we returned to smashing things or each other.

My fascination with television got me my first publication when I spotted an error in a TV show about a bear and sent a letter about it to the Bloopers section of a west coast television guide. My nitpicking was published, and my addiction to the printed word officially began.

We saw the peace movement of the 1960s on TV but had no homegrown hippies, except for one surly-looking guy with shoulder-length hair and a T-shirt that read *Nice guys wear Levi's*. He ran off with both of a local minister's daughters at the same time.

Television quickly became part of my boyhood rites of passage. When I turned eleven, I was allowed to stay up until nine on Sunday nights to watch *Bonanza* without having to resort to whining or begging or threatening glares. TV ownership also brought civic responsibilities, like hosting neighbourhood kids on Saturday mornings to watch cartoons and eat hot dogs until they got TVs of their own. My friend Donny Glasgow got a TV, out past the edge of town, but watching it was a bigger production at his place. His father had to crank up a generator half an hour before *Bugs Bunny* and *Bonanza* so that he could tune in.

But TV was limited, and Donny had a far-reaching mind. He made his own entertainment most of the time. He got himself a telescope and gazed up at the stars, connecting his tiny, remote valley with the solar system.

Peter Edwards

CHAPTER 32

RESIDENTIAL SCHOOL REVELATIONS

He would look out the window and "disappear."

RESIDENTIAL SCHOOL STUDENT DEALS WITH SEXUAL ASSAULT

IN 1987, TERRY ALECK of the Lytton area stepped forward and told a
horrific story of rape, beatings and torture to local RCMP. His story had
been festering in his memories for decades. At its core was Derek Clarke,
a dormitory supervisor, and Anthony William Harding, the principal of
St. George's Residential School.

Clarke was single and in his mid-twenties when he arrived in
November 1965 to work at St. George's as a live-in student supervisor.
He got the job without an interview or a check of his references. So it
went unnoticed that he himself hadn't gone past grade eight. As did the
fact that he had never recovered from repeated sexual abuse at a Catholic
orphanage in England and had spent four months as a student in the
St. Christopher's School for Emotionally Disturbed Children in North
Vancouver.

His new employers did know that he had recently been asked to leave a position as a child-care worker at another Anglican institution because he was unqualified. His old bosses referred him for the Lytton job anyway. They still considered him good enough to work at St. George's with young Indigenous boys. Besides, he would be getting paid well. When his job fell under federal jurisdiction three years later, he was classified as a level 1 child-care worker, at a salary of $5,363 a year, equal to a little more than $50,000 in today's terms.

Clarke came to St. George's at a time when the religious school was blending more with the mainstream education system. Students in grades seven and above were now sent to public school in Lytton, although they still lived at the residential school. By 1970, St. George's didn't offer classroom teaching any longer, except for religious training. Clarke's new job at St. George's was to supervise the junior and intermediate boys. Kids usually stayed there for about two years before moving on to the senior dormitory. For those two years, the poorly qualified young man loomed like a 24-7 god in their new world.

Clarke oversaw all the boys' activities outside class, from the moment they awoke until bedtime. He got them up in the morning and made sure their beds were properly made before breakfast. If a coin did not bounce off the top blanket, the bed had to be remade. Only when all the beds were perfect could anyone eat. He also made sure they got on the school bus to Lytton. Clarke supervised homework, play times and chores. He sorted their clothing. He escorted students to meals, enforced discipline and took the children on outings. He got to decide who was sick and who needed special attention. Anyone who failed to follow daily prayers or attend religious services could expect to feel the leather of the strap from him, either in the dormitory or in the principal's office, on their hands or on their buttocks.

Clarke was the closest thing the boys had to a parent while at St. George's. In a 2000 legal decision rendered by Madam Justice Janice Dillon of the Supreme Court of British Columbia, which determined what institutions, including the Anglican Church and the federal government, were responsible for Clarke's crimes, the judge described Clarke's place in the social hierarchy of St. George's:

> The social architecture of the school, reinforced by the Anglican
> hierarchical ethos, ensured that Clarke would be viewed not just
> as a parent, but as the most powerful influence in the children's lives.
> Through the principal, the employer conferred upon the dormitory
> supervisor absolute power over a child's daily life. He was to be given
> the respect demanded within the religious, militaristic hierarchy . . .
> The structure also made it unlikely that a child would complain. The
> nature of the intimacy ensured that the child would be too ashamed
> to tell anyone. It should also not be overlooked that Clarke was white
> as were all the staff, making the supervisor even more unassailable.

Clarke lived in a room off the dormitory, where he kept a large record collection. His favourite students got to listen to music in his room. If parents sent treats for their children, Clarke stored them in his room and handed them out when he saw fit. His power was most evident in the evenings, when he inspected the boys after they bathed and were wrapped only in towels. He checked to see if they were clean, right down to their penises. If a boy was sent to the back of the line, that meant he had been chosen to spend time alone with Clarke. That meant sex. Sometimes Clarke took a boy into his room in the early morning too. One former student later recalled that Clarke would whisper in his ears, "It's okay, it's okay," as the student cried into his pillow.

Madam Justice Dillon wrote:

> Clarke would bring one boy into his room in pyjamas while the others
> watched TV. Sometimes he took a boy into his room in the early morn-
> ing. At other times, he kept a boy in his room ostensibly to be cleaning.
> There, he kissed, caressed, sexually stimulated, performed oral sex,
> forced oral sex on himself and sodomized the boys.

His assaults sometimes took place in the main dormitory, when he fon-
dled children under their blankets while claiming to be "looking for
things." Clarke told his targets to keep their encounters secret. Favoured
boys got chocolates, pop, gum and weekend trips, with permission from
the principal. The sexual assaults continued in motel rooms. Boys who
got such favours were mocked by other students as "Clarke's boys."

Clarke cleaned up well in public. He was a former Boy Scout leader
and outwardly caring. His defence lawyer claimed that "in every other
aspect of his life, he has been productive and a model citizen." Though
even Clarke's counsel had to admit, "Mr. Clarke is a very sick man."

Years later, a former student identified as "E.R.M." told a courtroom
how he was sexually abused two or three times a week by Clarke for a
couple of years. Madam Justice Dillon wrote:

> E.R.M. testified that during these incidents, he would look out the
> window and "disappear" by which he said he meant that in his mind,
> he would go away so as not to have to be here. He said he felt confused
> and scared and ashamed and that he didn't want to tell anyone because
> he feared if he did, they would not have anything to do with him, that
> they would feel it was his fault.

E.R.M. recalled that he was about six in 1961 when he began his eight-year stay at St. George's, when the school had 160 students. He was from a particularly remote community, and his extended family had been largely self-sufficient, with four vegetable gardens. They also dried and canned salmon. He said that his parents and grandparents spoke to him mostly in their traditional language and rarely in English.

As an adult testifying before Dillon, E.R.M. recalled how he did not understand what was happening the first day he attended St. George's. Once he realized that he would be left there alone, he started crying, saying he wanted to go home. Some of the teachers and staff were kind, but others definitely weren't. Once, when he arrived back at St. George's after summer vacation, E.R.M.'s skin was darker than it had been the previous school year, because he had been out in the sun a lot. A teacher refused to believe that he was clean, and scrubbed him hard with a brush until his arms hurt, while telling him he was a "dirty Indian."

Years later, E.R.M. recalled how Clarke had a bristly beard that felt like sandpaper when he molested him. He said he was too confused, too scared and too ashamed to tell anyone. If he did say something, others might shun him and blame him, he thought.

E.R.M. never wanted to return to St. George's after summers at home with his family. Dillon wrote:

He said that when he was away from the school, and was returning, he'd cry as soon as he came over the hill and saw the school. He told his parents and his extended family that he didn't want to go to the school but he never told them why.

Like other students, E.R.M. didn't like the food at St. George's, telling Dillon, "I guess I was always hungry." Sometimes he would break into the root cellar for something to eat. Other times he would jockey to help the bakery truck driver, hoping he'd be paid in doughnuts.

E.R.M. finally left St. George's in 1969, and didn't return to the site until 1999. By then, the old school and residence had been burned down by an unknown arsonist or arsonists. The Lytton Indian Band Seniors Complex had been put up on the old school property. The chapel stood empty and dirty. E.R.M. found himself "looking over my shoulder" at the site and expecting a priest to chastise him. He testified before Dillon that his time at St. George's had affected him deeply, long after he left the school:

> I hate people in authority . . . In the residential school we were always
> told what to do. We had chores and we had to do it seven days a week,
> ten months a year and it was every day, we never got a rest. We always
> had chores we had to do. We had to do it. We had to do it. And I hated
> it. I hated it because they were—they'd tell us when to go to bed, they
> would tell us when to wake up. They would tell us when to eat, what
> to eat, what to wear, what to do in school—I—it's pissing me off just
> talking about it.

The abuse E.R.M. suffered at St. George's haunted him as a husband and as a father, he told Dillon:

> In the relationship that I have with [my wife] it's everything that I say
> has got to be my way. No compromise, no middle ground or nothing.
> It's my way or the highway. And it's been like that throughout the
> 18 years that we've been together. And for my children, my oldest
> daughter is 13. It really hurts, it really hurts when I see other men
> playing with my kids. It really hurts because I can't do that with my
> children. Because I'm always scared that I'll harm them or I'll abuse

them. That when my kids ask me for a hug I—it makes me feel uncomfortable. Or when they ask me for help I tell them go see mom or I ignore them. And it's hard. It's hard because everything that I'm doing to my children has been done to me. And I see that. But I don't know how to stop.

The St. George's experience also scarred his relationship with his mother, who spoke little English. He said that her traditional language was not passed on to him because of his time in the residential school system. He told the court that his two sisters who had attended residential schools had both attempted suicide. E.R.M.'s mother was asked in court through an interpreter why she sent her children to St. George's. She replied that "the Indian Agent had come to her and told her that they all had to go and that if they didn't, she risked going to jail."

E.R.M.'s mother also told the court that he seemed to be all right at first, during his time at St. George's, but then there was a profound change. "She said that he didn't listen to his family members anymore," Dillon wrote. "She said 'that's when I lost my son.'"

CHAPTER 33

BUSTED

Your past services in the field of practical Child Care
have been appreciated and we trust that your
personal problems will soon be cleared up.

ANGLICAN CHURCH WRITES SUPPORT LETTER
FOR SERIAL CHILD MOLESTER

IN MARCH 1973, a thirteen-year-old female student went missing from her dormitory at St. George's. She was found a short time later in bed with her dormitory supervisor, and the student acknowledged that they had had sex. St. George's principal, Anthony Harding, wrote an explanatory letter to the federal co-ordinator of student residences, pointing out that the supervisor had been previously warned about "the dangers of the emotional attachment that he thought was forming between them." The supervisor resigned on May 20, 1973. He wrote in his letter of resignation that he was leaving St. George's for reasons that were "personal to myself." Harding played along, writing two days later to advise him that "your resignation is accepted." He also expressed hope that the younger man would "soon find a type of employment that will give greater scope to your undoubted abilities." The positive parting letter was written even though the student said the dormitory supervisor had forced her to have intercourse with him, while he was under the influence of alcohol.

That same month, a relatively new teacher at Lytton Elementary School overheard St. George's boys on the playground talking about a supervisor "doing things to boys." The boys talked of "bum-holing," rode each other like dogs engaged in sexual acts, and grabbed at other boys' genitals. Some of the boys seemed to know of sexual assaults upon others. There was ridicule and jokes.

The teacher was alarmed. She alerted Joe Chute, the principal at Lytton Elementary and the face of white normalcy in town. Chute had become somewhat of a fixture in Lytton since moving there in 1950. He served as principal in the village for thirty-five years and would spend another fourteen years as mayor. He had been a member of the local Anglican church for the past twenty-three years. His friends included Reverend Harding, a fellow parishioner and the principal at St. George's. Chute's wife, Peggy, was a popular community organizer.

Chute told Harding of the serious issues raised by the junior teacher. It later struck a judge as odd that Harding had to be told what was going on at his school. Justice Janice Dillon charged:

> If Harding did not become aware of [Derek] Clarke's sexual misconduct, he ought to have . . . The administrator should have been aware of the behavior of children on the playground and childhood gossip which was apparent to a relatively novice teacher at the local school who acted swiftly to deal with the matter. If he was not, then he was willfully blinded by his own desires to avoid detection of lax moral conduct and sexually abusive behavior.

St. George's boys were then called, one by one, into Chute's office at Lytton Elementary School, as Harding waited outside. One of the boys was later described in court only as E.A.J. He had started at St. George's at age six. Before that, he lived with his family on a ranch outside Lytton. E.A.J. testified that some months after he moved to the intermediate dormitory, Clarke arranged a work task that required him to go to Clarke's room. That's where Clarke sexually assaulted him for the first time. Many similar assaults followed. They included fondling by Clarke, forcing E.A.J. to fondle Clarke, and anal rape. He described the latter as "making me scream—he just treated me like a dog." He testified that when Clarke "was done fucking me," he gave him a Chiclet and told him not to tell anyone.

E.A.J. said that after the first incident, he left and went to his bed, lay down and cried. As he wept, he looked out the window and watched the other kids having fun. "He testified that he felt confused and scared," BC Supreme Court Justice Paul Williamson wrote, after hearing a civil suit against the Church and government over abuses at St. George's. "He said that he felt hatred for Derek Clarke and, importantly, for his own mother. Questioned as to why he felt hatred towards his mother, he said that he hated her for 'bringing me to that school.'"

Chute heard from another student, refered to later in court as "G.B.S.," who also told of repeated sex with Clarke and how he finally simply stayed home and refused to go back to St. George's. The first time he had sex with the supervisor was particularly difficult for G.B.S. "He said that afterwards Clarke gave him a towel, told him to clean up, and let him go," Dillon later reported. "He said he went back to the dormitory, lay on his bed and cried himself to sleep." G.B.S. testified that he would go blank during the assaults. He said, "I went to a different place—I wasn't there—my mind wasn't there." Dillon noted that when G.B.S. gave this testimony decades later, he was literally shaking in the witness box.

After Chute heard all their accounts, the principal didn't call the police. He also didn't contact the boys' parents or arrange for counselling or call for a further investigation. No spiritual assistance was offered to the young victims at the religious school. "Chute did nothing as a result of these reports," Madam Justice Dillon of the Supreme Court of British Columbia later wrote, continuing:

Chute explained in testimony at trial that Harding told him that it was unnecessary to report the matter to police because the Department of Indian Affairs "had ways of dealing with such cases." Harding later told him not to worry about it. Chute said that he did not consider it his role to report because the incidents had not occurred at his school. However, he was assured by Harding that proper procedures were undertaken and said that he would have reported to police if he had thought that this was not the case.

Years later, the federal government's Truth and Reconciliation Commission reported that Harding told Clarke that if he didn't leave St. George's voluntarily, he would tell police of the abuse allegations. When Harding wrote to Clarke to accept his resignation, the letter didn't refer to the multiple sexual assaults on children at St. George's. Instead, it added: "Your past services in the field of practical Child Care have been appreciated and we trust that your personal problems will soon be cleared up."

And that was that. Police, Indian Affairs, counsellors, spiritual advisers and the boys' parents weren't told of the repeated sexual abuse. It was the boys' problem, to handle alone. Harding did write to the Department of Indian Affairs to tell them of Clarke's "resignation," but gave no reasons for the departure. As he left, Clarke was given a refund of pension credits for time spent at the residential school. No investigation followed.

Harding was promoted within the Church, rising to deacon that October and then priest in 1975, when St. George's had 101 students.

"The affair was cleansed," Dillon declared, adding:

> It can be concluded from Harding's failure to report to federal or police authorities that he did not want an investigation at the school. Following so closely upon the sexual misconduct of another staff member, this would most likely have occurred. These events took place at a time when other residences were being closed and concern had already been expressed by diocesan authorities that this not happen to St. George's.

After leaving St. George's, E.A.J. drank heavily and abused drugs until he was twenty-eight. He had difficulty trusting intimate partners and could be abusive with them. The first woman he had an intimate relationship with died by suicide. Another partner "threw it in his face" when she learned of his abuse at St. George's and said he must be gay to have gone along with it. He found another partner who was more understanding, but his problems still bubbled up. "He has outbursts of anger against his wife and against his children which he says are brought on by nothing which is their doing," Justice Dillon wrote. "He ends these by leaving the house for some time until he cools down and eventually coming back and apologizing."

Lytton remained a dark presence for E.A.J. long after he left St. George's. His mother and other family members lived there still, and he struggled to find excuses to avoid the village or limit his time visiting. As he moved into adulthood, he had trouble with authority and no real desire to get a full-time job. After he stopped drinking, E.A.J. sat down with his mother one evening and spoke to her about the sexual abuse he had suffered at St. George's. This was the first time they had discussed it. E.A.J. needed to make peace with her. It didn't feel right that he had told her he hated her for "bringing me to that school" and for "signing me in and leaving me." He said he was wrong to blame her. "He said that that marked a change in his relationship with his mother, that he realized that he loved her and should not have treated her as he did," Justice Williamson wrote. "He said they now get along better."

The hills around Lytton also offered some healing. About three times a year, E.A.J. ventured into the mountains alone. He would stay there for three to five days, long enough to cry without having to explain himself, to "clear my head—to shout out my anger—to feel at peace with myself."

E.A.J.'s sister was later sent to St. George's too—she was literally dragged there. She remembered Harding as always angry. She said he banged doors and would frequently become red in the face. A supervisor told her that she had to be at St. George's because her family was too "isolated" where they lived. She said she was told that if she did not go to the school, her parents would go to jail and she would never see them again.

> My aunt Virginia told me how they were always hungry
> at St. George's and the food was always terrible. She would
> look out the window of the girls' dormitory and she could
> see the smoke from her mother's cookstove rising up over
> the treetops only a few kilometres away. But even though
> she was so close, she could never go home.

> *Kevin Loring*

The Truth and Reconciliation Commission's report described in detail the degradation of even the children's traditional foods:

E.A.J.'s sister testified that the staff at St. George's called the students "savages" and "heathens." She said that occasionally at the beginning of the year students would bring things, in particular, food. She said her group would bring dried fish, natives from further south would bring smoked dried fish, and that children from the north would bring dried seaweed. They would trade them back and forth. She testified that if they were caught, what they had brought was thrown in the trash can and they were told "... that is where it belongs," that such food was what heathens ate, and that was not what they were at St. George's to learn.

E.A.J.'s sister recalled fainting and throwing up at St. George's, perhaps because of an allergy to incense. The Truth and Reconciliation final report noted:

She said that when she fainted, a supervisor dragged her out and told her that she was evil and had the devil in her and that was why she could not stay in church. She testified that the supervisor asked her if she had ever been burned and she said she had been burned once in the foot, around a fire when she was younger. She said that supervisor told her, "That's what it feels like when you burn in hell, except it's all over and that's where you're going." She testifies that to this day she worries about "the devil in her."

A civil suit before Justice Williamson of the BC Supreme Court heard that a student referred to as T.W.N.A. was sent to St. George's for grade one. He arrived at St. George's with his cousin, mother and aunt. He and his cousin both cried for a long time when they were left at the school, confused about why they were at St. George's and how long they would have to wait to return home. T.W.N.A. was first assaulted by Clarke when he was nine years old.

T.W.N.A. sometimes wet the bed, and he recalled that Clarke "would stuff my face in the wet sheet" in front of laughing students. Other punishments from Clarke included being forced to clean stairways from the basement to the fourth floor with a toothbrush, sitting in the corner in front of the class wearing a dunce's cap, and having gum stuck to his nose in front of the class while the teacher beat him on his hands and arms.

In describing the daily routine of the residential school, T.W.N.A. sounded as if he were talking about a military boot camp—but much worse. The food was poor. Generally, they had mush for breakfast, served with sour milk, with lunches of baloney sandwiches on white bread or peanut butter and jam sandwiches. Suppers didn't generally smell or taste good, and sometimes he threw his dinner under the table.

Worst of all were the four years of repeated sexual abuse. T.W.N.A. said he never told anyone about that. He didn't know how to talk about it. He also felt a sense of fear, telling the court that Clarke was "our supervisor, and if you said anything against the supervisor you got punished." Like E.A.J., he carried an irrational fear of authority figures into adulthood. His wife noted that he was shy about his body and that he showered compulsively. She said he sometimes woke her in the middle of the night with "a strange scream" and that, in his sleep, he would sometimes say "Help me" and "No."

Clarke's crimes were not investigated until 1987—fourteen years after he left St. George's and began abusing boys in Vancouver. His initial conviction was for sexual assaults on seventeen different boys, aged between nine and eleven. At least one of them killed himself before the trial began. Clarke had committed at least 140 illegal sexual encounters, the trial judge concluded, adding that the real number might be as high as 700.

Forensic psychologist Dr. Stanley Semrau told the court that Clarke had been emotionally scarred from living in British orphanages until the age of eight. He was repeatedly abused during those early years and never matured sexually, Semrau said. "It [boyhood] is a stage he's fixated at rather than regressing to," added the psychologist. He noted that Clarke was not abusing drugs or alcohol.

Clarke was initially sentenced to twelve years in prison. Before his sentencing, a character witness for Clarke turned on him and said she had just learned that he had molested her son too. In 1996, he had two years added to his sentence for four additional charges.

St. George's had been closed for ten years by the time Clarke went to prison in May 1989, at age fifty-two. Harding, the principal who'd allowed his crimes to go unreported, had gone on to run the local Anglican hospital after St. George's stopped operating as a residence in 1979 and dropped to just forty-five students. Harding was charged in 1989 with three counts of gross indecency and one count of buggery involving two former St. George's students between 1969 and 1976.

Harding put up a spirited fight in court. His lawyer called one of the complainants a liar. Another former resident was labelled an "upset young man" whose serious problems came from the abuse he had endured at the hands of Clarke. The tactics worked. Harding was found not guilty on all charges on June 8, 1989, after the jury had deliberated for six hours. But evidence continued to bubble up. So did legal action, including a negligence civil lawsuit laid in 1998 by seven former St. George's students against Clarke, Harding, Chute, the Anglican Church of Canada, the district school board and the federal

Department of Indian Affairs. Former students said Harding provided senior students with alcohol in his room before having sex with them.

No award from the civil suit could ever make up for the human cost of bringing justice to those in charge of St. George's. At least eight men are believed to have killed themselves when they were subpoenaed to testify. Suddenly, the former students were victims again. If they lost in court, it would mean they had not been believed, yet again. If the suit was victorious, on the other hand, they faced possible ridicule for accepting what some called "arse money."

Justice Janice Dillon heard from a former student identified in court as "J.M.," who testified that he was taken by Harding to Kamloops. Madam Justice Dillon wrote:

> Harding secured a motel room with one bed. Alcohol was left for
> the underage youth while Harding went out for a while. When
> he returned, Harding came to bed naked and attempted to fondle
> J.M. who grabbed his hand and said "stop." Nothing further happened.
> There were no more trips for J.M. He told nobody.

By that time, Harding was an Anglican deacon. "Harding had oral sex and sodomized the boy," Justice Dillon wrote. "He came another time to the boy's room to do the same thing but the boy started to cry and told him not to."

Justice Dillon found the Diocese of Caribou guilty by vicarious liability and awarded restitution. Hit with the bill, the tiny diocese declared bankruptcy. Harding died in 1992 before the court cases cleared.

Justice Dillon wrote that she believed Harding misled the Lytton Elementary School principal, Chute, and the federal government. She wrote:

The involvement of Harding in sexual misconduct and his failure to
do anything for the boys as a result of their disclosures leads to the
obvious inference that he did not care about Clarke's behaviour as long
as it was not known. The fact that he did not tell the department about
the reason for the "resignation," even though he told Chute that he
would do so, indicates that Harding did not want an investigation at
the school.

Dillon wrote of "rampant evil" and called Clarke's tenure at St. George's
an "eight-year reign of terror."

The Truth and Reconciliation Commission found that the events at
St. George's represented much more than the misdeeds of two men. "The
prosecutions at the Lytton school reveal a callous pattern of behaviour in
which abuse was excused and covered up in an effort to protect both the
system and the perpetrators," Commissioner Murray Sinclair wrote.

It seemed that almost everyone in Lytton was touched by this evil,
with its legacy of alcohol and drug abuse, depression and suicide.
Former Lytton area resident Christ'l Roshard recalls that she was often
reminded of the fallout of residential schools as she worked as a court
worker, a journalist and mayor of neighbouring Lillooet. "I saw the
end result, sitting in the courts . . . A lot of these kids just killed themselves, just jumping off bridges or in front of a train. It's a really ugly
part of our history."

Catherine Morrison, an Anglican priest who ministers in Lytton,
said this sense of the residential school's lingering impact is backed by
statistics. "The Church here keeps the burial registry and we have had
two hundred suicides in the last ten years," she said. "In a community of
seven hundred people, that's devastating."

Rosalin Miles of Lytton First Nation was born in 1965. She cringes
at the thought that she could have attended St. George's if her family

hadn't moved away to Langley. They had lived on the west side of the river, near the Earlscourt ranch. Her father attended St. George's for ten years but didn't talk about it as she was growing up. Still, she saw that something was very wrong in the area. "We became the suicide capital of Canada," Miles told us in an interview.

It wasn't until she was thirty years old that the silence around St. George's started to break. Miles was hearing stories about life at St. George's that were almost too much to comprehend. She heard of boys being held down while they were raped by priests, and of priests watching as boys were raped. "There's a lot of losses," she says. "There's a lot of shame. There's a lot of trauma." The stories haunted her. "The trauma—you think of someone who's raped. You think of someone who's five years old who's raped . . . Every night he has this trauma."

Aside from the suicides, former students faced plenty of other sad ends to their lives. "My dad died when he was fifty-two because of addictions," Miles says. Sometimes she wonders what her dad and his friends were like there as little boys. "I just think of them as little broken spirits."

It wasn't a great mystery why the school burned down after it was closed in 1979. "There was this rage in the community," Miles recalls. "A lot of men tore it down brick by brick."

> When we were children, my cousins and I used to play in the ruins of St. George's. The dairy barns and horse stables, we'd even break into the school itself. We'd smash windows and graffiti it. Under the wooden stairs at the entrance of the main building was a secret little cubbyhole with all these inscriptions carved or scribbled into the wood that read "so and so was here" and the date when they made their mark. One time we were playing in the old coal mound that was used to feed the boiler and my uncle

Buster saw us and scolded us. He told us not to play in that coal mound because underneath the coal was where they buried the suicides.

Kevin Loring

The fears stuck around even after the school was gone. "Am I going to be a good parent?" Miles wonders. "What's my worth? What's my value?" She found her work in healing. She studied kinesiology and earned her PhD, advocating traditional Indigenous health and well-being as part of the UBC Indigenous Studies in Kinesiology program. Healing meant tackling intergenerational trauma—as adult children felt angry at their parents for making them attend the school instead of somehow hiding them. "What the residential school system did was absolutely destroy families—break the ties of the teachings of the parents," Miles says.

There were more specific questions too. How many children died on site or after running away? The Truth and Reconciliation Commission names thirty-five children who died while in the custody of St. George's, but the number is believed to be far higher. How could anyone ever know? Anything seemed possible in the chaos of St. George's. Stories circulated of bodies being disposed of in an incinerator and of bones being found behind the nurse's house. "In Lytton, they would just throw them in the incinerator," Miles says. How could those bones ever be identified? Where should they be reburied? "It's miraculous if someone can move forward," Miles states. "I say 'move forward' rather than 'healing.'"

Residential schools across the country had a sorry record, and St. George's was among the worst of the worst. "From its opening until the end of the 1930s, the school was in a constant state of crisis," Sinclair wrote in his report.

Inspectors, students, and parents all raised issues about the quality of education, overwork, poor health, inadequate diet, sanitation, building maintenance, fire safety, discipline, truancy, sexual impropriety, and conflicts between staff members. While not unique, the problems of this school serve as an example of the inevitable outcomes of a poorly managed, underfunded, and misdirected system in action.

Trauma from St. George's Residential School continued long after it closed in 1979. Many Nlaka'pamux began to reach out to their traditional beliefs and practices. Lytton First Nation brought in healers to try to find ways to revitalize the traditional knowledge of the Nlaka'pamux to heal the people.

The hero of this sad story is Aleck, the first of the seven former students who provided accounts of abuse at the hands of Clarke and Harding. He and several of the other former students were offered settlements, the highest of which was $256,000. Aleck refused to settle out of court and pursued justice against their abusers, the Anglican Church and the federal government in the case *Aleck et al. v. Clarke et al.*, 2001 B.C.S.C., 1177. He was ultimately successful in his court case, bringing about the first such win against the Government of Canada and the Anglican Church for the abuses suffered at a residential school. When the judge asked Mr. Aleck if there was anything that he'd like to say now that he had won his case, he replied: "Yes, your honour, I want an apology from the guy who runs this country."

On June 11, 2008, Prime Minister Stephen Harper apologized on behalf of Canada, in the House of Commons, for the atrocities committed at the residential schools against Indigenous children, including those at St. George's in Lytton.

On July 25, 2022, Pope Francis apologized in front of school survivors and Indigenous community members at the former Ermineskin

Indian Residential School south of Edmonton. He called the schools a
"disastrous error" that was incompatible with the Gospel and which
bore "catastrophic" results. "I am deeply sorry," Francis said. "I hum-
bly beg forgiveness for the evil committed by so many Christians
against the Indigenous peoples." Four Chiefs then presented him with
a traditional feathered headdress, making him an honorary community leader.

Ruby Dunstan thrived after escaping from St. George's. As a thirteen-
year-old, she had been punished for speaking her Indigenous language
and she'd fled. She was a seventy-four-year-old grandmother in 2015
when she received an honorary doctorate from the University of
Victoria.

Dunstan had done much to earn the honour. She had worked as a
social worker and then as the first female Chief of Lytton First Nation.
She had also successfully fought clear-cut logging in the sacred Stein
Valley, and helped set up the band-operated Stein Valley Nlakapamux
School, serving as school board president.

As she received her honorary PhD, Dunstan told attendees at
her convocation ceremony about her experiences as a little girl at
St. George's, including how she was struck for speaking her language
and for showing signs of rebellion. She told those assembled of her
feelings as a five-year-old student after first arriving at St. George's.

> I had this thought in my head forever that I was just a dumb Indian
> because of the residential school. And it took a long time to get rid
> of that thought and that feeling. It's a shame that those people that
> did that to all of us are not here to witness something like this today,
> because it would be them that would be put to shame for what they
> did to us.

Dunstan told reporter Lindsay Kines of the *Vancouver Sun* in an interview before the ceremony, "I never, ever got a whupping when I was at home and then all of a sudden I was put into an environment where whupping was the thing. When I tried to fight back, they gave it to me worse . . . There was nobody around that you could talk to. Everybody thought you were crazy if you talked about being raped or sexually abused."

There was no better place to reclaim cultural identity than the Stein River Valley, on the west side of the Fraser River from Lytton. Something just felt right there. "There's a real deep presence," Miles says of the valley. "It's very easy for us to connect with our land." She thinks of how her great-great-great-grandparents were there and she feels the same way. She can see a rock and know they saw it too, and she somehow feels better and more whole. "That part energizes you—your ties to who you are."

The establishment of the Stein Valley Nlakapamux School in 2009 helped too, with its vision statement of helping students "to be confident, immersed in Nlakapamux way of life and excel academically so they will be self-reliant." A connection with the languages is also nourished there. "That whole area has been known as a very spiritual place," Miles says. "A lot of people are thriving now."

My play *Where the Blood Mixes*, which is set in Lytton, deals with the intergenerational trauma from St. George's Residential School. Many of the scenes are set in the Buds and Suds bar of the Lytton Hotel and along the riverbank. The play premiered on June 11, 2008, in Vancouver on the same day that Prime Minister Steven Harper apologized in the House of Commons for the atrocities of the residential school system. It wasn't planned that way, it was just one of those uncanny, magical coincidences that happen somehow. Terry Aleck has been a mentor to me throughout my life. Knowing that his fight for justice contributed directly to the official apology in the House of Commons is truly humbling and inspiring. His brave work helped open the door for other survivors to share their stories, which ultimately led to the establishment of the Truth and Reconciliation Commission of Canada.

Kevin Loring

CHAPTER 34

BATTLE FOR THE STEIN VALLEY

This valley is Indian land.

CHIEF RUBY DUNSTAN TO THE
WILDERNESS ADVISORY COMMITTEE, 1985

ONE OF THE MOST SIGNIFICANT events that happened in Lytton was the environmental conflict over the Stein Valley. The Stein is a gla-cier-fed river that originates in the Coastal Mountain Range between Lytton and Mount Currie, to the west. The valley is a sacred place to the Lytton Nlaka'pamux and Mount Currie Lil'wat peoples, a site of medicine and food gathering, vision seeking and cleansing. For centu-ries it was used as a place to commune with the ancestors and the Creator and to connect to Mother Earth and gain insight. All through the valley, pictographs, petroglyphs and culturally modified trees mark the dreams and visions of the Nlaka'pamux. Today, it remains the last unlogged watershed in the region and is celebrated as a model of co-stewardship between First Nations and the government. That situation didn't come about easily. The battle over whether to log the Stein or save it was a very divisive one in Lytton, setting neighbour against neighbour and even family members against each other.

Back in the 1960s, tourism was beginning to create jobs in the area, with the success of rafting companies taking people down the Thompson and Fraser Rivers. But the best-paying jobs were still in the railways and, in particular, forestry. Lytton Lumber was a family-owned and -operated lumber mill founded in 1964 by Lewis (Lew) MacArthur. Lew was a large, charismatic, patriarchal figure who built the company from the ground up. The MacArthurs' business philosophy was rooted in a desire to keep the local economy thriving. As competing mills moved towards more automation, Lytton Lumber maintained a more labour-intensive process that was less efficient but meant they could employ dozens of local workers. Instead of building an automated green chain— essentially a conveyor belt that outputs the fresh-cut lumber—they continued to operate with a manual green chain, employing a half-dozen or more workers piling the lumber by hand, sometimes running in two shifts. The MacArthurs knew that those jobs kept the town going.

In the 1970s, people were beginning to worry about the impacts of the logging industry in the region. British Columbia's economy was fuelled by resource extraction, and lumber was the province's number one export. Huge multinational companies with head offices in faraway countries and no connection to the local environments or communities were clear-cutting larger and larger parcels of old-growth forest, often selling the logs wholesale overseas, where they were then manufactured into products and sold back to Canadians at a premium. Lytton Lumber was a tiny mill in the grand scheme of the economy. These industry leaders were growing quickly, buying up the smaller mills or outcompeting them into extinction. The pressures on the MacArthurs if they were to remain competitive were enormous, and ultimately impossible to withstand.

Loggers turned their attention to what was potentially one of the most profitable stands of old-growth forest left in BC. The biggest hurdle to getting men and machinery into the Stein Valley was the Fraser River. The only access to the west side was over the local reaction ferry, which was not a viable means for logging trucks to ford the river. A bridge would have to be built, and then a new road would have to be cut into the Stein to get the trucks through the steep and rocky valley. Even at the planning stage, it was clear that the costs of building the necessary infrastructure to get into the Stein and extract the timber would be far too high, many times more than the potential profits that might come from logging the valley. But the culture in BC at the time was to log everything, regardless of profitability. The hunger for timber and the power of the logging industry politically and culturally were overwhelming. A commonly seen bumper sticker at the time read: *EARTH FIRST we'll log the other planets later.*

At the same time, the nascent environmental movement was emerging in British Columbia. People were becoming concerned about the devastation that large-scale industrial logging was causing to the environment. The tourist industry was beginning to market the natural amenities of the province. People didn't want to camp next to a clearcut; they wanted the untamed, undeveloped "Super Natural BC" that was being pitched to them in government pamphlets and commercials. Hikers and backcountry enthusiasts who had navigated the old pack trails of the Stein began to worry that it would become just another logged-out valley, and the natural and cultural treasures it protected would be erased from the world.

At the start of the Save the Stein movement, the most vocal advocates and those who had any agency in the matter were people from outside Lytton: hippies, typically from the Kootenays and southern BC, academics from the cities, the lower mainland and Vancouver Island,

and backcountry enthusiasts—all predominantly white. The movement to protect old-growth forests and stave off the collapse of ecosystems ran headfirst into the need of locals to put food on the table.

The Nlaka'pamux in the early days of the movement were largely on the periphery of the conversation. The BC government wasn't much interested in working with the First Nations and often ignored their concerns. The environmentalists, too, had their own agendas, as well as a growing sense of entitlement to the valley. The Nlaka'pamux began to feel suspicious of the urban environmentalists. Those outsiders were beginning to speak with authority about the future of the Stein, even in the presence of the Nlaka'pamux leadership.

As the movement evolved and concerns about the possibility of the valley being logged became more real, tensions between the environmentalists and the local Indigenous leadership grew. For the Nlaka'pamux, the issue of the Stein was not just an environmental concern; it was also cultural, spiritual and, ultimately, an issue of sovereignty and land rights. It became increasingly clear to the Indigenous leadership from Mount Currie and Lytton First Nation that they would have to lead the efforts and the environmentalists would have to learn to play a supporting role. A growing awareness about the issues of the Stein, through public relations campaigns and rediscovery initiatives that connected people to the valley, was beginning to have an impact on public opinion. But Indigenous land rights and title claims had deep legal and constitutional implications, for the Nlaka'pamux and for the government. Nothing was as simple as deciding whether trees stood or fell.

The conflict over the Stein was intensifying at the same time as the revelations and fallout from the abuses at St. George's Residential School and the re-emergence of Nlaka'pamux cultural values, language and assertion of land rights. It was as if all the traumas experienced by the Nlaka'pamux since the Canyon War were culminating in this fight to save the valley from the outsiders. Whether industrial loggers or tree huggers, everyone seemed to think they had the authority to decide the future of the sacred valley of the Nlaka'pamux.

For many Nlaka'pamux in Lytton, their healing journeys began in relationship to the Save the Stein movement. For the first time in generations, traditional teachings were being shared openly, and Nlaka'pamux culture, language and ceremonies were normalized and practised more in the community, as well as being taught in public schools. Sharing circles, smudging and Sweat Lodge ceremonies became more common.

> Hunting, fishing and foraging was quite simply a way of life. Every season has its food. And we spent every season out in the mountains and on the river harvesting those foods. We'd fish for salmon with rods and nets. The traditional way was to use dip nets and gillnets and in the river eddies as the sockeye and spring salmon made their way home. We also fish for steelhead and spring salmon with rods. In the summer, we pick berries in the mountains. In the fall we hunted for grouse, deer and moose and foraged for pine mushrooms to sell and to eat. In the winter we'd ice-fish for trout and burbot on lakes all through the Interior of BC. In the spring we'd pick wild horse celery, called *stweta7*, devil's club and wild asparagus along the riverbanks. There are hundreds of healthy traditional foods that grow all through the territory that the Nlaka'pamux would harvest. Which was another reason the starvation of kids at St. George's was such an outrage. They were literally surrounded by food.

> *Kevin Loring*

By the 1980s, there was a very high rate of suicide and domestic violence in the community, and efforts were being made to reach back to traditional spiritual medicine and ways of dealing with these kinds of emotional, psychological and spiritual wounds. Many of the pathways to healing for the Indigenous people involved connecting to the land in a spiritual sense. At the centre of that awakening was the fight over the Stein.

> I learned about the eagle feather, sage and sweetgrass and the four directions. I learned about the salmon and the bears and the eagles and their importance. I asked questions about the old stories. And the people, Elders, would tell me whichever story or fragment of a story they wanted to share or could remember. All the old Spetakwl creation stories start with a place, a location within the territory, and that context is key to understanding them. They describe the origins of landscapes, features and animals and how certain events caused things to exist as they are today. How the bald eagle got its white head. Or why the fish are located at and spawn in certain rivers. Why certain large rock features look the way they do and are located in the places that they are found. All these things have fantastical corresponding stories that are funny and violent and supernatural. All stories are connected to the land.

> *Kevin Loring*

Ever since the gold rush, the Nlaka'pamux have been fighting for sovereignty over their lands, and against colonialism and erasure. When the environmentalists came into the community, they too began to talk as though they had authority over the land and could speak on behalf of its future. This frustrated the Indigenous community members and instilled distrust. Chief Ruby Dunstan made it clear that they were not going to be spoken over by *shamas* (a derogatory term for white people) who thought they knew better, well-intentioned or not.

In time, the factions in the movement were able to align around the Indigenous leadership from Mount Currie and Lytton First Nation. Crucial to making this happen was the first Stein festival. The Voices of the Wilderness Festival, as it was called, was held deep in the alpine headwaters of the Stein Valley just as British Columbia Forest Products was getting ready to begin to survey the potential access road into the valley. The festival was held at Brimful Lake, which is a couple of days' hike from the junction of the Stein and the Fraser, just upriver from Lytton. Many people from the community and around the province, both settler and Indigenous, gathered, shared knowledge and learned about the deep cultural and spiritual importance the valley holds for the St'at'imc, Lil'wat and Nlaka'pamux peoples.

Artists performed and locals shared their knowledge about the area, the ecosystem and their relationships to it. Elders were flown in by helicopter to share their knowledge and help guide the activities of the gathering. This festival galvanized the movement and allowed the settler environmentalists to understand the importance of rooting their actions in the Indigenous leadership of the movement and not outside agendas.

The Nlaka'pamux were fighting for the integrity of the land as well as the cultural and spiritual integrity of their people, but there was also an internal, communal battle with each other. The economic future of the community was tied to logging and the jobs it provided. Even in Indigenous households, it was Loggers versus Steiners.

On the one hand, my dad was the bush foreman for the
mill, basically middle management overseeing operations
in the field. On the other, my mom, who is Indigenous,
loves the Stein and wanted to keep it pristine. For a kid,
it was very confusing. The Stein was the last untouched
watershed in the region and the importance of keeping it
intact was clear to me. I had seen what a clear-cut looked
like and I didn't want that for the Stein. It made sense to
me to at least leave this one valley alone. And I know my
mom also didn't want the Stein to be logged, but she would
never contradict my father about it—or her brothers, who
also worked at the mill. Leaving the Stein alone would
affect their well-being too. Logging paid our bills.

Kevin Loring

To further add to the conflict, the BC government offered Lytton
Lumber 30 percent of the timber from the valley. This would be a huge
win for the tiny mill. Small and mid-sized mills were closing down, and
Lytton Lumber was like a rowboat on the ocean trying to stay afloat
in a raging sea of environmental protests, Indigenous road and rail
blockades, cross-border softwood lumber disputes, and giant companies from overseas bullying local companies out of business. The stakes
were high. Tensions were high. Thousands of years of Nlaka'pamux
cultural heritage were being weighed against the tenuous economic
well-being of the community. This was the era of Clayoquot Sound,
Haida Gwaii and the Meares Island blockade, to name a few memorable protests from the time. Mistrust and antipathy were high between
Indigenous groups and the government across the province. Added

into this volatile mix was the ecological integrity of a chinook salmon–bearing river system that could easily be ruined by development.

> As the Share the Stein/Save the Stein battle carried on,
> my dad seemed to become more aware of the implications
> of what the fight was about. One time, while we were
> driving through one of the areas that he was working up
> in Thompson, he asked if I could tell the area had been
> logged. I was surprised, because we were surrounded by
> trees. They had been selectively logging the area. He was
> proud that, other than the road we were on, I couldn't even
> tell. I thought that was pretty cool.
>
> *Kevin Loring*

In the summer of 1985, the BC government gave loggers the go-ahead. Construction could now begin on the road into the Stein Valley, which would pass right through the lower corridor, the exact route identified as the most culturally and environmentally sensitive in the valley. But that 30 percent of timber that would go to a local mill was putting enormous pressure on the community to support the efforts to log the valley.

Pressure was being felt on both sides of the conflict, though. In the face of the increased demands on the BC government to address Indigenous land rights and environmental issues across the province, including the Stein Valley conflict, the government created the Special Advisory Committee on Wilderness Preservation.* But the fight over

---

* Soon known as the WAC (Wilderness Advisory Committee).

the Stein only intensified. Competing archaeological surveys came to opposing conclusions regarding the significance of the archaeological impacts of the road development and logging. Then came the first Stein Valley concert. More were planned in the following years, with celebrities such as Martin Sheen, David Suzuki, Gordon Lightfoot, Blue Rodeo and others bringing international awareness to the cause.

To counter the public relations momentum of the Save the Stein movement, the former mayor of Lytton, Chris O'Connor, who at the time was the Professional Forester at the mill, rebranded the pro-logging movement. Its new slogan, "Share the Stein," was a friendlier way to say "Log the Stein."

After years of delays, environmental and archaeological assessments, picketing, road blockades and public demonstrations, the logging of the valley was now delayed indefinitely, until more assessments could be conducted. The campaign to educate the public on the importance of an intact Stein Valley won out.

The Stein Rediscovery Program was a very influential movement that had a lasting impact on the community and for the cause of saving the Stein. Based on the Haida rediscovery program, Stein Rediscovery brought youth into the valley to learn about its ecology and cultural significance, revitalizing Nlaka'pamux cultural practices and language and providing an incredibly rich land-based experience for youth. With the work that was done on the trail, making it easier to hike through the valley, the Stein Rediscovery Program brought youth up to the glacial headwaters, where they participated in outdoor activities and cultural sharing. Many kids from Lytton and youth from outside Lytton got a chance to experience the valley and teachings from Elders and knowledge keepers. For many, this program was a source of healing, self-discovery, and mental, emotional and spiritual growth, as well as awareness about the valley and the need to save it.

Chief Ruby Dunstan made the case for permanently putting control of the Stein in Indigenous hands to a WAC panel exploring suitable ways to manage several natural resources in the province, of which the Stein was one:

> The Valley is Indian Land. We have been in continuous occupancy
> and use since time immemorial. We have never ceded, sold nor lost
> this land in conflict . . . We will no doubt seek a just and fair share of
> our traditional lands, of what was ours before settlement, it should be
> land we value, that we have used and which has not been exploited,
> nor occupied by others. It should include the Stein Valley.*

In 1995, the Stein Valley was declared a Class A provincial park to be co-managed by Lytton First Nation and the BC government. This co-management regime between a First Nation and a provincial government was the first of its kind in the country. The Stein had been saved. A little over a decade later, Lytton Lumber would shut down operations indefinitely. It remains closed today.

---

* Madeline Wilson, "Co-management Re-conceptualized: Human–Land Relations in the Stein Valley, British Columbia" (MA thesis, University of Victoria, 2011); citeseerx.ist.psu.edu/document?repid=rep1&type=pdf&doi=8db931911bcf55a47b e08d697ecad2044c605430.

CHAPTER 35

MORE LYTTON GOLD

After a long time of my frantic waving, he spotted me.

FORMER LYTTON RESIDENT MARK REBAGLIATI SEES
HIS ATHLETE SON ROSS AT OLYMPIC CEREMONY IN JAPAN

FORMER LYTTON RESIDENT Mark Rebagliati had plenty on his mind on the morning of Thursday, February 5, 1998. His job was challenging: he was working between Mexico City and the resort town of Acapulco as exploration manager and chief geologist for the Campo Morado gold-silver-zinc-lead project. Then there was his mother, Sylvia, a long-time Brown Owl (girls' Brownie leader) in Lytton, who had moved to Vancouver, where she maintained her own apartment. Friday was her eighty-fourth birthday. On top of that, there was Mark's son Ross. He was competing in the giant slalom snowboard on the opening day of the 1998 Winter Olympics in Nagano, Japan.

Mark came from a long line of Rebagliatis who liked to travel and accomplish big things. His grandfather was the original Bernardo Rebagliati who came to Lytton in 1886. Like Bernardo, Mark seemed to be always busy. He received the 1998 Prospector of the Year award from the Prospectors and Developers Association of Canada for his role in the discovery of three ore deposits: Mount Milligan and Kemess South, both in northern central British Columbia, and his current project at Campo Morado, Mexico. His Mexican job was a 24-7 affair and there was little downtime, as he oversaw a crew of about a hundred people. It was in a remote area, and so to see Ross live at the Olympics, he had to fly back to Vancouver and then catch a red-eye to Japan.

Once he had completed that journey, Mark strained to see Ross in the sea of joyous athletes from around the world as they paraded into the Olympic stadium. "Trying hard as I could, I was not able to spot Ross among the Canadian contingent from my seat," Mark recalls. When the opening ceremonies ended, Mark moved to a lower section of the enormous stadium, but even then he needed his camera's zoom lens to finally spot his son among the other athletes.

Ross couldn't see his father at first, but he had already spoken to his beloved grandmother. He'd called her on his cellphone as the Canadian team were marching into the stadium. She was looking after his little dog, Patches. As the thousands of athletes gradually left the stadium floor, Ross lingered behind, scanning the stands. "After a long time of my frantic waving," Mark remembers, "he spotted me."

Ross was competing the next day. Breakfast was at 6 a.m., followed by a bus ride to the snowboard venue at Mount Yakebitai. Mark wished Ross good luck after he'd checked out the course.

The first run was good but not great, with Ross in eighth spot. He got a chance to chat briefly with his dad again and told him, "I can't lose, Dad, I'm at the Olympics."

"Slay them on this run," Mark told his son, who was known on the World Cup circuit as the Slayer.

Ross hit a top speed of 108 kilometres per hour on the second run and, in a flash, he was in first place.

Father and son then stood together, watching the other racers descend the slope. When the last of them had crossed the finish line, Ross's two-run combined time was 2:03.96, putting him in first place, narrowly ahead of Thomas Prugger of Italy at 2:03.98 and Ueli Kestenholtz of Switzerland at 2:04.08. The Italian media immediately adopted the Canadian as one of their own. They wanted to know where in Italy the Rebagliati family was from, and why and when they had emigrated to Canada. The answers to those questions would have required whole books, anchored in the appeal of dusty Lytton.

Ross did his urine test and then set off with his father to the medal ceremony. It was Canada's first medal, and on the first day of competition.

Mark was in his hotel room a day later when all hell broke loose. He recalls, "At about 3 a.m., I woke thirsty and found I'd left the Olympic TV channel on." He was getting a drink of juice from the fridge when he heard, "Snowboarding gold medal–winning Canadian Ross Rebagliati has tested positive for cannabis." It wasn't until half a day later that Mark was able to connect with Ross on the phone. "The conversation was awkward," Mark says. "Ross sounded reluctant to say much, so I asked him if he was alone and had privacy." All his son could reply was, "No."

Mark reassured him that, whatever the outcome, they both knew he had won the event. The trauma would pass, and there was a lot more life to live in front of him. Then he flew back to Mexico to resume his work. Only later did he learn that Ross had called him from the Nagano jail washroom, in the presence of a policeman and a Canadian Olympic official. Though Ross was stripped of his medal after testing positive for THC, the active ingredient in marijuana, he eventually got the medal back, after arguing that he must have inhaled second-hand smoke at a send-off party.

Ross has deep Lytton roots, even though he never lived or snow-boarded there. "We have half the graveyard," he says. His grandmother was an early lifeguard in Lytton, and his father, Mark, was a champion high school runner. He remembers posing for a photo as a tot on Kenny Glasgow's giant Harley-Davidson statue in Botanie Valley during a visit. "We would pass through on the way to the Okanagan," Ross recalls. He remembers going into the Copper Kettle restaurant on Main Street and seeing how the town's men gathered there at 6:30 a.m., and how his dad seemed to know everybody. There was something about the tone of the place that stood out. "You go there and people are much more laid-back," Ross says.

After the Olympics, Ross transitioned into home construction, developing housing in the Okanagan that is cool during the hot Interior summers and warm in winter, and which doesn't burn down in any season. That helped him appreciate the challenges of building in Lytton. "I've been to Lytton when it was hot—so hot I didn't think the air conditioning was working," he says.

He has a particularly fond memory of visiting his father's old house and meeting its current occupant, who quickly treated him like an old friend. "We had cookies," Ross recalls. "Kids had ice cream. They had cannabis growing in the front yard."

He maybe never lived in Lytton, but reflecting on this last point, he proves he has the locals' sense of humour. "She was doing her best," he says. "I gave her some pointers."

CHAPTER 36

HOLLYWOOD VISIT

A fucking nightmare.

ACTOR-DIRECTOR SEAN PENN ISN'T
ENTHRALLED WITH HIS LYTTON EXPERIENCE

ACTOR JACK NICHOLSON trekked out to tiny Lytton in the winter of 2000. So did actor-director Sean Penn, who had chosen Lytton as a prime location for the noir mystery thriller *The Pledge*, which began shooting there in February 2000. Penn later reflected on his Lytton experience, remembering it as "a fucking nightmare."

Lytton had attracted Hollywood before. *The Winds of Chance*, starring Victor McLaglen, Ben Lyon and Anna Nilsson, was filmed there in 1925. Nilsson refused to risk her life in a scene where she was to be tied up and placed on the deck of a boat heading down the Fraser River. A local man acted as her stand-in and apparently survived. Lytton had also served as a location for *The Rainbow Boys*, starring Donald Pleasence and Kate Reid, which was filmed in the 1970s in the old Earlscourt mansion.

But back to Penn and Nicholson. *The Pledge* was based on a 1957 novella of the same name by Swiss writer Friedrich Dürrenmatt, and featured sixty-three-year-old Nicholson in the role of an aging police detective. Penn's on-again, off-again real-life partner Robin Wright Penn was cast as Nicholson's love interest. There were cameos from a star-studded cast that also included Vanessa Redgrave, Helen Mirren, Sam Shepard, Mickey Rourke, Benicio del Toro and Harry Dean Stanton. Some locals got to be extras. As did the Raphael family's G'wsep Gas & Food stop, sort of. Sonny Raphael ran the service station, the name of which translates to "sunrise." The movie people decided his business didn't have quite the right look, so they built a more rustic, rundown service station on Raphael's property.

At one point, a big white Samoyed dog crashed the set. Locals later noted wistfully that the Lytton canine's appearance had been left on the cutting-room floor.

The movie shoot generated considerable local excitement. "A lot of people wanted to be part of it," Donny Glasgow recalls. Donny's son Angus got a part that involved smashing a window, which was tougher than it sounds, as the window was made of non-breakable plastic. He also got to yell at Jack Nicholson. Like the scene with the white dog, that one remained on the cutting room floor.

> I just remember being in the thick of this hard-core theatre
> conservatory training program, working my butt off,
> pulling sixteen-hour days, six days a week, living the life
> of a starving artist to train to be a professional actor down
> in Vancouver and hearing that everyone back home in
> Lytton was working with the greatest actors in Hollywood.
> Sometimes the universe has a sick sense of humour.
>
> *Kevin Loring*

Word drifted out that Penn wasn't a happy camper in Canada's hot spot. The film was over budget and he had to fight to complete it. In the end, it was a critical success, but it didn't do as well at the box office as hoped.

G'wsep Gas & Food enjoyed the extra attention from its new-found fame, and the Raphaels kept the fake gas station sets. "They've set it aside," Donny says. Pieces have since been added to the real gas station, only adding to its value as a tourist attraction.

> There was a drive-in movie theatre down near G'wsep Gas & Food in the 1960s. It was socially acceptable and almost expected to sneak friends in in the trunk of a car to save a few bucks' entry fee.
>
> We could also see movies in the small downtown Legion hall, where a no-drinking rule wasn't strictly, or even lightly, enforced. My big brother Jim was a projectionist there. Jim was unflappable, a quality that benefited him when he later went on to become a physican, like our father, Uncle Cliff and my other brother, David. When Jim routinely didn't change the reels fast enough, people screamed at him. He never seemed rattled at all.
>
> My strongest memory at the theatre was when one of the toughest kids in town relieved himself into the large popcorn tub of an enthusiastic eater a couple of seats over from me. The kid hadn't been sharing his popcorn, so I wasn't particularly sympathetic. It was just one more layer to the Saturday afternoon entertainment, sort of like surround sound. The public urinator had sniper-like precision, so I felt safe.

I can't forget the expression of the kid when he suddenly stopped eating his popcorn and realized he was under attack. It was like a freeze-frame of a moment of total horror. I took this as a graphic life lesson on the hazards of being selfish.

Peter Edwards

CHAPTER 37

ANNIE'S FAREWELL

I didn't go to school. That's why I know so much!

AREA RESIDENT ANNIE MUNRO

WARRIORS FROM THE 1858 Canyon War were still alive when Annie Munro was born in Siska, near Lytton, in the final years of the nineteenth century. She thought it was probably 1896. Annie managed to avoid going to residential school, for which she was always grateful. "I didn't go to school," she told an interviewer. "That's why I know so much!"

Siska's nearly ten kilometres south of Lytton, on the isolated west side of the Fraser River. It's under the steep cliffs where the Canadian Pacific and Canadian National Railways run out of space and cross the river.

Annie was brought up to speak Nlaka'pamux cin and had to learn English, decades later, in order to talk with her grandchildren. Nlaka'pamux people were moving out of their pit houses during her youth. Life still centred around the salmon runs on the Fraser River. Dip nets were still used to catch salmon in the eddies. Men caught the fish while women split and boned the catch, hanging the meat over racks to dry.

Some of it was flattened and baled for use in trade. Some was roasted, dried and then ground into a powder for pemmican, with oil or fat and dried berries mixed in. Women wove durable, eye-catching baskets to carry plants, berries, wild onions, roots, lilies and balsam, and also wove blankets from mountain goat wool.

Annie grew up at a distance from white society, as the Cariboo wagon road had been shut down in 1891 between Yale and Spences Bridge. Annie was in her thirties when a new road was finally built, in 1927, between the coast and the Interior.

As she grew older, Annie was known for her hugs and warm, welcoming smile, as well as for her knowledge of traditional medicines and healing practices. Known in her native tongue as Ya-Yae, or Grandmother, she could often be found weeding and planting her garden and tulips, close to her cherry and apple trees and strawberry patch. As she grew deep into old age, Annie moved in with her daughter Emily Martin, but the arrangement became difficult. Annie's health was declining and eventually Emily could no longer cope. Emily was in her mid-seventies herself. By age 104, Annie was in the care of St. Bartholomew's Hospital in Lytton.

In May 2002, Emily got a notice saying that 109-year-old St. Bartholomew's was shutting down, to be replaced by what was euphemistically called a "wellness centre." If a family member couldn't care for Annie, she would be transferred to a facility in Ashcroft, eighty kilometres away. Annie didn't have many family members to care for her. Her husband, William, thirteen of her fourteen children and nine of her grandchildren had all died before her. Transferring to Ashcroft would take her far from her community and remaining family as well.

Annie wept and pleaded to stay where she was. Emily's stress level shot up. It just wasn't right for this to be happening to her mother, but she didn't know what else she could do. Emily died on May 14, 2002, of heart failure. Her body was found in a chair in her small trailer. On her lap was a letter about her mother's condition.

The government had given the hospital a three-month reprieve, but that wasn't good enough for Annie. Her mind was set. She didn't want to live in fear of another negative decision. Hospital staff members were already accepting offers to work elsewhere. Annie reportedly told a friend: "I don't want to die ugly. I don't want to die afraid. I don't want to leave."

Annie made a decision. She stopped taking her medication. A week later, she died in hospital, on June 26, 2002.

Candles and crosses decorated Lytton Memorial Hall as Annie's funeral ceremony blended Nlaka'pamux and Christian traditions. Some two hundred mourners—about half the population of Lytton at the time—were led by Nlaka'pamux spiritual leader Terry Aleck and Anglican Reverend Mike Watkins. That was the same Terry Aleck who had championed the fight against widespread abuse at St. George's Residential School, ultimately winning an apology from the prime minister and the Pope.

The hall reverberated with the sounds of traditional drumming. An Indigenous mural featured winged birds and a warrior's mask. In a way that made perfect sense in Lytton, someone gave a reading from the familiar Psalm 23, which begins, "The Lord is my shepherd, I shall not be in want. He restores my soul. He guides me in paths of righteousness for his name's sake. Even though I walk through the valley of the shadow of death, I will fear no evil, for you are with me; your rod and your staff, they comfort me."

Annie's simple grey coffin was placed in the back of a canopied green pickup truck for the trip across the Fraser River, along a rough hydro access road and back towards the plain wooden house where she had raised her family with her husband, William. The drive ended at the traditional Kwiekw cemetery, where William had been buried thirty-four years earlier. Mourners tossed handfuls of dirt and tobacco onto her casket, as well as two dozen floral arrangements, as she was lowered into the earth. Annie had lived to witness three centuries from the perspectives of two cultures, and now she was returning to the land of her ancestors.

CHAPTER 38

THE MUNKSTERS

I was Lytton born
I am Lytton living
And I will Lytton die
Is there any part of life i am missing?

KENNY GLASGOW, FACEBOOK

IN THE EARLY DAYS of the new millennium, Lytton came up, as it does, during a discussion around whether the time might be right to look for a new centre for their universe. The discussion was taking place among a group of monks from the Lions Gate Buddhist Priory of Vancouver, followers of the Serene Reflection Meditation tradition of Sōtō Zen and T'sao-tung Chan Buddhism. Guiding much of this deep thought was a monk whose ordained name was Reverend Koten Benson, a former Maritimer who was ordained in Shasta Abbey in the US in 1978. Another of the monks was from Saskatchewan. There were also a couple of Czechs and a former computer programmer from Silicon Valley.

"We are rather dull, if the truth be told," Koten states in an interview. "Our form of Buddhism is called 'farmer's Zen'—very ordinary."

Vancouver was becoming the wrong size for the monks. "We began to have people who wanted to be monastics," he says. "We felt it would be better to become monastics out of the city. We had no money. By no money, I mean no money. That expands one's horizons. When you have no money, one can look anywhere. We asked a real estate agent. He said, 'There is this piece of land up near this place called Lytton.'"

Almost immediately, Koten heard from Vancouverites all the reasons why Lytton would never work. It was too far away. Who would want to go there? But then Koten saw photos of the place, and they triggered something. "The mountain reminded me of pictures of the Chinese mountains."

The monks took a drive up the canyon in 2001. "When we drove down and saw the rivers coming together," Koten recalls, "that really struck me in a very, very strong way."

The monks were impressed but not convinced. So their search continued for the new centre for their universe. "Wherever we went looking for land, we always thought of Lytton," Koten says.

A man named Leyton Budd from the Lytton area made contact with the monks. Leyton said he knew he wouldn't live forever and he wanted his land to go to them. For some reason, he wanted this very badly. He even dreamt about it. "He thought he was dying and it turned out it was just his medication needed changing," Koten says.

Koten kept checking out the photos they'd taken when they were in Lytton. He was trying to be practical, but something about those pictures kept drawing his attention. The monks wanted a place with a well and electricity and buildings that were in good shape. Roads were also important. Lytton lacked all those things. Still . . .

Koten asked neighbours in Lytton if Leyton had also spoken to them about his dreams of monks settling on his property. "We're not supposed to be cynical, but we wondered," Koten shares. The neighbours confirmed Leyton's story; he had told others of his dreams of monks moving onto his land.

Koten went back for a look at Leyton's property. There was a little snow on the ground as he walked up a hill in Botanie Valley and then looked down. "I thought, 'Gosh, I'm not imagining this. I'm not off my rockers. This is it.' When I saw it, I thought, 'This is exactly what I'm looking for.' We fell in love with the land."

The monks hoped to raise some of the money for the land through a donations box in their Vancouver temple, where people dropped off quarters and loonies. They also sent off fundraising letters. Ben Metcalfe, founder of Greenpeace, said he'd like to help. He had become a Buddhist years before, and he dropped a folded-up cheque into the donations box. "I thought, 'I'm going to succumb to temptation and take a look,'" Koten remembers. He saw a long number on the cheque. He wasn't used to large sums of money. "I couldn't figure it out," he says. "It's got too many zeros."

The monks weren't penniless any longer. Soon, with Metcalfe's $50,000 donation and their box of coins, they were able to go to a bank and start signing forms. A woman in the Chinese community co-signed for him. It felt surreal. "I personally had no money. It felt really ridiculous," Koten admits.

Leyton Budd was waiting when the three monks and some lay residents arrived at their new home on 160 acres on the slopes of Botanie Valley, near Donny Glasgow's place. "He [Budd] said he had dreamt of Buddhist monks in brown robes walking on his land, but not so many!" Koten says.

Koten got familiar with the local sights, including a trip to the Lytton Museum in 2001, where he saw a coin on display. It was from the old Chinese joss house on Main Street, once located right where he now stood. "That really struck me," he says. "This was quite flabbergasting to me. I never expected to find a link—a Buddhist link to Lytton."

Whenever they went into the village in their brown robes, Koten and his fellow monks were made to feel welcome. "People would always say something like, 'Welcome back,'" Koten says. Once, a little Nlaka'pamux boy earnestly screwed up the courage to approach the strangers and ask them a question. "He looked up at us with some level of awe and said, 'Are you Jedi knights?'" he asked. During another visit, a woman saw the monks in their brown robes and asked, "Are you here for the healing festival?" Then she began talking about the Asking Rock in the Stein Valley, across the river from Lytton. Indigenous people would stop at the rock to ask for permission to enter the valley, as well as good weather and good fortune. Red ochre images of sacred events had been painted there, generations ago. "I'm a very non-New-Agey person," Koten insists. "I didn't know what an asking rock would look like." He decided to check it out. "It was unmistakable," he says.

A feeling about their new home was clear and strong. "There's something very, I hesitate to say, 'sacred' about that place," Koten shares when describing Lytton.

They started conducting ceremonies in a Main Street parking lot before it was built into a new Chinese temple. They weren't the only ones drawn to the location. Chinese people would come into town and pray there.

With the help of Lorna Fandrich from the Lytton Museum, Koten started to research the site, and found himself drawn to the works of Teit and how the Nlaka'pamux considered this area the centre of their world—the place where all stories began. "I really wanted to honour that temple and that site . . . that we were continuing something that the Chinese had started in the 1880s," he says. "We were drawn here because of the welcome we received from all the people and also because there was a Chinese temple here in the 1880s that was dedicated to Kwan Yin—the female Buddha of Mercy."

Koten became fascinated by the long history of intermarriage between newcomers and the Nlaka'pamux, and how that had come about because Lytton is a natural gathering place. "There's a sense here as if there are overlapping worlds, like concentric circles that overlap each other. Where it's possible to cross boundaries . . ." The sacred sense of the rivers coming together extended to the bloodlines of the people who called ltKumcheen home.

He heard a legend about the Valley Curtain woman, who took a basket of fruits and created a valley for her family. "I think it's one of the major sacred places in all of the province," he says. "If this was in India, there would be thousands of pilgrims washing themselves in the river." But it wasn't India. The land here reminded him of someplace more familiar and the effect that land had on people he'd known growing up. He thought of his Newfoundland roots. "Newfoundlanders relate to the rock beneath them. Good, solid rock . . . It's so powerful a place."

He appreciated the strength he heard from one local woman, when someone too strongly suggested "improvements" that could be made in the village. She replied: "We came here to get away from the city. We chose to come here. We do not feel it needs improvement." He found something solid and reaffirming in this prevailing local attitude. "This place is untameable," Koten enthuses. "That's what—excuse me—gets up some people's noses." He liked sending "stick-in-the-muddish" visitors down to see Kenny Glasgow so that they could tour his outdoor art park, with its two-storey-high Harley-Davidson motorcycle statues and two satellite discs painted to resemble women's breasts.

Koten was enchanted when he learned the story of the reconstruction of the joss house. It began shortly after long-time residents Lorna

Fandrich and her husband, Bernie, who used to run Kumsheen Rafting, bought a vacant property at 145 Main Street. Shortly after purchasing the land, Lorna, an amateur historian, saw a 1934 article from the Vancouver *Province* that detailed how there had once been a Chinese meeting hall on the lot. At the time, Lorna was a grandmother nearing retirement age. She couldn't stop thinking about the people who used to worship on their newly acquired patch of land, and she became determined to build a replica joss house, summoning the glory of the old building with its wood frame construction and wooden siding.

Work began in 2014, and by 2017 the site had been transformed into the Lytton Chinese History Museum. Koten and his fellow monks began to use the rebuilt joss house for Meditation Tuesdays, followed by walking meditation and tea. Each June, the monks held a ceremony dedicated to Kwan Yin, the deity of mercy, the Buddha-Mother of Great Compassion, at the rebuilt wooden joss house on Main Street. The priory even prepared a hundred-page, spiral-bound cookbook that could only have come from Lytton. *Kwan Yin Loves Pie* includes recipes such as Kwan Yin Pie, Grant's Politically Incorrect No-Nonsense Pancakes, Kheer (Rice Pudding), veggie burgers, Ohio buckeyes, Don't Be Afraid of Tofu, Kamal's Yoghurt, Mountain Tseweta Corn Bread and Botanie Valley Honey Cake.

Michele Feist was at loose ends after the death of her husband, Grant. She had been a nurse for thirty years. That job was over. She had had a loving marriage. Now that was over too. "I knew I had to start over," she says. She needed to get out of the Lower Mainland. But to where? She had friends at the Buddhist temple in Lytton but would need convincing to consider such a remote little place. She talked with her friend Koten. Looking back on her conversations with him, she thinks he might have found the *Four Quartets* of T.S. Eliot useful in describing it: "A place 'where prayer has been valid' for ten thousand years."

She and Grant had visited Lytton after hearing Koten say positive things about the place. "We both kind of went, 'Holy God, why did they move here?'" Then she gave it some thought. "There must be something about the place because of the way he talked about it," she recalls thinking at the time. She was almost fifty-one when Grant died. "I just didn't go back to work. We had been very close." She kept looking for her new home. "I drove everywhere in my car . . . Nothing stuck."

An avid backpacker, she went for a hike in the mountains around Lytton and found something. It was a feeling, and a very strong one. "There was something about just walking there. I felt I had reconnected with something important."

She was fifty-two when she moved to Lytton in March 2016, buying a hundred-year-old home at 3rd and Fraser Streets, just down the street from the Chongs' old store. She painted her new home bright yellow, with turquoise trim, and planted lots of bright flowers. Koten advised her not to ask too many questions of her new neighbours; they'd tell her what they thought she should know, when they thought she should know it. "They could take people as they are," she says, recalling her early months in Lytton. "It was sort of a refuge. You could go there and reinvent yourself."

Michele joined a yoga class in the elementary school library. The instructor there would watch videos and then interpret them for the class. "It was a community event." Michele was particularly impressed with the women she met in Lytton. They seemed to be unapologetic survivors. "The place breeds fearless women."

There were lots more hikes in the hills, where she found herself increasingly loving her new home. She had hiked through the Tetons in the Rocky Mountain Range, and in the Himalayas, but felt something unique around Lytton that she had never experienced in those more famous locales. "There's space to be yourself there . . . It's bigger than us. It's bigger than the people involved." It felt right to move Grant's ashes there too. He would have understood.

She quietly connected with local people. "I've never been so welcomed. I never really felt pressured to be anything but myself. I could actually sort of recover." She knows everyone might not feel that way about Lytton, and it doesn't really matter. "There's this little aspect of the weird and the wonderful. People either get it or they don't."

And to really get it, Michele soon learned you had to get up early. "From my kitchen window I could watch the alpenglow, the pinkish tinge, climb over the tops of the mountains across the Fraser. The mornings were clear, and quiet. I could hear birds in the old elm in the front yard. Usually there would be juncos and cedar waxwings. Lots of starlings making their distinctive call. I looked across the road at the Totem Motel and the Bains house, as well as Lorna Thom's house, with her beautiful flower garden and peach tree. She often gave me peaches." As the day progressed, the sound of trains became more distinct. "They were a constant background noise, and kind of became incorporated into the day. I used to sleep right through the trains, and in fact found it soothing after a while. Across the Fraser were the greener, treed mountains, some with scars of old fires. In winter, the snow would creep down the mountains till later in the season we would be all in white."

The scenery around Lytton was breathtaking, and Michele could soak it in from her tiny bright-yellow house. "If the weather was right," she says, "I had the best view in the universe."

CHAPTER 39

SHRINKAGE

*The day started out as uneventfully as any other, and continued
thus to midday and from there it was nothing at all to ease
into an evening of numbing, undiluted monotony that survived
unmarred by even the least act of momentary peculiarity—in fact,
let's skip that day altogether and start with the day after.*

"DISHONORABLE MENTION" WINNER BY JON STARR OF
RUMFORD, MAINE, IN BAD WRITING CONTEST INSPIRED BY
LYTTON'S NAMESAKE, SIR EDWARD BULWER-LYTTON

THE COMPLETION OF the massive Coquihalla Highway project in
1987 bypassed Lytton. Soon businesses were pulled away from a community that had once vied to become the capital of the province.

When a mill shut down, the town's largest remaining employer
became Kumsheen Rafting, a whitewater rafting enterprise. Belinda
(Lindy) Watkinson, the youngest child of Tom Sr. and Edith Watkinson,
was a valued employee. Like her parents, she thrived on work. "It was
loads of fun," she recalls. "I booked trips, helped organize meals, packing trip boxes. We would rotate weekends setting up and breaking

camps depending on length of the trip. Shuttle rafts/trailers from drop-off to pickup point. Tons of fun, but heavy work . . . The Europeans love it."

The village area also still attracted rockhounds panning for gold and looking for jade, and birdwatchers hoping to photograph eagles.

The owners of Kumsheen Rafting, Lorna and Bernie Fandrich (whom we met in the previous chapter), purchased a shack and some land on Main Street in 1980 as a place to store rafting equipment. Then they read a newspaper article about how their new property was historically and spiritually significant. They learned that from the 1880s until 1928, when Guiseppe Taverna finally acquired it, the site had been home to a joss house.

They learned about the supporting role the property had played in the lives of Lytton's earliest Chinese, and its significance to Chinese Canadians more broadly. The shack had held a representation of Shen Nong, the god of cereals and medicine, who taught how to cultivate land and look for medicinal herbs. The largest representation was that of Kwan Yin, the goddess of mercy, the one who takes away fear and hears the cries of the needy. They were accompanied by a representation of Zhu Rong, the goddess of fire. During the Great Depression, hobos riding the rails would slip into the joss house and take away food that had been left as a gift to the gods. They camped out in Hobo Hollow, at the end of Main Street.

The Fandrichs were soon hooked on learning about the history of their newly purchased property. There was much study and travel to Buddhist temples in California. They pulled together experts to help out and received exhibits from a private collector. They set lofty goals for the little site. They announced on the website they created for the Lytton Chinese History Museum that the new building

will be a reconstruction of the 1881 Chinese Temple. Although not
a functioning temple, it will be respectful of the religious significance
of the earlier temple and will include an altar and area for study and
meditation. Historical displays will bring recognition to the early
Chinese influence in Lytton and the Fraser and Thompson Canyons,
and will create a greater awareness of the historic links between
the Chinese community, the First Nations community and other
local residents.

The museum built up a collection of some 1,600 artifacts, which
were carefully catalogued and digitally archived. The collection helped
tell the stories of the Chinese who moved to the Fraser Canyon to mine
for gold, do dangerous work on the railways or become merchants, like
the Chong family right there in Lytton. It also provided a physical
reminder of the connections and contributions of Chinese Canadians
across the country.

The Lytton Chinese History Museum was blessed by Koten and
other local Buddhist monks when it opened on May 13, 2017. Guests
included the Vancouver Shaolin Lion Dance Troupe. That grand
opening attracted some two hundred people, no small feat for a town
of just 250.

Soon there were local visitors as well as tourists from mainland
China. In 2019, the museum won a Heritage BC Award of Outstanding
Achievement, meant to recognize "special projects and accomplish-
ments in the field of Education and Awareness." There was also the
Drs. Wallace B. & Madeline H. Chung Prize for Chinese-Canadian
community archiving.

Lytton was shrinking. Its role as a gateway to the Interior had been
usurped by a massive highway. But the spirit of the place always seemed
disproportionate to the size of its population. Though small in number,

new ventures and people were quietly finding a home in a place that had long welcomed those who just didn't seem to fit in anywhere else.

Lytton drew some two hundred people on August 30, 2008, for a literary debate. That was pretty good for a community that had never had a bookstore or a public library. It was also 80 percent of the population, roughly equivalent to two million people attending a civic event in Toronto, or 16,109,600 in Mexico City. No wonder Lytton produced at least two authors.

At issue that day was nothing less than the literary reputation of the community's namesake, former colonial secretary Sir Edward Bulwer-Lytton, of "It was a dark and stormy night" fame. Defending Bulwer-Lytton's good name was his great-great-great-grandson, the Honourable Henry Fromanteel Lytton-Cobbold, a screenwriter and aristocrat. On the attack was Professor Scott Rice of the English Department at San José State University, the guiding hand behind the annual Bulwer-Lytton Fiction Contest (BLFC), which encourages writers "to compose the opening sentence to the worst of all possible novels." The BLFC allowed writers of a variety of skill levels to compete in a number of categories, including purple prose, romance and science fiction. An earlier "dishonorable mention," from 2008, is given as the epigraph to this chapter.

A press release for the outdoor event was headlined TOFF AND PROF DUKE IT OUT AT GREAT EDWARD BULWER-LYTTON DEBATE. When the debate was over, the toff had won by a large margin over the visiting American. It was the first major showdown between Canadians and Americans in the area since the Canyon War, and once again, the home side triumphed.

Speaking of the Canyon War, which could have been much bloodier than its dozens of casualties, 2018 marked the 160th anniversary of the peace accord forged by Chief Cexpe'nthlEm with the miners' leader, Henry Snyder. In attendance at the ceremony honouring the leaders was historian Daniel Marshall. "Cexpe'nthlEm was as much a father of BC as James Douglas," Marshall told the *Ashcroft-Cache Creek Journal.* "If he and Snyder hadn't made peace, it's very possible that the US would have moved in. Cexpe'nthlEm needs to be recognized for the courageous stance he took in ending the Fraser Canyon War."

By the summer of 2020, plans were in place to use new technology to finally solve the mystery of Cexpe'nthlEm's burial place. Not even his cause of death, in 1887, was known for sure. He was believed to have been about seventy-five when he died. There were reports he was buried near a stone memorial erected in his honour, close to the Anglican church and parish hall. Other reports suggested his body was laid to rest somewhere overlooking the village. If his burial site could ever be determined, the town had the idea to build a suitably impressive memorial complex celebrating the great Chief, overlooking the spot near the train station where he had made peace with the Americans.

The plan was called the Chief Cexpe'nthlEm Memorial Precinct Restoration Project, and it was a partnership between Lytton First Nation, the Village of Lytton, the Anglican parish and the New Pathways to Gold Society. "This is an important first step in building a fitting memorial to a great leader," Lytton First Nation Chief Janet Webster told Barbara Roden of the *Ashcroft-Cache Creek Journal.* "We're very eager to see the results of the survey and whether or not we find any human remains—be they Chief Cexpe'nthlEm's or any of our people," Webster said.

> We lived a block or so from the modest stone monument
> to Chief Cexpe'nthlEm. The Chief was a mystery to me, as
> we learned nothing of him in our classes at school, even
> though he played a major role in the history of the area,

especially by keeping out American invaders who certainly would have marched north if there had been a sustained war with the gold miners in 1858. The year 1966 was the Centennial Year of British Columbia's founding as a British colony, and 1967 was Canada's Centennial, so my school years certainly would have been a good time to point out just how significant the Chief was.

One day, when a town road crew had been digging up the street beside our house, I went down in the hole to explore. I was about eleven years old. In a dirt wall of the hole, I found a skull, wrapped in some sort of curled-up bark. I told my parents about it. There was an earnest discussion between adults and I heard no more of it. Another time, I found a cardboard box in a crawl space of our house. Inside was a human skull and some bones. I told my parents again, and the box was gone.

Again, I heard no more about it.

Peter Edwards

Lytton mayor Jan Polderman heralded a new phase of reconciliation with an upbeat quote for the press, signalling a happier future than the downturn inflicted years before by the new highway. "It's a great example of how people can, even in times of great stress and turmoil, find common ground and work together to build something that can benefit everyone," he said. "We're excited to see the results and look forward to creating a new heritage tourism asset for Lytton and the Fraser Canyon."

And then things exploded again.

CHAPTER 40

CLIMATE CHANGE

In Canada, there was a town called Lytton.
I say was because on June 30 it burned to the ground.

PRIME MINISTER JUSTIN TRUDEAU ADDRESSES
GLOBAL WARMING CONFERENCE IN SCOTLAND IN 2021

BC'S 2021 WILDFIRE SEASON began on June 17, 2021, when a fire was reported on George Road, seven kilometres south of Lytton. An Environment Canada weather warning on June 23 announced that the weather was about to get dangerously hot. Residents were urged to check on friends and neighbours and make sure they stayed cool and were drinking enough water. A further alert issued on June 24 stated:

NEVER LEAVE PEOPLE OR PETS INSIDE A PARKED VEHICLE.

WATCH FOR THE SYMPTOMS OF HEAT ILLNESS:
DIZZINESS/FAINTING; NAUSEA/VOMITING;
RAPID BREATHING AND HEARTBEAT; EXTREME THIRST;
DECREASED URINATION WITH UNUSUALLY DARK URINE.

OUTDOOR WORKERS SHOULD TAKE REGULARLY
SCHEDULED BREAKS IN A COOL PLACE.

Then, on June 27, Lytton, which billed itself as "Canada's hot spot," set Canada's all-time maximum high for temperature with a reading of 46.6 degrees Celsius, eclipsing the old record of 45 degrees set on July 5, 1937, at Yellow Grass and Midale, Saskatchewan.

That was hot enough for eighteen-year-old Swedish environmental activist Greta Thunberg to take notice of the tiny Fraser Canyon community from across the ocean. She retweeted a message from meteorologist Scott Duncan, which referenced Lytton's dubious new record. "It is only June," Duncan said. "Annual highest temperature is normally in late July!" Thunberg warned: "The heat-wave is just getting started."

Unfortunately, they were right. Less than twenty-four hours later, on June 28, Lytton smashed its new temperature record with a reading of 47.9°C. Lytton was on the map again, and it was far from finished making news. On June 29, the temperature hit 49.6°C. Lytton's old record for that day was 40.0°C, set in 2008. And its brand new all-time record was already obsolete, by a margin of nearly two degrees.

A bulletin sent out by Environment Canada that day at 4:26 p.m. warned:

A DANGEROUS LONG DURATION HEAT WAVE IS AFFECTING B.C.

THREAT: DAYTIME HIGHS RANGING FROM
40 TO 48 DEGREES CELSIUS COMBINED WITH
OVERNIGHT LOWS OF 18 TO 24 DEGREES CELSIUS . . .

THERE IS LITTLE RELIEF AT NIGHT WITH ELEVATED
OVERNIGHT TEMPERATURES. THIS RECORD-BREAKING
HEAT EVENT WILL INCREASE THE POTENTIAL FOR
HEAT-RELATED ILLNESSES AND INCREASE THE RISK
OF WILDFIRES DUE TO DROUGHT CONDITIONS.

Lytton was shockingly, dangerously hot. On Wednesday, June 30, Environment Canada noted: "Yesterday's record at 49.6 C set a new world record of the highest temperature ever recorded above latitude 45 N, beating the previous record of 49.4 C (121F) set in Steele, North Dakota in July 1936." The forty-fifth parallel passes through the Piedmont region of Italy, just south of Turin, and along the Quebec–Vermont border. "The official highest recorded temperature [anywhere] is now 56.7 C (134F), which was measured on 10 July 1913 at Greenland Ranch, Death Valley, California, USA."

About half an hour before Environment Canada sent out that bulletin, flames had shot into the home of seventy-four-year-old Eric Siwik, engulfing it within seconds. Siwik hid outside behind a large metal rubbish bin. There was nowhere safe to go. Thick smoke blocked his sight and made it tough to breathe. He thought he was about to die before paramedics rescued him.

Downtown, Lytton's RCMP station exploded in flames.

> I was in my backyard in Metcalfe, Ontario, just outside
> Ottawa, with my wife and we were planning our annual
> summer trip to Lytton. We go back every summer to fish
> and put on a play based on our creation stories for the
> community with my theatre company and our ensemble
> of families and children. I opened my phone to check
> Facebook when I saw a livestream of Lytton on fire.
> Someone from across the river was livestreaming the whole
> thing. I ran to my computer and watched in horror as my
> childhood home burned in real time. My mom's house and
> the houses of my friends and relatives all catching fire. The
> wind was blowing the flames horizontally. Cars exploding,

houses exploding. I saw my brother's work van ignite and
then explode in my mom's backyard. I didn't know if
anyone was home or where any of my family was. I didn't
know if they made it out. And then the thick black smoke
obscured everything. And I knew that if anyone was
in town, they wouldn't be able to survive that. I felt like
I was burning. Like I was on fire. And there was nothing I
could do.

Kevin Loring

Tricia Thorpe and her husband, Donny Glasgow, a school bus driver,
felt their home was safe, a few kilometres away in Botanie Valley, and
drove into Lytton to help their friends and neighbours. All they could
see was smoke. The fire had jumped the Thompson River. The entire
village was in flames, from one end to the other. Behind them, a ridge
of flames was consuming their house and barn. While they were trying
to help, they lost everything—even their observatory, atop the barn,
which was outfitted with an $1,800 Russian telescope so that Donny
could see Venus and star clusters and other spots light years away. The
flames swallowed up their newly completed workshop, chicken coops,
gardens, $35,000 worth of spinning wheels and a loom, and their pets
and livestock, including alpacas, sheep, peacocks, chickens, a Great
Pyrenees dog named Thunder and two puppies. Even Donny's wallet
and identification were gone. The rest of Thunder's litter and their
mother, Sunshine, were rescued, along with a particularly tough cat.
All of it hurt, but losing the animals was the worst.

Something massive and global was happening, and Lytton seemed at
the centre again. The inferno was among more than two hundred active

fires burning across British Columbia. Meanwhile, in Europe, the climate change problem wasn't so much fire as flooding, which killed more than two hundred people in Germany, Belgium and neighbouring countries throughout July. Lytton had a long history of fires, but nothing like this. The picturesque little town in the mountains was suddenly a poster child for global climate disruptions. A report from the Latin American news agency CE Noticias Financieras began:

> The heat wave in the northern hemisphere is breaking records in 2021.
>
> A clear example of this is the case of Lytton, a small town in British Columbia, Canada, which recorded in early July the highest temperature in history in the country at 49.5 °C.
>
> That sparked wildfires that engulfed the town in flames and its 250 inhabitants had to flee for their lives.
>
> Less dramatic but no less troubling news is repeated throughout the west coast of North America in the face of the alarmingly high temperatures recorded since the beginning of the boreal summer.

The report went on to note that the planet has warmed by about 1.2°C since the industrial era began, and scientists are warning that things will get hotter—and worse—unless dramatic changes are made to cut CO_2 emissions.

"It's dire," Thunberg tweeted quoting Mayor Polderman. "The whole town is on fire. It took, like, a whole 15 minutes from the first sign of smoke to, all of a sudden, there being fire everywhere."

Sadly, she was right again. Lost to flames that day were 124 structures in the village of Lytton and 45 in the adjacent Lytton First Nation, as well as 34 nearby rural properties. That meant 90 percent of local buildings had been ruined in a flash. Most of those properties, including that of

Glasgow and Thorpe, were either uninsured or underinsured, as it was tough to get coverage in such a hot, dry location with no full-time fire department.

The destruction included the village hall and official records. Gone also were Lytton's two grocery stores, the farmers' market, pharmacy, bank, medical centre, coffee shop and outdoor benches, as well as Michele Feist's bright-yellow house with the turquoise trim and the cheerful flower garden.

The day after the fire, the BC SPCA was allowed to enter the village for four hours to rescue forty-one animals.

In Botanie Valley, most of the motorcycle statues built by Kenny Glasgow had survived, since they were made of steel, with just the tires burning off. Just down the road, Koten and the other monks were also spared.

A week after the fire, Prime Minister Justin Trudeau met with Lytton mayor Jan Polderman, Janet Webster, Chief of Lytton First Nation and chair of the Nlha7kápmx Nation Tribal Council, and Chief Matt Pasco, hours away in Coquitlam to talk about how the community might recover. By that time, Lytton's now-former residents were harbouring strong suspicions that the fire wouldn't have spread so fast if grass and bushes hadn't been allowed to grow so close to the railway tracks. Dry as it was, the vegetation was just kindling waiting for a spark. The trains and the scalding hot metal rails threw off plenty of those.

An image captured by the engine camera of the CP coal train that passed through Lytton on the CN line at approximately 4:30 p.m. was posted on the Transportation Safety Board's website, as part of a report on their investigation into the possibly train-related origins of the fire. The photo shows tinder-dry brush all along the edge of the track. Also in the image, a young mother, identified as KR, is seen standing beside the track with her young child on the path leading to the walkway across the bridge. As the train passes, KR and her child are covered in coal dust from the train. She films the train with her phone as it passes.

Afterwards, KR walked across the bridge to her home on the west side. Halfway across the bridge, at approximately 4:45, she noticed a fire had started at the edge of the track, so she called the fire department. By the time she was across the bridge, people were arriving and trying to put out the flames, but the fire spread rapidly uphill and along the banks of the railroad. At the time the fire started the wind was blowing at around 35 kilometres per hour with gusts up to 50 kph. As the fire drew in the extremely dry canyon air, the winds suddenly reached upwards of 75 kilometres an hour, with gusts reaching hurricane force. Within minutes, Lytton was engulfed in flames.

Warren Brown, a water technician for Lytton First Nation was one of the brave locals helping to battle the blaze alongside the Lytton Volunteer Fire Department. When the fire knocked out the power to the water system feeding the hydrants, Warren was able to fill two of the seven systems by redirecting a local creek. "We were thinking, just get the hydrants up and running for the fire fighters." Residents ran for their lives with nothing but the clothes on their backs. The volunteer fire fighters fought for as long as they could, but it wasn't long before they had to evacuate as well.

Jeff Chapman was visiting with his parents, Jeanette and Michael, when they noticed smoke down at Hobo Hollow. What they thought was a grass fire quickly spread to their yard. They tried to put out the flames, but within ten minutes their house was on fire. Michael and Jeanette sought shelter in a trench on their property, and as Jeff was overwhelmed by the speed of the fire, he ran down the train tracks. He filmed himself as he ran for his life. In the video, the town burns around him, the footage capturing the shock and horror of the fire. Jeff made it out alive, but tragically his parents were the two fatalities of the fire.

The TSB's investigation found no "anomalous" indicators on the train itself that would indicate an ignition source. However, the investigator in charge, James Carmichael, speaking at a streamed media information session after the report's release, stated that the TSB's investigators believed the Lytton Creek fire originated "within five feet" of the centre of the track. Train cars are typically ten feet wide.

The year before the Lytton Creek fire in July 2020, the CNR had paid a sixteen-million-dollar penalty for starting a wildfire ten kilometres down the line six years earlier. On June 11, 2015, the Cisco Road Fire was started by workers cutting a rail. It burned 2,400 hectares and took four months to extinguish. A few years later in 2016 another fire was ignited by the railroad near Spapium, threatening the home of former Chief Ruby Dunstan and others on the west side of the Fraser near Nikaia Creek. Structures were burnt, and an evacuation was ordered for Lytton and surrounding areas. So folks were familiar with the dangers of dry summer heat and trains, but nothing could prepare them for the ferocity they would face on June 30, 2021.

The Lytton Creek Fire burned until August and destroyed 83,000 hectares. The CNR Thompson Bridge at Lytton was extensively damaged, shutting down rail traffic along that critical line. The CP railroad was still intact, so traffic along that line continued. The pace of trains through the canyon slowed temporarily, but the rail lines are economic arteries to the Pacific. The wealth of the nation passes in and out of the Fraser Canyon every day. By July 13, the CNR had repaired the Thompson Bridge and rail traffic resumed.

Residents and journalists were allowed to tour what remained. They saw the grey ruins of houses, and trucks with melted wheels. The post office and a church still stood. So did the memorial to Chief

Cexpe'nthlEm. The brightly coloured rainbow crosswalk, optimistically painted in June 2019, also somehow remained. It had been painted to honour the local 2SLGBTQ+ community on the suggestion of Lytton RCMP commander Sergeant Curtis Davis, and local high school had agreed to pay for the paint. Tangled power lines lay on the ground. All that remained of the Fandrichs' museum was its database.

The heat warnings hadn't let up. On July 5, a warning let people in the area know their troubles weren't over:

> A DANGEROUS LONG DURATION HEAT WAVE CONTINUES
> WITH ELEVATED OVERNIGHT LOWS.

The latest heat warning finally ended on July 7, when Fraser Canyon residents were warned of a new weather-related threat:

> THUNDERSTORMS ARE EXPECTED TO BE SHORT-LIVED
> BUT HAVE THE POTENTIAL TO PRODUCE PEA TO
> NICKEL SIZE HAIL AND 5 TO 15 MM OF RAIN . . .
>
> LIGHTNING KILLS AND INJURES CANADIANS EVERY YEAR.
> REMEMBER, WHEN THUNDER ROARS, GO INDOORS!
>
> SEVERE THUNDERSTORM WATCHES ARE ISSUED WHEN
> ATMOSPHERIC CONDITIONS ARE FAVOURABLE FOR THE
> DEVELOPMENT OF THUNDERSTORMS THAT COULD PRODUCE
> ONE OR MORE OF THE FOLLOWING: LARGE HAIL, DAMAGING
> WINDS, TORRENTIAL RAINFALL.

Heat warnings continued to pop up until July 16, cautioning that

> ABOVE SEASONAL DAYTIME TEMPERATURES AND ELEVATED
> OVERNIGHT TEMPERATURES WILL MEAN LITTLE RELIEF FROM
> THE HEAT. THIS HEAT EVENT WILL INCREASE THE POTENTIAL
> FOR HEAT-RELATED ILLNESSES.

The long-range forecast from Environment Canada was frightening: "Over the next 30 years, the number of extremely hot days in a year is expected to more than double in some parts of Canada."

Tiny Lytton was referenced by Trudeau in his opening statement to the Conference of the Parties to the UN Climate Convention in November 2021 in Glasgow, Scotland, before 120 world leaders, including US president Joe Biden and German chancellor Angela Merkel. "In Canada, there was a town called Lytton. I say *was* because on June 30 it burned to the ground," Trudeau said. "What happened in Lytton can and has and will happen anywhere. How many more signs do we need? This is our time to step up—and step up together."

Then Trudeau committed to cap emissions from Canada's oil and gas sector. "We'll cap oil and gas–sector emissions today and ensure they decrease tomorrow at a pace and scale needed to reach net zero by 2050," he declared. "That's no small task for a major oil and gas–producing country. It's a big step that's absolutely necessary."

Thunberg was at the meeting. She wasn't impressed by the earnest words of the world leaders. Instead, she sang, "You can shove your climate crisis up your arse," outside the meeting. Then she told supporters, "We say, 'No more blah, blah, blah. No more exploitation of people and nature and the planet.'"

Meanwhile, Lytton people, wherever they were staying, were taking a different angle on outrage. They didn't want to be referred to in the past tense.

> The smell of the seasons in the canyon, the wind, the
> rivers, the mountains. The sound of the coyotes howling
> on the west side on cold winter nights. The rhythm
> of the trains rumbling by. The big trucks buzzing by on

the Trans-Canada Highway. I played here, learned here, loved here. My history is here, on these streets, buried in this ground.

You dig anywhere in this town and you'll find artifacts from thousands of years of Nlaka'pamux. Now this charred layer that was the Lytton of my entire life is just another layer in the geography, and the Lytton I remember a slowly fading hologram in my mind.

Kevin Loring

CHAPTER 41

THE FUTURE

It shouldn't be a symbol of anything. These are real people.

FORMER LYTTON RESIDENT MICHELE FEIST

THE MONKS FROM the Lions Gate Buddhist Priory held a memorial on July 23, 2022, for animals lost in the fire. One was a dog named Gilbert, who was somewhat of a local fixture and whose bones were found in the village's ashes. Some people who could not attend the memorial in person sent photos and names of animals to be read aloud.

Among those attending was retired nurse Michele Feist. "It was wonderful. Buddhist ceremonies mean business," she says. "There were about eighteen people there, which is big for us . . . Pretty much everyone who attended had lost at least one animal. Some many more . . . We had two single-spaced pages of names which were recited as part of the ceremony."

As Feist sifted through the ashes, she knew Lytton was becoming a symbol of climate change. That left her uneasy. "It shouldn't be a symbol of anything. These are real people." Then she felt a sense of calm as she thought of the mountains surrounding the village. "They don't care.

They're implacable. They're there before me. They're there after me. They don't go anywhere."

As she spoke, a year after the fire, some 1,200 area residents remained displaced. Frustrations were understandably high. Their community still looked like a war zone. Weeds were growing amidst the charred and crumbled buildings. Insurance claims remained unresolved. The federal government pledged $77 million in June 2022 for Lytton to help rebuild as a more fire-resistant community. The BC government promised another $21 million, added to $9.3 million to hire recovery staff and $18.4 million for debris removal and repairs.

Still, there was plenty of red tape and precious little rebuilding. The money didn't seem to be getting to the real people on the ground. The global pandemic was adding to the inertia, as were landslides in November and heavy snowfalls in December. A fence went up around the town, presumably to keep people from falling into holes that had once been basements. And if that wasn't enough, the village records had been destroyed.

Donny Glasgow recalled a few times in the past when he'd thought of leaving Lytton. A few decades earlier, when he was forty-eight, he was visiting Vancouver, but then felt the irresistible pull back to the mountains. "It was a vast culture shock." He's a fourth-generation Botanie Valley resident. Living there just feels right. He returned to cherish the land where he was born. "Now that I'm an older guy . . . if I won 100 billion trillion dollars, I'd stay here," Glasgow says. "The Natives say we are part of the land. We're not separate. They're right."

A year after their farm burned to the ground, Glasgow and Thorpe rebuilt while nearby Lytton remained flattened. The soil beneath the village of Lytton and Lytton First Nation was designated toxic by government inspectors. Further, the entire village was classed as a heritage site, with high archaeological importance. That meant extra time was now spent sifting through the rubble, in an effort to respect artifacts and human remains—of which there would be no shortage, after several millennia of human habitation. The Glasgows were spared because their farm was on regional land and escaped the toxic and archaeological designations.

On the downside, they couldn't get fire insurance because they relied on wood heat in the winter. Federal assistance also wasn't available. They couldn't wait for a government saviour. They instead drew upon generations of goodwill and community support. Neighbours put them up when they had nowhere to stay and then pitched in with the reconstruction.

The Glasgows weren't naive. They knew they had to rebuild in a way that prepared them for future fires. So they planned a cement house with a metal roof and sprinkler systems throughout the property. Over time, they hoped to move from the electrical grid to solar power, once their budget could support it. As they were rebuilding, their farm was already home to eight prehistoric-looking guinea fowl from Africa, three peacocks, two roosters, twenty-three chickens, four goats, six sheep and four alpacas. Glasgow is also personally rebounding after a heart attack. "I feel good. I slow down pretty quick."

The fire reinforced their sense of community. Glasgow and Thorpe took their puppies to the local fire station one day, to give firefighters a snuggle break and remind them that they're appreciated.

There was a 68.25 percent turnout for Lytton's municipal election in October 2022. That contrasted sharply with 36.3 percent in Vancouver and 29 percent in Toronto, which also held elections that month. Part of the reason for Lytton's high turnout was Donny Glasgow, who estimates he went to some nine hundred places to drop off flyers and drove 4,390 kilometres campaigning for his wife, Tricia Thorpe, who was elected as a new Thompson-Nicola Regional District director. That makes her rural even for Lytton.

While campaigning, Thorpe and Glasgow filled a thick notebook with voter concerns. Topping the list was wildfire mitigation. He noted that weeds are no longer cleaned up the way they used to be alongside rail tracks. "It's not just railroads," Glasgow says. "It's everywhere." That also meant trimming trees. "People want fire mitigation. A proactive approach."

Access to health care was another big issue. Thorpe didn't have to be briefed on that one either. If Tricia hadn't been there to quickly drive Donny to hospital in Lillooet, he wouldn't have survived his heart attack in the spring of 2022.

Elected as the new mayor of Lytton was retired local principal Denise O'Connor, who also lost her home to the fire. She was also president of the Lytton and District Chamber of Commerce. She had two challengers for the mayor's job, a jump in interest from the previous election, when Jan Polderman and all four councillors won by acclamation. O'Connor topped the polls with 87 votes. There were 129 of 189 eligible votes cast.

Thorpe herself won with 228 votes to 123 cast for incumbent Steven Rice, who had served three consecutive terms as director for the regional district of Blue Sky Country. The high voter turnout came despite obvious complications. Residents were scattered. Some were driven to advance voting day at Kumsheen ShchEma-meet School in Lytton, where general voting also took place. Mail-in votes were also accepted.

Two years after the fire, on June 29, 2023, the state of emergency was finally lifted, meaning residents were allowed back onto their properties. Some of their sites were contamination-free and no longer subject to archaeological work, meaning reconstruction could finally begin. On August 6, there was a wildfire on Stein Mountain, north of Lytton, which brought evacuation orders for more than a dozen homes across First Nations reserves. Lytton was once again Canada's hot spot, with temperatures hitting 42°C by the middle of the month. On August 17, heavy smoke from another fire poured across the area, fanned by high winds and the heat.

Donny Glasgow isn't fazed. "We are ready for anything, two sprinklers on the barn and one on the house," he says. But he does remain frustrated by the lack of progress in rebuilding, which he calls a joke. He ridicules the cost and purpose of the fence around the village, which is becoming just a string of vacant lots while rebuilding is under way on many properties outside town.

Work continues on checking for Indigenous remains and artifacts. It's still a mystery where Chief Cexpen'nthlEm is buried, although his stone monument still stands.

Meanwhile, the Glasgows have four alpacas now, including Autumn, who was born on the first day of fall after the fire. The birth was a hopeful sign, coming as Donny and Tricia were well into construction of their new home. They're optimistic that their community is worth rebuilding, yet again.

"It'll return," Donny says.

NOTES

CHAPTER 1 | CENTRE OF THE UNIVERSE

Hanna, Darwin, and Mamie Henry, eds. *Our Tellings: Interior Salish Stories of the Nlha7kápmx People.* Vancouver: UBC Press, 1995.

Hume, Stephen. *Simon Fraser: In Search of Modern British Columbia.* Madeira Park, BC: Harbour Publishing, 2008.

Hutchison, Bruce. *The Fraser.* Toronto: Clarke, Irwin & Co., 1950.

Laforet, Andrea, and Annie York. *Spuzzum: Fraser Canyon Histories, 1808–1939.* Vancouver: UBC Press, 1998.

Lamb, W. Kaye, ed. *Simon Fraser: Letters & Journals, 1806–1808.* Toronto: Macmillan, 1960.

York, Annie, Richard Daly and Chris Arnett. *They Write Their Dreams on the Rock Forever: Rock Writings in the Stein River Valley of British Columbia.* Vancouver: Talonbooks, 1993. Re the five ancient villages around Lytton and archaeologists.

CHAPTER 2 | GOLD FEVER

Marshall, Daniel. *Claiming the Land: British Columbia and the Making of a New El Dorado.* Vancouver: Ronsdale Press, 2019.

Teit, James. "Mythology of the Thompson Indians." In *The Jesup North Pacific Expedition.* Edited by Franz Boas. Memoirs of the American Museum of Natural History. Vol. 8, pt. 2, 412. Leiden, Netherlands: E.J. Brill, 1912.

Also see Laforet and York, *Spuzzum*, 54–55.

CHAPTER 3 | CANYON WAR

Hunter, Justine. "1858: How a violent year created a province." *Globe and Mail*,
November 18, 2008.

Hutchison. *The Fraser.*

Laforet and York. *Spuzzum.*

Marshall. *Claiming the Land.*

Walkem, W.W. *Stories of Early British Columbia.* Vancouver: News-Advertiser, 1914.

Wickwire, Wendy. *At the Bridge: James Teit and an Anthropology of Belonging.*
Vancouver: UBC Press, 2019.

Wright, Eric. "Fraser Canyon War." *The Canadian Encyclopedia.* Published online
April 10, 2019.

CHAPTER 4 | WATKINSONS ARRIVE

Tom Watkinson Jr. wrote an excellent, thoroughly researched family history, which
was invaluable.

Tom Watkinson Jr's 2021 Christmas newsletter to his grandchildren was also
extremely useful.

Lorraine Harris's *Halfway to the Goldfields: A History of Lillooet* (Vancouver:
J.J. Douglas Ltd., 1977) also helped with the Watkinson farm, and detail
about horse races down the main street of Lytton. I am especially grateful
for her details on the romance between Billy Kane and Susan Watkinson.

Caroline Watkinson was born May 23, 1884, at the ranch, the eleventh child of
Joe and Catherine. Her husband, Charles Norman McCaffery, drove the
stagecoach from Lytton to Lillooet. He died of undisclosed causes at age
thirty-five and was also buried in the ranch cemetery.

CHAPTER 5 | THE HARANGUING JUDGE

Begbie Correspondence, F 142-C, Begbie to Colonial Secretary, Oct. 25, 1860.

Begbie Correspondence, F142-C, Begbie to Douglas, April 30, 1860. bcgenesis
.uvic.ca/B59136.html.

Begbie, Matthew Baillie. Bench books, Vol. 7, July 10, 1872.

Crawford, Tiffany. "Justice Matthew Begbie, B.C.'s first chief justice, was responsible for the hanging deaths of six Tsilhqot'in chiefs." *Vancouver Sun*, July 6, 2019.

Foster, Hamar. "Was Begbie really a 'hanging judge'?: B.C.'s first chief justice was fairer than stories imply, historians say." *Times Colonist* (Victoria), September 2, 2018, D2.

Glavin, Terry. "The colonial history behind B.C. Day that can make us all proud: A colonial governor who was part black welcomed racial minorities and stood up for Indigenous people against marauding Americans: How was he airbrushed from the modern narrative?" *Maclean's*, August 1, 2018.

Hanna and Henry. *Our Tellings*.

Hauka, Donald J. *McGowan's War: The Birth of Modern British Columbia on the Fraser River Gold Fields*. Vancouver: New Star Books, 2003.

Hutchison. *The Fraser*.

Kumtuks (website). "Judge Matthew Begbie: British Columbia History." kumtuks.ca /judge-begbie/. Accessed December 13, 2023.

Lake Country Calendar (Kelowna). "What's in a name? The story of Revelstoke's Mt. Begbie." February 16, 2020.

MacDonald, Esther Darlington. "Patrick Kilroy—the bullying Butcher of Lytton." *Ashcroft-Cache Creek Journal*, March 24, 2015.

Marshall, Daniel Patrick. "Claiming the Land: Indians, Gold Seekers, and the Rush to British Columbia." Phd diss., University of British Columbia, 2000.

North Kamloops News Advertiser. "Stealing flour, beans in 1866 was SERIOUS." August 31, 1966.

Pettit, Sydney G. "'Dear Sir Matthew': A Glimpse of Judge Begbie." *British Columbia Historical Quarterly* 11, no. 1 (January 1947): 1.

Times Colonist (Victoria). "Law society ditches Begbie statue." June 4, 2017, A5t.

Walkem. *Stories of Early British Columbia*.

Williams, David R. *". . . The Man for a New Country": Sir Matthew Baillie Begbie*. Sidney, BC: Gray's Publishing, 1977.

——. Various articles on Sir Matthew Baillie Begbie. Published online January 24, 2008; last edited July 24, 2015.

CHAPTER 6 | THE CHURCHES

Christophers, Brett. *Positioning the Missionary: John Booth Good and the Confluence of Cultures in Nineteenth-Century British Columbia*. Vancouver: UBC Press, 1998.

Fisher, Robin. *Contact and Conflict*. Vancouver: UBC Press, 1977.

Friesen, Jean. "Duncan, William." In *Dictionary of Canadian Biography*, vol. 14. Toronto and Québec: University of Toronto/Université Laval, 2003–. biographi. ca/en/bio/duncan_william_14E.html. Accessed December 13, 2023.

Hanna and Henry. *Our Tellings*.

Harris, Cole. "The Fraser River Encountered." *BC Studies* 94 (Summer 1992).

Harris, Douglas. "The Nlha7kápmx Meeting at Lytton, 1879, and the Rule of Law." *BC Studies* 108 (Winter 1995–96).

Laforet and York. *Spuzzum*.

Tennant, Paul. "Aboriginal Peoples and Politics." *BC Studies* 94 (Summer 1992).

Wickwire, Wendy. "To See Ourselves as the Other's Other." *Canadian Historical Review* 75, no. 1 (1994): 1–20.

Williams, Cyril E.H., and Pixie McGeachie. *Archbishop on Horseback: Richard Small, 1849–1909, Missionary at Lytton, Chaplain at St. Bartholomew's Hospital, Lytton and Archdeacon of Yale*. Merritt, BC: Sonotek Publishing, 1991. Deals with Gammage's arrival in Lytton.

York, Geoffrey. *The Dispossessed: Life and Death in Native America*. Toronto: Lester & Orpen Dennys, 1989.

Fisher, Tennant, Cole Harris and Douglas Harris all deal with the 1889 meeting in Lytton in which Indigenous people made a serious attempt to adjust to governance under white law and were undermined by the provincial government and ignored by Ottawa. The thesis is that the rule of law didn't protect Indigenous people from newcomers.

The explanation of the name Amor De Cosmos comes from *The Canadian Encyclopedia*.

CHAPTER 7 | HOSPITALITY BUSINESS

Hutchison. *The Fraser*.

Lytton & District Centennial Society. *Lytton: A Story in Pictures, 1966–67, Told by the Older Ones for the Young People of Lytton*. Lytton: Freedom Graphics, 1966–67.

Smith, Jessie Ann, as told to J. Meryl Campbell and Audrey Ward. *Widow Smith of Spence's Bridge*. Merritt, BC: Sonotek Publishing, 1989.

Louis Hautier died in 1886, and his hotel business was taken over by his son, Alphonse, who died in December 1939 at the age of eighty-five. The hotel burned to the ground in 1896 and was rebuilt in 1910. When it was destroyed by fire again in 1937, it was not rebuilt.

CHAPTER 8 | PLAGUES

Boyd, Robert T. *The Coming of the Spirit of Pestilence: Introduced Infectious Diseases and Population Decline among Northwest Coast Indians, 1774–1874*. Seattle: University of Washington Press, 1999.

Ostroff, Joshua. "How a smallpox epidemic forged modern British Columbia; In 1862, smallpox killed thousands of Indigenous people in B.C.—and what ensued sparked issues that the province still grapples with today." *Maclean's*, August 1, 2017.

Teit, James, and Franz Boas. *The Thompson Indians of British Columbia*. Andesite Press, 2015.

Walkem. *Stories of Early British Columbia*.

Wickwire, Wendy. *At the Bridge*.

The *British Colonist* passage comes from: "The Small Pox and the Indians." *Great Unsolved Mysteries in Canadian History*. canadianmysteries.ca/sites/klatsassin /archives/newspaperormagazinearticle/99en.html. Accessed December 14, 2023.

CHAPTER 9 | ARRIVALS

Also arriving in Lytton during the gold rush were the five Oppenheimer brothers, David, Charles, Meyer, Isaac and Godfrey. They were merchants who grew up in Blieskastel, Germany, and immigrated to the United States in 1848, stopping first in New Orleans. They sold miners' supplies, first during the California gold rush and then during the Fraser Canyon gold rush of 1858. The brothers were running stores in Fort Hope and Lytton by 1859. After Lytton, it was onwards and upwards for the Oppenheimers. They started Vancouver's first warehouse in 1885, in the Gastown district building where singer Bryan Adams built a recording studio a century later. David moved on to serve as Vancouver's mayor from 1888 until 1893.

George, Catherine. "Tracking the National Dream: A century after the last spike of the Canadian Pacific Railway was driven at Craigellachie, B.C., the legendary route through the Rockies continues to hold tourists spellbound." *Toronto Star*, July 12, 1997.

Liddell, Peter, and Patricia E. Roy. "Oppenheimer, David." In *Dictionary of Canadian Biography*, vol. 12. Toronto and Québec: University of Toronto/Université Laval, 2003–. biographi.ca/en/bio/oppenheimer_david_12E.html. Accessed December 13, 2023.

The Province (Vancouver). "Pay last tribute to real pioneer." April 2, 1921, 7.

Robinson, Noel. "The Story of My Life, No. 45." *Vancouver Daily World*, August 7, 1915, 12.

——. "The Story of My Life, No. 45." *Vancouver Daily World*, August 28, 1915, 9.

——. "The Story of My Life, No. 45." *Vancouver Daily World*, September 11, 1915, 11.

Thomas, Earl. *Vancouver Daily News Advertiser*, January 23, 1902, 3.

CHAPTER 10 | PROMISE OF RAILWAY

Berton, Pierre. *The Last Spike: The Great Railway, 1881–1885.* Toronto: McClelland & Stewart, 1971.

Chow, Lily. *Blossoms in the Gold Fields: Chinese Settlements in the Fraser Canyon and the Okanagan.* Halfmoon Bay, BC: Caitlin Press, 2018.

Hutchison. *The Fraser.*

Marsh, James. "CPR welded Canada together—but at a high cost." *Vancouver Sun*, November 10, 2003, E6.

National Post. "On this day: A snapshot from Canadian history." May 14, 2004, A2.

The Province (Vancouver), magazine, May 19, 1956.

Roberts, Mike, and Bill Barlee. "Gold Trails and Ghost Towns: Lytton." YouTube video, 24 min., uploaded by Colin M, March 15, 2016. youtube.com/watch?v=U6lyliK2Lqg.

Turner, Robert D. "Onderdonk, Andrew." In *Dictionary of Canadian Biography*, vol. 13. Toronto and Québec: University of Toronto/Université Laval, 2003–. biographi.ca/en/bio/onderdonk_andrew_13E.html. Accessed December 14, 2023.

Washington Post. "Men who smile at danger: Bridge builder must be a combination of daring, skill and courage." From *Railman's Magazine*, June 16, 1912.

Wickwire. *At the Bridge.*

Lasha story from *Lytton: A Story in Pictures*

Hotel story from *The Province* (Vancouver), October 23, 1927.

CHAPTER 11 | BISHOP ARRIVES

Gowen, Herbert H. *Church Work in British Columbia: Being a Memoir of the Episcopate of Acton Windeyer Sillitoe, D.D., D.C.L., First Bishop of New Westminster.* London, UK: Forgotten Books, 2018.

VirtualMuseum.ca. "Colourful Characters in Historic Yale." communitystories.ca/v1
/pm_v2.php?id=story_line&lg=English&fl=0&ex=00000517&sl=3984&pos=1&
pf=1. Accessed December 14, 2023.

Weir, Joan. *Catalysts and Watchdogs: B.C.'s Men of God, 1836–1871*. Victoria: Sono
Nis Press, 1995.

CHAPTER 12 | ANTHROPOLOGIST FRIEND

Banks, Judith Judd. *Comparative Biographies of Two British Columbia Anthropologists:
Charles Hill-Tout and James A. Teit*. Vancouver: UBC Press, 1970.

Campsie, Alison. "The lost story of a Shetlander who became a champion of First
Nation Canadians." *The Scotsman*, November 27, 2019. scotsman.com/heritage
-and-retro/heritage/lost-story-shetlander-who-became-champion-first-nation
-canadians-1401241.

Marshall, Daniel. "#575 The late, great, James Teit." *Ormsby Review: Serious writing
about B.C. culture*, July 9, 2019. https://thebcreview.ca/2019/07/09/575-the-late
-great-james-teit/.

Smith. *Widow Smith of Spence's Bridge*.

Thompson, Judy. *Recording Their Story: James Teit and the Tahltan*. Vancouver/
Toronto, Gatineau, and Seattle: Douglas & McIntyre, Canadian Museum of
Civilization, and University of Washington Press, 2007. Material about escaping
35-year-old woman.

Wickwire. *At the Bridge*.

Wickwire, Wendy. "Teit, James Alexander (Tait)." In *Dictionary of Canadian
Biography*, vol. 15. Toronto and Québec: University of Toronto/Université Laval,
2003–. biographi.ca/en/bio/teit_james_alexander_1884_15E.html. Accessed
December 14, 2023.

CHAPTER 13 | VIVA LYTTON

Mark Rebagliati was invaluable here.

Wickwire. *At the Bridge*, 43–44.

CHAPTER 14 | SETTLER GROWTH

Hanna and Henry. *Our Tellings.*

Hill-Tout, Charles. *The Salish People: The Local Contribution of Charles Hill-Tout.* Vol. 2, *The Squamish and the Lillooet.* Edited by Ralph Maud. Vancouver: Talon Books, 1978.

Laforet and York. *Spuzzum.*

Truth and Reconciliation Commission of Canada. *Canada's Residential Schools: The History.* Part 1, *Origins to 1939,* and Part 2, *1939 to 2000.* Montreal and Kingston: McGill-Queen's University Press, 2015.

Williams and McGeachie. *Archbishop on Horseback.*

CHAPTER 15 | ENTERING THE TWENTIETH CENTURY

Interview with Dr. Rosalin Miles.

"The Diocese of New Westminster and the Indian Residential Schools System." Updated by Melanie Delva, archivist, Diocese of New Westminster, Ecclesiastical Province of BC and Yukon, June 25, 2014. (For additional information, visit the Truth and Reconciliation section of the Anglican Church of Canada's website.)

Friesen, Jean. "Hills, George." In *Dictionary of Canadian Biography*, vol. 12. Toronto and Québec: University of Toronto/Université Laval, 2003–. biographi.ca/en/bio /hills_george_12E.html. Accessed December 14, 2023.

Hanna and Henry. *Our Tellings.*

Hitchin, Neil. *"Come Over and Help Us": The New England Company and Its Mission, 1649–2001.* Ely, UK: St. Pancras Books, 2002.

Milloy, J.S. *"Suffer the Little Children": The Aboriginal Residential School System, 1830–1992.* Submitted to the Royal Commission on Aboriginal Peoples, 1996. https://www.vancouver.anglican.ca/diocesan-ministries/indigenous-justice /pages/indian-residential-schools-summary.

Teit, James Alexander. "The Thompson Indians of British Columbia." Edited by Franz Boas. Memoirs of the American Museum of Natural History. Vol. 2, pt. 4. New York: AMNH, 1900.

Truth and Reconciliation Commission. Vol. 1, 663–68. Vol. 2, 384–85, 428.

York. *The Dispossessed.*

CHAPTER 16 | THE MYSTERY OF THE THREE DEITIES

Chow. *Blossoms in the Gold Mountains.*

CHAPTER 17 | ALL HALLOWS' WEST

Weir. *Catalysts and Watchdogs.*

CHAPTER 18 | BOOM TOWN AGAIN

Ashcroft Journal. "Jimmy Teit the marksman." February 11, 1986.
Eckert, Fred J. "Cruising Rockies: Looking down on the world." *Washington Times,* October 6, 1996, E1.
Fairfax, Ted. "Railway pay Lytton's lifeblood." *The Province* (Vancouver), May 15, 1948.
Hill-Tout, Charles. *The Salish People.*
Laforet and York. *Spuzzum.*
Vancouver Daily World, May 11, 1914, 1.
Vancouver Sun, May 12, 1914, 8.
Wickwire. *At the Bridge.*
Williams Lake Tribune. October 20, 2005, 14.

CHAPTER 19 | SUFFERING LITTLE CHILDREN

Baker, Simon. *Khot-La-Cha: The Autobiography of Chief Simon Baker.* Compiled and edited by Verna J. Kirkness. Vancouver: Douglas & McIntyre, 1994.
Diocese of New Westminster. "The Diocese of New Westminster and the Indian Residential Schools System." https://www.vancouver.anglican.ca/diocesan-ministries/indigenous-justice/pages/indian-residential-schools-summary.
Milloy. "Suffer the Little Children."
Truth and Reconciliation Commission of Canada. *Canada's Residential Schools.*

CHAPTER 20 | INROADS

The Rebagliati transportation links also included three generations of railroaders. Peter George (Pete) started with the railway in 1914 and rose to become the roadmaster, the boss for all track maintenance, by the time he retired in 1955. His son, Raymond Keith, carried on the tradition and became a roadmaster too. In 2000, Raymond's son, Peter Ronald, became a roadmaster, or operations superintendent, from Vancouver to Fort Nelson.

CHAPTER 21 | WORLD'S FASTEST MAN

Butler, Don. "Our need for speed: Men's 100-metre race has enthralled us for more than 2,700 years." *Edmonton Journal*, August 21, 2004, A13.

De Long, Jack. "On the Sunbeam." *Vancouver Sun*, June 8, 1952.

Frayne, Trent. "Sprinter may have been ahead of times." *Ottawa Citizen*, September 4, 1987, C10.

Hawley, Samuel. *I Just Ran: Percy Williams, the World's Fastest Human*. Vancouver: Ronsdale Press, 2001.

McDonald, Archie. "A reluctant hero is bid farewell." *Vancouver Sun*, December 4, 1982.

Oliver, Brian. "Gold Coast 2018 owes a debt to 'Bobby' Robinson, the Pierre de Coubertin of the Commonwealth Games." insidethegames.biz, April 1, 2018.

Simmons, Steve. "Canada's greatest runner's dead." *Calgary Herald*, December 9, 1982, 37.

Stewart, J.D.M. "A history of Olympic triumph and despair: No one can forget Bailey's gold medal in '96, writes J.D.M. Stewart. But we should also consider the big Summer Games moments beyond recent memory," *Ottawa Citizen*, August 11, 2012, B7.

CHAPTER 22 | DOWNTOWN FIRES

Calgary Herald. "Jury in Lytton fire tragedy recommends escapes for hotels." September 21, 1931, 9.

Capital Journal (Salem, Oregon), September 11, 1931, 7.

Chilliwack Progress. "Charles Morrow has narrow escape in Lytton fire." September 17, 1931, 1.

Edmonton Journal. "Rites are held for fire victim." September 23, 1931, 13.

Find a Grave. "Colonel Joseph Victor Norman Spencer." January 14, 2016. findagrave.com/memorial/157069746/joseph-victor_norman-spencer.

Higgs, Canon Stanley. *That They Might Have Life: An Autobiography.* Lytton: Freedom Graphics Press, 2009.

Lytton Museum and Archives. "Newsletter, The First Five Years."

The Province (Vancouver). "Lytton fire victim is dead." September 11, 1931, 1, 6.

——. "Another man is dead from injuries received in Lytton Hotel." September 15, 1931, 1.

——. "Lytton fire victim to be buried Thursday." September 16, 1931, 30.

——. "Mrs. Thibodeau expresses thanks for public's aid." September 20, 1931, 32.

Vancouver Sun. "Lytton fire injuries fatal to local man." September 11, 1931, 1.

The September 12, 1931, issue of the *Ashcroft-Cache Creek Journal* contained the headline "Village of Lytton swept by fire Thursday a.m."

CHAPTER 23 | GLASGOWS ARRIVE—WATKINSONS SURVIVE

MacKenzie, Hector. "Were you there the night Dingwall snubbed The Beatles?" *Ross-shire Journal,* November 20, 2015. ross-shirejournal.co.uk/news/were-you-there-the-night-the-beatles-underwhelmed-dingwall-154663/.

The Great Depression was also a tough time out at the Watkinson ranch and all the other ranches in the area and across the continent. The Lytton-area land still had promise, but things weren't working out anywhere. "There the soil was a fine, rich, sandy loam, well adapted to the growth of cereals, corn, beans, potatoes and alfalfa," Joe's great-grandson Tommy Watkinson recalled. "Alfalfa was the principal crop, and yields were high when it was properly irrigated."

Joe Watkinson had worked the family farm he founded on the Lytton–Lillooet road until his death on January 29, 1914. His son Frederick R. Watkinson (the grandfather of author Peter Edwards's friends Tommy and Harvey Watkinson) then ran the ranch with the help of a number of sons until he passed away at the age of seventy-six, in 1939.

CHAPTER 24 | ESCAPE TO LYTTON

Hutchison. *The Fraser.*

Wilson, Ethel. *Hetty Dorval.* Toronto: Macmillan, 1947.

——. "A night in Lytton." *The Province* (Vancouver), October 19, 1940, 44.

——. *Swamp Angel.* Toronto: Macmillan, 1954.

CHAPTER 25 | THE PRINCIPAL

Interview with Dr. Rosalin Miles, member of Lytton First Nation, Research Associate, Indigenous Studies in UBC School of Kinesiology.

Agence France Presse. "Protesters demand probe into Canadian Indigenous schools." July 31, 2021.

Hanna and Henry. *Our Tellings.*

Hives, Canon C.F. "A defense of St. George's, the work of one Indian school." *Vancouver Sun,* April 12, 1948, 4.

Kines, Lindsay. "Honorary degree beyond dreams of residential-school fighter: They gave her a standing ovation and draped the ceremonial hood around her neck, and Ruby Dunstan stayed composed through all of it Tuesday." *Vancouver Sun,* June 10, 2015.

Marsh, Elsie. "Lytton beefed at 12-cent steak." *Vancouver Sun* magazine supplement, November 5, 1949, 60.

Truth and Reconciliation Commission of Canada. *Canada's Residential Schools.*

CHAPTER 26 | ROOTS

Arizona Daily Star. "Lytton, B.C. has severe fire loss." June 14, 1949, 5.

Mackie, John. "B.C.'s oldest company has a familiar name: David Oppenheimer was both a businessman and a politician who changed the face of B.C." *Vancouver Sun,* July 11, 2008, B3.

——. "Oppenheimer laid the city's foundation." *Vancouver Sun,* May 2, 2017, A4.

Marsh. "Lytton beefed."

——. "This day in history: December 14, 1911: Thirteen years after his death, the City of Vancouver unveiled a memorial to David Oppenheimer at Stanley Park." *Vancouver Sun,* December 14, 2013, A2.

The Province (Vancouver). "$150,000 fire sweeps Lytton." June 13, 1949, 1.

——. "Lytton rises again from big fire ashes." July 12, 1949, 23.

Vancouver Sun. "Lytton hard-luck town." June 13, 1949, 2.

——. "Lytton citizens roll sleeves before rolling out barrel." July 16, 1949, 19.

Victoria Daily Times. "$150,000 Lytton fire: Five stores burned." June 13, 1949, 1.

Tom Alexander Watkinson did excellent research on his family, some of which
appears in his book *A Spirit of Generosity: The Story of Catherine Edith Campbell
Watkinson.* He generously shared his research.

James Teit's life and work at Spences Bridge are featured in Wickwire, *At the Bridge.*

CHAPTER 27 | ENTERTAINMENT OPTIONS

Interview with Charles Melanson.

Maki, Allan. "Sportsman helped to bring CFL to B.C." *Globe and Mail*, September 10,
2015, S8.

CHAPTER 28 | BIG ON SPORTS

"Earlscourt a first at Royal Winter Fair." *Vancouver Sun*, November 25, 1953, 48.

Interviews with James Baker and Robert Bolan.

CHAPTER 29 | DOWN ON THE RANCH

Interviews with Donny Glasgow.

Lorraine Harris's *Halfway to the Goldfields: A History of Lillooet* (Vancouver: J.J. Douglas
Ltd., 1977) helped with the Watkinson farm, and detail about horse races down
the main street of Lytton.

Watkinson, Tom Alexander. *A Spirit of Generosity.*

The Watkinsons held a family meeting in 2000, when the siblings turned the ranch
over to Fred, who ran it with his wife, Barb. Fred had come to Canada as a two-
year-old in a kilt. "We did not want the ranch to be split up or sold to someone
outside the family," Tom Jr. later explained. Fred loved ranching and his son Kelly
seemed a good successor when Fred decided to move on. "It was really Fred that
brought the ranch forward, where it had some great years and he was able to
make a living there," Tom Jr. said.

CHAPTER 30 | THE CHONGS

Chow. *Blossoms in the Gold Mountains.* This deals with the Chongs and their
neighbours, as well as Chinese heritage families throughout the province.
A valuable work.

Adrienne Fairburn was invaluable, providing correspondence and David Chong's
eulogy at his brother Peter's funeral. Many of her documents were destroyed,
however, in the June 2021 fire. She also provided the Carson Mak recorded
interview.

Interview with Peter and David Chong. drive.google.com/drive/folders/1aGGE
reEz8csinbkYM43X9d6A8DgqmJmp?usp=sharing.

CHAPTER 31 | CENTENNIAL YEAR

Interviews with Kareen Zebroff.

The Province (Vancouver). "Ferry is just a focal point of Indian anger." August 4, 1967, 5.

Vancouver Sun. "Four Lytton houses razed by runaway forest blaze." August 6, 1970, 1.

CHAPTER 32 | RESIDENTIAL SCHOOL REVELATIONS

INTERVIEWS

Interview with Dr. Rosalin Miles of Lytton First Nation, who works within the
UBC Indigenous Studies in Kinesiology program as a research associate.

Interview with former Lytton area resident Christ'l Roshard.

ARTICLES

Blair, Kathy. "Church, school officials must have known of rampant evil, judge says."
Anglican Journal, October 1, 1999.

Cariboo Observer (Quesnel), October 18, 2000.

Morton, Brian. "Appeal unfair, abuse victim says: I can't get on with my life, says
native awarded $250,000 in damages against Anglican church." *Vancouver Sun,*
September 22, 2001, B9.

Siemon-Netto, Uwe. "Sex scandal imperils Canadian church." United Press
    International, May 15, 2001.

REPORTS

Diocese of New Westminster. https://www.vancouver.anglican.ca/diocesan-ministries
    /indigenous-justice/pages/indian-residential-schools-summary.
Truth and Reconciliation Commission of Canada. *Canada's Residential Schools.*

COURT CASES

Terrance Wayne Nelson Aleck v. Derek Clarke, Anthony William Harding, Her
    Majesty the Queen in Right of Canada as Represented by the Minister of Indian
    and Northern Affairs. Supreme Court of British Columbia, Reasons for Judgment
    of the Honourable Mr. Justice Williamson, August 8, 2001.
T.W.N.A., E.A.J. and G.B.S. et al., plaintiffs, v. Clarke et al., 2001 BCSC 1177. Docket:
    C886397, Vancouver, Supreme Court of British Columbia, 2001. BCSC 177,
    Docket: C886397.
T.W.N.A. v. Clarke, 1999. CanLII 15172 (BC SC), 1999-11-16, Docket: C886397,
    Vancouver, Supreme Court of British Columbia.
F.S.M. v. Clarke et al., CanLII 9405 (BC SC), 1999-08-30.

CHAPTER 33 | BUSTED

This chapter drew from the same sources as chapter 32.
The quote from the explanatory letter written by St. George's principal Anthony
    Harding to the federal co-ordinator of student residences comes from a report
    by the Truth and Reconciliation Commission.

CHAPTER 35 | MORE LYTTON GOLD

Interviews with Mark and Ross Rebagliati.
Mark Rebagliati's family history.

CHAPTER 36 | HOLLYWOOD VISIT

Interview with Donny Glasgow.

CHAPTER 37 | ANNIE'S FAREWELL

Hume, Stephen. "Reverend native elder at heart of care controversy dies at 106."
     Vancouver Sun, June 28, 2002, A1.
Laforet and York. *Spuzzum*.
McInnes, Craig. "New system splits more aged couples." *Vancouver Sun*, June 25,
     2002, A4.
Mitchell, Penni. "B.C. runs roughshod over rights." *Winnipeg Free Press*, July 8,
     2002, A10.
Sandler, Jeremy. "Lytton buries elder Annie Munro: Like the life she lived, the service
     to honour the centenarian Siska elder spanned two worlds." *Vancouver Sun*,
     July 2, 2002, A4.
Vancouver Sun. "Another harrowing encounter with the health care system."
     February 1, 2003, A27.
——. "Health care in Lytton: The tortuous saga continues." March 9, 2005, A13.

CHAPTER 38 | THE MUNKSTERS

Interviews with Rev. Koten Benson, Michele Feist and Donny Glasgow.
Email interview with Belinda Watkinson.
Roden, Barbara. "New Lytton Chinese Museum opens." *Ashcroft-Cache Creek Journal*,
     May 16, 2017.
——. "Goddess of Mercy: Amid the devastation in Lytton, some glimmers of hope
     remain." *Ashcroft-Cache Creek Journal*, July 14, 2021.
Whitehead, Christine. "Stein Valley Asking Rock." Gold Country Geotourism Program.
     exploregoldcountry.com/pdf/caches/The%20Stein%20Valley%20Asking%
     20Rock.pdf. Accessed December 15, 2023.

CHAPTER 39 | SHRINKAGE

Interview with Lorna Fandrich.

Email interview with Lindy Watkinson.

Ashcroft-Cache Creek Journal. "After the Lytton joss house—Chinese Gods in a Lytton woodshed." February 9, 2016, 3.

Slava. "2008 Bulwer-Lytton Results." AlphaDictionary.com, March 15, 2009. alphadictionary.com/bb/viewtopic.php?t=3805.

Young, Ian. "Inferno destroys Chinese-Canadian heritage museum." *South China Morning Post*, July 9, 2021, 9.

CHAPTER 40 | CLIMATE CHANGE

This draws from hundreds of pages of Environment Canada records obtained under the Access to Information and Protection of Privacy Act, with file number A-2022-00217.

CE Noticias Financieras. "Climate change: What a 'heat boss' does, the unprecedented position created in Miami to fight a 'silent killer.'" July 27, 2021.

Quote from TSB investigator James Carmichael at a streamed media information session about results of the TSB investigation. Global News Hour at 6 B.C., October 14, 2021. https://globalnews.ca/video/8267746/global-news-hour-at -6-bc-oct-14.

CHAPTER 41 | THE FUTURE

Interviews with Donny Glasgow.

Dulisse, Anna. "4 lessons learned from Lytton wildfire survivor." Living Here, September 8, 2022. livinghere.ca/4-lessons-learned-from-lytton-wildfire-survivo r/?fbclid=IwAR3ViFBU0udY6dwJfWyxVbvsrKj4dQlbjhvgEJK6fC1QOp18lJb9N O9MKDg.

Parmar, Tarnjit. "Dog rescued from Lytton wildfire welcomes new litter of puppies nearly 1 year later." *CityNews*, June 14, 2022. https://vancouver.citynews.ca/2022 /06/14/dog-lytton-wildfire-litter-year-later/.

Roden, Barbara. "Lytton residents mark two years since the fire destroyed town." *Ashcroft-Cache Creek Journal*, July 4, 2023.

BIBLIOGRAPHY

BOOKS

Chow, Lily. *Blossoms in the Gold Fields: Chinese Settlements in the Fraser Canyon and the Okanagan.* Halfmoon Bay, BC: Caitlin Press, 2018.

Hill-Tout, Charles. *The Salish People: The Local Contribution of Charles Hill-Tout.* Vol. 1, *The Thompson and the Okanagan.* Vancouver: Talonbooks, 1978.

Lytton & District Centennial Society. *Lytton: A Story in Pictures, 1966–67, Told by the Older Ones for the Young People of Lytton.* Lytton: Freedom Graphics Press, 1966–67.

Marshall, Daniel. *Claiming the Land: British Columbia and the Making of a New El Dorado.* Vancouver: Ronsdale Press, 2019.

Smith, Harlan. *Archaeology of Lytton, British Columbia.* Memoirs of the American Museum of Natural History, vol. 2, pt. 3. Publications of the Jesup North Pacific Expedition, vol. 1, pt. 3. (New York: AMNH, 1899).

ARTICLES

London Daily News, July 14, 1859, 5.

Times-Colonist (Victoria), February 11, 1874, 4.

Richmond Dispatch. "After Many Years." December 1882.

Oshkosh Northwestern, February 9, 1900, 1.

Topeka State Journal, February 9, 1900, 2.

Victoria Daily Times, February 12, 1900, 5.

Washington Post. "Men who smile at danger: Bridge builder must be a combination of daring, skill and courage." From *Railman's Magazine*, June 16, 1912.

Vancouver Daily World, May 11, 1914, 1.

Vancouver Sun, May 12, 1914, 8.

The Province (Vancouver). "One man dead as fires rage." March 7, 1915, 18.

Robinson, Noel. "Last 'forty-niner' of province laid to rest." *Vancouver Daily World*,
     August 28, 1915, 9.

Vancouver Daily World, September 11, 1915, 11.

The Province (Vancouver), February 15, 1921, 19.

The Province (Vancouver). "Cariboo Road." February 22, 1921, 12.

Robinson, Noel. "The story of my life—No. 45." *Vancouver Daily World*, April 2, 1921, 7.

The Province (Vancouver), September 13, 1924, 22.

The Province (Vancouver), October 23, 1927.

Chilliwack Progress, May 28, 1931, 10.

Moore, John F. "Hurly burly of history flows quietly by Lytton." *Vancouver Sun*,
     September 10, 1931.

Wade, Dr. M.S. *Vancouver Sun*, September 10, 1931.

The Province (Vancouver), November 18, 1933, 45.

The Province (Vancouver). "Tourist trade helped tavern keepers, garage owners
     and retailers." November 2, 1936, 1.

Nanaimo Daily News, July 29, 1939, 1.

The Province (Vancouver), July 29, 1939, 1.

Langley Advance, December 5, 1946, 7.

Hives, C.F. *Chilliwack Progress*, January 1, 1947, 9.

Hives, Rev. Canon C.F. "A defense of St. George's, the work of one Indian school."
     Vancouver Sun, April 12, 1948, 4.

Times-Colonist (Victoria). "150 down with 'flu." January 24, 1949, 1.

Vancouver Sun. "Lytton beefed at 12 cent steak." November 5, 1949, 60.

Dalrymple, A.J. "Farm and ranch." *The Province* (Vancouver), November 9, 1949, 39.

Dalrymple, A.J. "Farm and ranch." *The Province* (Vancouver), July 15, 1951.

Vancouver Sun. "Bought cow Freetown Buttermaid at Hereford sales in England."
     July 6, 1953, 2.

Vancouver Sun, November 25, 1953, 48.

The Province (Vancouver), May 19, 1956, 54.

Times-Colonist (Victoria), July 10, 1958, 29.

Vancouver Sun, October 27, 1959, 10.

The Province (Vancouver). "Ferry is just a focal point of Indian anger." August 4, 1967, 5.

The Province (Vancouver), September 12, 1969, 4.

Vancouver Sun, March 29, 1971, 6.

The Province (Vancouver), September 8, 1977, 37.

Vancouver Sun, March 28, 1978, 10.

Nanaimo Daily News, February 21, 1979, 22.

The Province (Vancouver), January 27, 1983, 16.

The Province (Vancouver), July 10, 1983, 33.

Times-Colonist (Victoria). "Canyon Bridge spans century." June 9, 1984, A9.

Ashcroft-Cache Creek Journal, February 23, 1988, 15.

Times-Colonist (Victoria), April 5, 1992, 20.

Leung, Wendy. "Graves of Chinese pioneers give up their secrets: Canadian burial sites a reminder of early migrants' big role." *South China Morning Post*, July 20, 2008, 12.

Ashcroft-Cache Creek Journal. "After the Lytton joss house—Chinese Gods in a Lytton woodshed." February 9, 2016, 3.

South China Morning Post. "Inferno destroys Chinese-Canadian heritage museum." July 9, 2021.

Roden, Barbara. "A history of Lytton, from First Nations to the Gold Rush to disastrous fires." *Ashcroft-Cache Creek Journal*, July 6, 2021.

Abbotsford News. "Goddess of Mercy: Amid the devastation in Lytton, some glimmers of hope remain." July 17, 2021.

REPORTS

Truth and Reconciliation Commission of Canada. *Canada's Residential Schools: The History*. Part 1, *Origins to 1939*, and Part 2, *1939 to 2000*. Montreal and Kingston: McGill-Queen's University Press, 2015.

COURT CASES

Terence Wayne Nelson Aleck v. Derek Clarke, Anthony William Harding, Her Majesty the Queen in Right of Canada as Represented by the Minister of Indian and Northern Affairs, Supreme Court of British Columbia, Reasons for Judgment of the Honourable Mr. Justice Williamson, August 8, 2001.

T.W.N.A., E.A.J. and G.B.S. et al., plaintiffs, v. Clarke et al., 2001 BCSC 1177, Docket: C886397, Vancouver, Supreme Court of British Columbia, 2001 BCSC 177, Docket: C886397.

T.W.N.A. v. Clarke, 1999 CanLII 15172 (BC SC), 1999-11-16, Docket: C886397, Vancouver, Supreme Court of British Columbia.

F.S.M. v. Clarke et al., 1999-08-30, CanLII 9405 (BC SC).

ACKNOWLEDGEMENTS

PETER EDWARDS:

James Baker, Rev. Koten Benson, Robert Bolan, Lori Chong, Lily Chow, David Edwards, Adrienne Fairburn, Lorna Fandrich, Michele Feist, Juliet Forrester, Craig Pyette, Darwin Hanna, Patrick Manders, Charles Melanson, Dr. Rosalin Miles, Melanie Ready, Mark Rebagliati, Ross Rebagliati, Christ'l Roshard, Tricia Thorpe and Don Glasgow, Belinda (Lindy) Watkinson, Tom Watkinson Jr., Kareen Zebroff.

KEVIN LORING:

Freda Loring, Juliet Forrester, Guy Neufeld, Jody-Kay Marklew, John Haugen, Terry Aleck, Craig Pyette, Dr. Ruby Dunstan, Dave Walkem, Bryan Loring, Doris Loring.

All photos are in the public domain, ie. postcards, community poster and magazine illustrations from 1860, covers of *Der Spiegel* magazine and *Montreal Star*; are personal property of the authors; or permission has been granted by photo owners: Rebagliati, Chong and Watkinson families, and Tricia Thorpe and Don Glasgow.

PETER EDWARDS is the organized-crime beat reporter for the *Toronto Star* and the bestselling author of seventeen non-fiction books and one young adult novel. His works have been published in four languages. Edwards is a member of Top Left Entertainment, a production development company, and an executive producer for the Citytv series *Bad Blood*, created by New Metric Media and aired on Netflix. His book *One Dead Indian: The Premier, the Police and the Ipperwash Crisis* was made into the Gemini Award–winning movie *One Dead Indian* by Sienna Films, which aired on CTV. Edwards was awarded an eagle feather from the Anishinabek Nation and a gold medal from the Centre for Human Rights. His book *Delusion* (published in Europe as *The Infiltrator*) is on the CIA's recommended reading list for staff and agents.

KEVIN LORING is a Governor General's Award-winning playwright, an actor, a director and the founding Artistic Director of Indigenous Theatre at the National Arts Centre of Canada. He is also the Artistic Director of Savage Society, a not-for-profit production company.

His three published works are: *Where the Blood Mixes*, *Thanks for Giving* and *Little Red Warrior and His Lawyer*. He comes from the Loring family from Botanie Valley and the Adams of Snake Flat. He is a Nlaka'pamux of Lytton First Nation.